LITERARY CRITICISM AND CULTURAL THEORY

Edited by

William E. Cain
Professor of English
Wellesley College

A ROUTLEDGE SERIES

LITERARY CRITICISM AND CULTURAL THEORY
WILLIAM E. CAIN, *General Editor*

SURVIVING THE CROSSING

(Im)migration, Ethnicity, and Gender in
Willa Cather, Gertrude Stein, and Nella Larsen

Jessica G. Rabin

Routledge
New York & London

Published in 2004 by
Routledge
270 Madison Avenue
New York, NY 10016
www.routledge-ny.com

Published in Great Britain by
Routledge
2 Park Square
Milton Park, Abington
Oxon OX14 4RN
www. routledge.co.uk

Copyright © 2004 by Taylor & Francis Group, a Division of T&F Informa.
Routledge is an imprint of the Taylor & Francis Group.

Printed in the United States of America on acid-free paper.

10   9   8   7   6   5   4   3   2   1

Library of Congress Cataloging-in-Publication Data
   Rabin, Jessica G., 1973–
     Surviving the crossing : (im)migration, ethnicity, and gender in Willa Cather, Gertrude Stein, and Nella Larsen / Jessica G. Rabin.
       p. cm.—(Literary criticism and cultural theory)
     Includes bibliographical references.
     ISBN 0-415-97118-7 (hardback : alk. paper)
     1. American literature—20th century—History and criticism. 2. Emigration and immigration in literature. 3. Women and literature—United States—History—20th century. 4. American literature—Women authors—History and criticism. 5. Stein, Gertrude, 1874–1946—Criticism and interpretation. 6. Cather, Willa, 1873–1947—Criticism and interpretation. 7. Larsen, Nella—Criticism and interpretation. 8. Immigrants in literature. 9. Ethnicity in literature. 10. Sex role in literature. I. Title. II. Series.

    PS228.E55R33 2004
    813.'52093552—dc22
                                     2004014245

To Toby
And in memory of my grandparents who made the crossing:
Robert Rabin
Susan and Henry Schurenstedt

Contents

Acknowledgments

Many thanks to Paul Foster Johnson, William Cain, and Routledge for giving me the opportunity to revisit, revise, and revitalize this text.

The insights and scholarship of Walter Kalaidjian, Julie Abraham, and Martine Brownley help set the foundations of this project; I appreciate the time and effort that they contributed in order to bring it to fruition. I am indebted, as well, to my mentor Merrill Skaggs who introduced me to the great (literary) love of my life and encouraged me in all my academic pursuits. I am also grateful for the support and enthusiasm of my other friends in Cather Studies, especially Marilee Lindemann, Susan Rosowski, and Joseph Urgo.

My family, like Vickie Templeton's friends the Rosens, set me on the path that "led toward the moon," by serving as a source of academic and personal inspiration. I've always been proud of my family, and I am grateful for the way they prepared me for the world and then welcomed me back to the parish—and will no doubt send me forth again with glad hearts when the time comes. Many thanks to my parents, Bernard and Debbie Rabin, and Joan Rabin and Barbara Slater; my grandmother, Rose Rabin; and my brother, Dan Rabin.

Thank you to my friends who listened, laughed, and reminded me to breathe, especially Pam Garrettson and Pierrette Stukes. I also appreciate my soccer teammates who helped me channel my excess energies and occasional frustrations into a socially acceptable and (relatively) non-destructive format.

For permission to reprint here a portion of an essay I first published in the collection *Willa Cather's New York,* I would like to thank the volume's editor, Merrill Skaggs, and Fairleigh Dickinson University Press.

Chapter One
Introduction: A Sense of Selves

Binarisms permeate the foundations of our western cultural and intellectual framework—native/foreign, black/white, man/woman, heterosexual/homosexual—but are the fixed essentialisms implicit in such models truly reflective of the reality of human experience (actual and literary)? It is my goal to join the ongoing scholarly complication of binaries by offering a more fluid conception of boundaries. In place of essentializing categories of identity, I explore the ramifications of using multiple subject positioning as a means of conceptualizing and representing identity. By examining the literature of three women modernists, I show how the dispersal of fixed identity is facilitated through language. In other words, I focus on the ways in which fiction unhinges identity, along with the consequences of such a process—both liberating and dislocating. Such a process does not take place in a vacuum. The transnational atmosphere of the interwar period in the United States facilitated a loosening of identity categories which was both created by and reflected in the literature of the period. Writers who had a complicated relationship to identity categories and who created characters whose lives could not be neatly compartmentalized found in this cultural climate the psychological space prerequisite to writing and the possibility of communicating with an audience. In my quest for a fuller, more useful paradigm of identity formation and perpetuation, I examine issues of ethnicity and race, nationality and geography, and gender and sexuality in the fiction of Willa Cather, Gertrude Stein and Nella Larsen.

The emphasis I place on how language facilitates the dispersal of fixed identity has its roots in post-structuralist philosophy. In particular, Derridian and post-structuralist critique of binarisms provides an important underpinning for my study. By emphasizing the instability of language, Derrida interrogates the idea of the unitary subject itself, as Terry Eagleton explains: "to use signs at all entails that my meaning is always somehow dispersed, divided and never quite at one with itself. Not only my meaning, indeed, but me: since language is something I am made out of, rather than merely a convenient tool I use, the whole idea that I am a stable, unified entity must also be a fiction" (130). In addition, Derrida uses the term "deconstruction" to describe "the critical operation by which [binary] oppositions can be partly undermined, or by which they can be shown partly to undermine each other in the process of textual meaning" (Eagleton 132). Although deconstruction is not my goal, I take up Derrida's dissatisfaction with binary paradigms in my approach to the texts under consideration.

By offering a critique of binary models, I participate in a series of ongoing explorations in literary and cultural studies. Eagleton points out, for example, that feminism and post-structuralism share some important goals and preoccupations: "for all the binary oppositions which post-structuralism sought to undo, the hierarchical opposition between men and women was perhaps the most virulent" (149). In addition to feminist critics, gender, queer, and race theorists have subjected binary models to intense scrutiny over the past fifteen years. Diana Fuss argued in 1989 that "the binary articulation of essentialism and difference can . . . be restrictive, even obfuscating, in that it allows us to ignore or to deny the differences *within* essentialisms" (xii). The following year, Eve Sedgwick suggested that binarisms in sexual orientation should be more fluid than the homo/heterosexual division implemented in the late nineteenth century (9–10), while Judith Butler urged feminists to avoid "totalizing gestures" (*Gender* 13) and noted that heterosexuality needs and creates "an oppositional, binary gender system" (*Gender* 22). In 1991, Jonathan Dollimore proposed that "the essentialist/anti-essentialist opposition is rather less stable than is often supposed in theoretical discourse" (26). Three years later, Lee Edelman opposed his own work to prior inquiries which looked for "'homosexual difference' as a determinate entity rather than as an unstable differential relation" (3), suggesting that he, too, disagreed with the notion of gay identity as coherent, totalizing, and completely separate from that of straight identity. In the 1995 collection *Social Postmodernism,* Anthony Appiah and Ali Rattansi offer race-oriented critiques of binarisms. Appiah, "the son of an African father and a European mother," argues that "identities are complex and multiple" (Nicholson and Seidman 14, Appiah 110). For his part, Rattansi works to complicate paradigms of race and ethnicity so that these terms might reflect multiplicity and complexity rather than simple binaries (256–58). To summarize, post-structuralist philosophy and the deconstruction of language have emphasized how language constructs the subject and how language is itself slippery. The flexibility thus offered to the concept of the subject has been particularly useful for members of so-called minority groups who have been traditionally and unfairly demarcated as inferior.[1] Hence, recent feminist, African-American, gender, and gay/lesbian theorists have used post-structuralism's tenets and adapted them for their own ends. I intend to do the same.

I have chosen to focus on three women writers whose best-known works were published during the interwar period in part because the issues that interest me, such as race, ethnicity, and sexual orientation, all interact with gender in complex ways (as black feminists like Patricia Hill Collins have proposed vis-a-vis matrices of oppression).[2] I am interested in women's writing because of its formative influence on modernist sensibility. As both Norman Cantor and Elizabeth Ammons have asserted, the early twentieth-century women's movement played a key role in the modernist movement (Cantor 122; Ammons 4). While I do not wish to imply that all women writers—or the three in my study, in particular—are feminists,[3] the concomitant development of early twentieth-century feminism and woman-authored modernist texts is compelling. The experience of being women writers during this time and writing provocative and multivalent texts constitutes a significant axis of comparison. Looking at these three writers in light of one another provides both a deeper understanding of individual accomplishment and a broader view of their participation in larger trends.

In arranging and discussing these three writers, I also draw on Iris Young's adaptation of Sartre's concept of seriality. In attempting to talk about "woman" as a category without resorting to essentialism, Young proposes "a way of thinking about women as a social collective without requiring that all women have common attributes or a common situation . . . [and one which] does not rely on identity or self-identity for understanding the social production and meaning of membership in collectives" (188, 197–8). A series, Young explains, stands in contrast to a self-conscious group, and "membership is defined . . . by the fact that in their diverse existences and actions [members of a series] are oriented around the same objects or practico-inert structures" (203). For the writers under consideration, "practico-inert structures" might include publication politics, societal expectations for women writers in the realm of genre or subject-matter, or residual Victorian standards of gender-appropriate behavior. Cather, Stein and Larsen have traditionally been studied within the framework of ostensibly non-overlapping literary movements (e.g., pioneer literature, avant-garde modernism, Harlem Renaissance), suggesting the inadvisability of arguing for a conscious communal relationship. At the same time, however, similarities in biography, commonalities in themes, and indirect contacts via reading and mutual friends meant that these three women were, to say the least, coming into contact with a similar set of cultural and social "objects."

Hence these writers, who were not part of a movement or a community, clearly have much more in common than a group of people waiting for a bus (one of Sartre's examples of a seriality).

In acknowledging both similarities and differences in experience and art, I move towards a paradigm that eases away from the polarities that require us to see literary movements and contextual constructivism as opposed. I also implement Young's suggestion that seriality can be usefully applied to race and nationality, as well as to gender (206). Ethnicity and nationality are central concerns in all three writers, and each offers novel conceptions about the relationship between identity categories and identity. The problem Young addresses in her essay, how to talk about "woman" without resorting to essentialism (188), has clear parallels with my goals here. Where I differ from Young, however, is in my ends. Young rejects "the attempt to theorize gender identity as multiple rather than binary" (193) and sees seriality as a way to "disconnect . . . gender from identity" (209). The iconoclastic modernists whom I am studying, on the other hand, seem to stop short of Young's postmodern dispersal. Although they destabilize categories and emphasize fluidity, gender is still a significant dimension of identity (as are ethnicity and nationality) for Cather, Stein and Larsen. When I look at the three women together, I do not consider them a strict seriality, "individuals [who] pursue their own ends with respect to the same objects conditioned by a continuous material environment . . . [and who] have nothing necessarily in common in their histories, experiences, or identity" (Young 199). Nor do I argue that these writers constitute a conscious community of purpose (a group). Rather, I interrogate patterns and analyze the presence of multiple solutions to similar problems.

COMING OF AGE IN TRANS-NATIONAL AMERICA

One major reason I see Cather, Stein and Larsen as participating in a seriality with important ramifications for the study of their work is the salience of the cultural climate constituting the backdrop for their literary emergence or coming of age. For all three, the time and place Randolph Bourne invokes with the appellation "Trans-National America" was formative in terms of personal and professional development. At the same time that Bourne's essay expresses a vision of multiculturalism which "looked forward to our own social diversity in the post-Vietnam era" (Kalaidjian 19), it provides a reflection of contemporary trends and strivings. The high point of the Modernist period, which Cantor identifies as 1900–1940, fostered trans-continental exchange, the movement of both ideas and of people across the ocean—immigrants and expatriates (1, 123). Furthermore, travel within America became easier around the turn of the century, and many intellectuals moved to the cities.

This demographic trend had important ramifications for the development of new modernist forms. Raymond Williams explains: "the most important general element of the innovations in form is the fact of immigration to the metropolis, and it cannot too often be emphasized how many of the major innovators were, in this precise sense, immigrants. . . . [T]he crucible of the metropolis [was] . . . no mere melting pot but an intense and visually and linguistically exciting process in its own right" (45–46). Cather, Stein and Larsen participated in both the transcontinental movement and the gravitation towards American urban centers characteristic of the early twentieth century.[4]

With more frequent physical and intellectual contact between America and Europe, political conditions in Europe became increasingly important for the United States. World War I precipitated Bourne's trans-national thesis, and it also clarified the need for emergent models of identity and identification. Noting that the war in Europe seemed to intensify nationalist feeling among immigrants rather than edifying their sense of themselves as Americans, Bourne offers the following explanation: "In our loose, free country, no constraining national purpose, no tenacious folk-tradition and folk-style hold the people to a line. The war has shown us that not in any magical formula will this purpose be found" (271). Rather, Bourne suggests, the idea of being or belonging to any cause or group exclusively was not a realistic way to view affiliations.

If the Great War highlighted the presence of nationalistic immigrant "movements [that] had been making great headway before the war even began" (Bourne 261), it also made a lasting impression on all three women writers under consideration. Cather engaged in much soul-searching and uncharacteristic struggle to write a war novel, the text she would always consider her favorite. *One of Ours* won a Pulitzer Prize, but its hostile reception by men who resented a woman's foray into male literary turf in some measure precipitated Cather's sense that "the world broke in two in 1922 or thereabouts" (Skaggs 6, *NUF* v). Stein did not write about World War I in its immediate aftermath, but her wartime experiences in France would become the basis for a significant portion of the novel which made her a household name in America, *The Autobiography of Alice B. Toklas*. Ten years after it ended, "the war" (*P* 154) additionally provides an important backdrop for both of Larsen's novels, though it is rarely mentioned explicitly. It conveniently disposes of Anne Grey's first husband in *Quicksand*, while in *Passing*, it provides a defining framework for Clare's European sojourn, as she relates tales of "wartime in France, of after-the-wartime in Germany" (170) for friends she has not seen in fifteen years. During the war years, Larsen herself was engaged in the crucial task of "finding a home," a prelude to "working for an education" and "becoming a writer" (Davis 110, 137, 154). World War I thus captured the imagination of all three writers.

One reason World War I had such an impact on contemporary artists and thinkers is that it raised questions about the future of an American nationality and led to the popularization of one of the most pervasive and long-standing symbols in American culture, the melting pot. Indeed, although the response of native-born Americans to immigrant loyalties during the war precipitated Bourne's essay, he takes the future as his main topic, exploring the question of national identity in a multi-national or international country. Bourne focuses on immigration and how it has changed (or should change) the definition of American selfhood. The great fact of immigration, the most important influence in turn-of-the-century American culture (R. Williams, qtd. in Ferraro 111), permeated literary and cultural discourse throughout the interwar period, additionally precipitating a cultural crisis about the nature of the American character or nationality. Bourne begins his essay by noting that "no reverberatory effect of the great war has caused American public opinion more solicitude than the failure of the 'melting-pot'" (260). And yet, despite being one of the concept's detractors himself, Bourne nevertheless unwittingly employs its rhetoric, suggesting the ubiquity of melting pot ideology. Indeed, Werner Sollors observes that "Bourne attacked the melting pot from the left, whereas Henry Pratt Fairchild did it from the right," pointing out the irony by which "the cosmopolitan dual citizens Bourne envisioned were described in clear melting pot language: 'America has burned most of the baser metal from them'" (*Beyond* 97). The metaphor initially seems pluralistic, but Philip Gleason similarly acknowledges that "with all its liberality and tolerance, the cosmopolitan version of the melting pot was still a theory of assimilation. The idea that the immigrants must change was basic; they were to become new people" (*Concepts* 82). On the other end of the political spectrum from Bourne, Henry Pratt Fairchild offers a substitute for the melting pot: "if we must have a symbol for race mixture, much more accurate than the figure of the melting pot is the figure of the village pound" (125). Fairchild further contends that "Unrestricted immigration. . . . was slowly, insidiously, irresistibly eating away the very heart of the United States. What was being melted in the great Melting Pot, losing all form and symmetry, all beauty and character, all nobility and usefulness, was the American nationality itself" (261).[5] More recent theorists have proposed symbols of their own: John Blair announces that "the venerable Melting Pot has given way to images legitimizing multiethnic diversity as in the homely *salad bowl* or the more elegant *mosaic*" (142), while Lawrence Fuchs offers the image of the kaleidoscope. Gleason, however, insists that the melting pot is an imperfect symbol, but the

best of the alternatives (*Speaking* 24). Whether or not the Melting Pot was or
is an accurate symbol for the creation and sustenance of an American nationality, it has been a persistent one for the past ninety-five years.

The subjects of my study could not help but be exposed to this symbol,
and they personally encountered the realities of (im)migration, as well.
Although none was a first-generation immigrant, each had split European and
American alliances. Cather "many times longed to be a European" (Lilienfeld
48), while Stein spent her entire adult life in France, and Larsen was of mixed
race and mixed nationality (her father was African-American and her mother
was Danish). As children, all came into close contact with immigrants and
European culture. Cather spent many Nebraskan childhood days riding her
pony from homestead to homestead, seeking out the "old farmwomen,
Bohemian and Scandinavian, [who] moved her imagination" (Brown, *Critical*
26); she would draw heavily on those memories in her Nebraska stories and
novels. Stein was exposed to European languages and customs at an even earlier age, as her family moved to Austria when she was an infant, returning to
the United States when Stein was four. Larsen did not travel abroad as a child,
but she grew up in an ethnically and racially diverse neighborhood with a
large number of European immigrants (Davis 33). In addition to growing up
in the midst of European society (in Europe or in America), Cather, Stein and
Larsen all took significant geographical journeys themselves. When Cather's
family moved from Virginia to Nebraska, "she felt the break cruelly" (E. Lewis
12). Later, her journeys from Red Cloud to Lincoln, from Lincoln to
Pittsburgh, and from Pittsburgh to New York heralded important changes in
her life. Stein was even more of a wanderer than Cather, living in Europe,
Baltimore, San Francisco, and East Oakland before attending the Harvard
Annex, returning to Baltimore, and then joining her brother Leo in France.
Larsen journeyed within the United States,[6] but her writing suggests that she
perceived movement between North and South as going between different
worlds or different countries. She grew up during the Great Migration, the
cultural backdrop which also serves as the context for her texts (Yohe 3). Born
in Chicago, she attended Fisk in Nashville and nursing school in New York,
the city she made her home for most of her adult life.

Cather, Stein and Larsen engaged with European culture, knew immigrants, and experienced migration themselves. None of them espoused melting pot ideology,[7] and none wanted to be melted herself. Cather believed it
unforgivable to deny immigrants their native language (Pers 24) and never
tried to assimilate to the mores and standards of the small prairie town that
became her home at age ten. Jane Lilienfeld observes that "as a teenager,
Cather shocked the Red Cloud townspeople by her absolute self-possession,

the conviction of her genius, and her flamboyant cross-dressing" (46). Nor had she shown any signs of becoming a proper Southern lady as a small child in Virginia.[8] Although Stein did not make such explicit displays of her sense of her own difference as a child, she was determined to meet the world on her own terms. Like Cather, she "had immense strength of ego," and she cultivated an "appreciation of difference" from a young age (Wagner-Martin, *Favored* 13–14). As an adult, Stein was interested in and amused by variation among Americans (particularly according to geography) and believed that neither her genius nor her de-facto expatriation rendered her less of an American. Larsen also engaged in a delicate balancing act, both seeking membership in elite African-American circles and trying to differentiate herself from such groups. Michael Kammen notes that "the melting pot is an inept metaphor, but it did work for the blacks in the sense that it turned many different kinds of Africans into one kind of African American" (qtd. in Gleason, *Speaking* 36). Larsen, however, did not want to be considered an ordinary member of a unitary group. Rebelling against such a blurring of individuality, Larsen continually emphasized her Scandinavian roots. Like her character Helga Crane, Larsen "position[ed] herself very strongly by asserting her difference" and needed to be thought unique (Clemmen 462).

At the same time that these writers held themselves apart and validated a view of a diverse, rather than a homogenous, body of Americans, all wanted to fit in: to be accepted, to achieve financial success, and to win critical acclaim. Although her overarching goal was to produce critically acknowledged great art, Cather did not disdain her paying audience (Lilienfeld 50). She was savvy about publishing and marketing, and switched publishers when she felt that her current firm was not doing its best to promote her work. Stein was famous for her propensity for self-promotion. She wanted to have her works published, though she spent years writing texts that most people did not understand, and when celebrity finally came, she thoroughly enjoyed it. Similarly, it was common knowledge that Larsen sought recognition (B. Williams 48). She wanted both her fame and her income to spring from her career as a novelist (Davis 2). For each woman, being an American writer constituted a key axis of identification and represented the road to success.

YOUR NATIVE LAND, YOUR LIFE[9]

Since Cather, Stein and Larsen all retained an American identity as a key aspect in their sense of self, it is important to understand the meaning of an American identity (race, culture, nationality, etc.) and to contextualize it among other identity categories—those which are imposed as well as those which are chosen.[10] Here I am specifically invoking Sollors's framework of "consent and descent" (*Beyond* 5–6), although modifying his approach because it, too, rests on an either/or distinction. Nevertheless, it is useful to take from Sollors—and others writing from a sociological or historical position—the point that the turn of the century through the 1920s constituted a crucial period in explorations of race, ethnicity, and American identity.[11] Writers of literature during the interwar period shared this preoccupation, and thus it is not surprising that the age of high modernism, with its paradoxical coupling of immigration and expatriation, contributes to the discourse of identity formation and perpetuation. Discussions of whether a so-called "American race" exists or whether Americanism is best conceptualized as a philosophy (Munsterberg), a way of life or a culture (Blair, Fuchs), or a nationality (Commons, Fairchild) also contribute to the difficulty of understanding the place of ethnicity in American life and letters. The ambiguous standing of African-Americans in most theories of Americanism leads to both dilemmas of definition and further entrenchment in binarisms, and the problem of "furnishing uncontentious definitions of ethnicity and racism" (Rattansi 252) and relating these terms to Americanism remains unsolved.

While only Larsen had a defining identification with a stigmatized group,[12] all experienced what it means to be "nonstandard, or, in America, . . . not fully American" (Sollors, *Beyond* 25). Although Cather was socially conservative and seemed to accept at least some Victorian views on sex and sexuality (Shaw, "Victorian" 25), critics have argued "that 'lesbian' did in fact capture Cather's self-definition" (O'Brien, *EV* 6). Furthermore, at the time Cather was publishing her first Nebraska novels, "'immigration and ethnicity must have struck writers as controversial subjects which had better be avoided in literature for fear of antagonizing important groups in society'" (Fryckstedt, qtd. in Pers 16). Even after years in cultured company, Cather retained a sense of being a country bumpkin in comparison to blue bloods who had the good fortune to be born in the northeast: "Years later, when Cather was traveling in sophisticated Eastern cultural circles, she still felt insecure because of her prairie background" (O'Brien, *EV* 117). Stein was not embarrassed by her background, but she had to continually fight the label "expatriate" which was invariably applied to her. She was also a Jew living in anti-Semitic times and a lesbian trying to establish herself in patriarchal circles. In addition to being black, Larsen was of mixed national origin, further complicating her American identity.[13]

In addition to occupying marginalized subject positions, all employed minority difference in their texts: Cather's characters include European immigrants, African-Americans, people with disabilities, and Jews; Stein writes about working-class immigrants and African-Americans, and she often speaks of Jews as if she were not one herself; Larsen's texts make distinctions between different classes of African-Americans, and her characters refer to Jews, as well. In the cases of Cather and Stein, however, use of ethnically or racially diverse subjects has garnered charges of appropriation and ethnocentrism. Ammons, for example, criticizes Cather's representations of the Cliff Dwellers in *The Song of the Lark* and *The Professor's House* and of African-Americans in *Sapphira and the Slave Girl.* Her unflattering assessment is that "when it comes to women of color, whether Indian women in Arizona or black women in Virginia, Cather does not subvert but instead becomes Jim Burden and Niel Herbert" (136). She passes a similar judgment on Stein, observing of "Melanctha" that "black people in this work are stupid, hypersexual, immature, and fundamentally Other in their feelings about human life" (103). Corinne Blackmer explains how subject position constitutes a crucial difference between Stein (and, by extension, Cather) and Larsen: "whereas for Stein racial identity was primarily, in the case of 'Melanctha,' a metaphor, for Larsen race was ontologically inseparable from day-to-day existence and, by extension, from literary aesthetics" (70). She concludes that such positioning had ramifications for each author's respective success, as she notes that "because Larsen, as both a woman and an African-American author, literally *inhabits* the mask of racial difference, while Stein *employs* the African mask as an artistic vehicle, their fates on the literary marketplace replicated the politics of racial inequality, and were radically different and unequal" (86).

Although Cather, Stein and Larsen occupied different social and political spaces in part due to their racial and ethnic backgrounds, all wrote both about people like themselves and about people who were somehow on the margins. In some cases, marginal figures are also the ones identified with the author. Hermione Lee observes that Cather, for example, often creates male narrators who conform to Robert Park's definition of "marginal man" ("Bridge" 40). She explains that such characters as Jim Burden and Godfrey St. Peter (both of whom have been read as Cather figures) "feel alienated and separate from their 'cultural milieu,' and that alienation has a great deal to do with an internalized conflict between different, opposing kinds of Americanness" (41). The same might be said of Stein's Melanctha Herbert and of Larsen's Helga Crane. Sollors connects this experience of marginality to national identity, noting that "in American, casting oneself as an outsider may in fact be considered a dominant cultural trait" (*Beyond* 31).

Indeed, these writers did not consider themselves completely outside or inside of any given identity category. Rather, their affiliations are complex and shifting. In addition to depicting category-defying characters in their work, Stein, Cather, and Larsen were themselves cosmopolitans and world-travelers.

Further, all were aware of the major movements and preoccupations of their time in a wide variety of fields—history, sociology, psychology, art, and science. Because of their broad knowledge and varied experiences, all can be considered (at some level) insider/outsiders in accordance with Alice Gambrell's paradigm, in which "insider-outsider intellectuals, whose value consisted in their simultaneous distance from and intimacy with the subjects of their own inquiry . . . performed their work atop one of the most volatile philosophical faultlines within present-day remappings of the field of 'modernism'" (4–5). Gambrell sees "affiliative issues" (22) as key to the subjects in her study, and notes "a strong impulse towards *self*-revision" (32) in their texts. Like the women modernists in Gambrell's study, Cather, Stein and Larsen retained privileged positions in social groups and had a pronounced strain of elitism. For example, Cather became a local celebrity to the people of the state of Nebraska, who commissioned a portrait of her for the Omaha public library. Stein, for her part, occupied her self-assigned position as the only woman in a community of male geniuses from her undergraduate days until the end of her life, while Larsen both enjoyed her status as a member of the black elite and tried to emphasize the uniqueness conferred on her by her Scandinavian roots. Also in line with Gambrell's theories, Cather, Stein and Larsen all offered several versions of themselves and their subjects, engaging in a process of "self-revision."

Where I differ most crucially from Gambrell, however, is in the nature of this recasting which she sees as a "double revision—directed both inward and outward," i.e., revising the self and the institution in which it functioned (32). Here Gambrell establishes yet another set of opposed binaries, and applies an anthropological term in a broader context. I hesitate to adopt this strategy because of the danger of attributing insider/outsider status to Cather, for example, and conflating such "native ethnographers" as Zora Neale Hurston with a strictly fictional writer. Cather has been praised for her sympathetic, detailed and realistic portraits of immigrants, but she has made no claims to scientific accuracy or even to realism as it is usually defined.[14] Cather did not set out to act as an intermediary between misunderstood Swedes and the outside world, and thus it would be inappropriate to view Cather's interest in immigrant farm wives as a form of self-nativism.

While I reject the essentialism and binarisms implicit in the insider/outsider paradigm, I do think such a framework provides an example of how models of identity can be loosened up to facilitate the transition to a discourse of both/and as opposed to either/or. Gambrell emphasizes the positive aspects of the insider/outsider's potential for inter-group mobility, and yet Cather, Stein and Larsen experienced the fluidity of permeable boundaries as sometimes liberating but sometimes dislocating. For example, Cather fluctuated between affirming and devaluing same-sex attraction (in herself and others), immigrant contributions, and ethnic stereotypes. As Robert Nelson has pointed out, Cather occupied an "ambiguous situation as a deeply spiritual offspring of the Virginia gentry transported to the harsh plains of the Midwest, as a woman artist with a cosmopolitan outlook, and as a lesbian" (21). She paradoxically provides some of the more sympathetic portraits of immigrants written by a non-ethnic American modernist, while retaining her status as a champion of American nostalgia. Thus she is inside and outside of multiple categories simultaneously. Similarly, Stein variously chose to empha-size and de-emphasize such aspects of herself as her lesbianism, her woman-hood, her Jewishness, and her status as an American citizen. She did not consider herself coherent, consistent, and unitary like a chemical equation. All water consists of two atoms of hydrogen and one of oxygen at all times—the proportions remain constant. It would be impossible, however, to write out a comparable equation for identity categories in a hypothetical, mono-lithic Gertrude Stein. Finally, wanting both acceptance and uniqueness, Larsen and her heroines moved uneasily between bohemianism and social propriety (in both black and white circles). Her ambivalence about both her sense of her place and her goals or aspirations makes it difficult to assign strict inside/outside demarcations to her social milieu either.

All were variously inside and outside an American identity, as well. Cather's sense of herself as an American remained crucial to her self-image, as she refused expatriation to resolve her feelings of not belonging (Shaw, "Victorian" 23–25). Furthermore, since critics such as Mona Pers (20), Nelson (56–7), and Lilienfeld (48) have suggested that Cather valorized Europeans at the expense of Americans, it is particularly significant that Cather chose to stay in America. At the same time that Cather identified with Americans as a group (whatever that might mean), her identity was region-ally-based. Trying to establish a link with her southern past, Cather insisted that she was named for her soldier uncle who died fighting for the Confederacy (a fancy that Lewis perpetuated in her memoirs). She also re-turns to her Virginia roots in her later stories and last novel. Cather simulta-neously maintains her connections with Nebraska, in spite of having moved east at the earliest possible opportunity. Cather lived most of her life in New York City, the consummate city and the epitome of otherness for many south-erners and mid-westerners alike. Yet she never felt completely at home among the sophisticated New York and Boston sets, and she is certainly never iden-tified with New York. But she liked good clothes and good food, and was quite cosmopolitan in her way, keeping abreast of the latest trends in litera-ture and art.

Having lived in several different countries and regions, Stein had a special relationship to the English language, almost like that of a non-native speaker. She preferred to live where English was not spoken in order to have the English language all to herself (Marren 174). In this way, Stein shared an attitude towards language which Williams connects with immigrants: "to the immigrants especially, with their new second common language, language was more evident as a medium—a medium that could be shaped and re-shaped—than as a social custom" (R. Williams 46). Ammons adds that Stein's propensity for linguistic dislocations "makes us start over" (88)—in other words, she puts her readers in the subject position of immigrants. In spite of her expatriate lifestyle and her immigrant relationship to language, Stein remained "convinced of the ineluctable impress of one's native land, [and] she happily affirmed her own American heritage" (Spencer 210). Indeed Susan Marren takes this observation one step further, noting of *The Autobiography of Alice B. Toklas* that "Stein reconstitutes herself as the quintessence of Americanness—a reconstitution that could not, the text suggests, have been accomplished on American land" (170). Hence Stein's world view affirms both her identification as an American and her cosmopolitan lifestyle.

Larsen similarly experienced the challenge of trans-nationalism throughout her life. Growing up in a mixed neighborhood and being the product of a multi-racial, multi-national marriage, Larsen came into intimate contact with different ways of being American. Furthermore, her novels suggest that she considered the rural South an entirely different country than the urban centers of the North in which she grew up (Yohe 21, Davis 4). David Lewis corroborates this view with his terminology when observes that southern migrants brought "religious fundamentalism and fervor to Harlem . . . [like] other immigrant groups, which gained psychological comfort and social stability from various orthodoxies and customs" (221). Beyond her views on regional or demographic affiliations, Larsen knew firsthand that "striving to be both European and black requires some specific forms of double consciousness" (Gilroy 1). Like other ethnic American writers, she faced the dilemma of "the double audience" (Sollors, *Beyond* 249), and she found herself pulled both by Africa and by white America (Huggins 8). Larsen did not want to be pigeonholed as a Negro novelist (Davis 282), and yet she sought recognition from African-American arbiters of culture as well as white critics. At the same time that she valued Carl Van Vechten's opinions on her work, she was thrilled when the Woman's Auxiliary of the NAACP gave a tea in honor of *Quicksand*'s publication. While W.E.B. DuBois spoke of a "dual consciousness" and James Weldon Johnson described a "dual personality" (Gilroy 131), Larsen offers Clare Kendry, whom Kristine Yohe has identified as a character with "dual status" (63). Hence Larsen's sense of herself as an American was complicated both by her ties to Europe and her status as an African-American woman.

Dual or multiple citizenship, a notion consistent with the insider/outsider concept, also appears as an important idea in Bourne's essay: "we may have to accept some form of that dual citizenship which meets with so much articulate horror among us. Dual citizenship we may have to recognize as the rudimentary form of that international citizenship to which, if our words mean anything, we aspire" (280). Bourne offers further endorsement for Cather's and Larsen's travels and Stein's residence abroad as compatible with an established American identity:

> Indeed, does not the cultivated American who goes to Europe practice a dual citizenship, which, if not formal, is no less real? The American who lives abroad may be the least expatriate of men. If he falls in love with French ways and French thinking and French democracy and seeks to saturate himself with the new spirit, he is guilty of at least a dual spiritual citizenship. He may be still American, yet he feels himself through sympathy also a Frenchman. And he finds that this expansion involves no shameful conflict within him, no surrender of his native attitude. He has rather for the first time caught a glimpse of the cosmopolitan spirit. (281)

Through their sojourns abroad and their engagement with European culture, Cather, Stein and Larsen all engaged with dual (if not triple or quadruple) citizenship.

IDENTITIES POLITICS

Such cosmopolitanism allowed these authors to create textured, nuanced, and sophisticated texts. And yet their cultivation and their engagement with multiple subject positions had a negative facet as well: "whoever is not [normative] has to be segregated or repressed or excluded, or to hide himself, or to play a double game one way or another. This is the latent condition which allows otherness or difference to become integrated within a 'total' ideology or hegemony" (Balibar 63). All had to variously submerge and accentuate parts of themselves to negotiate the social and professional turfs they wished to occupy, and all encountered resistance to the kind of work they were producing. When Bourne comments that "these people were not mere arrivals from the same family, to be welcomed as understood and long-loved, but strangers to the neighborhood, with whom a long process of settling down had to take place" (262), he is referring to non-Anglo-Saxon immigrants. His words are equally applicable, however, to African-American and women writers in the early twentieth century.[15] These writers had a problematic relation to modernism and canon formation. Much of Cather's later work was dismissed as nostalgic and anti-modern, a notion she helped to perpetuate with comments like the one she offers in the prefatory note to *Not Under Forty:* "it is for the backward, and by one of their number, that these sketches were written" (v).[16] Marianne DeKoven contends that the bulk of Stein's writing was not modernist for the opposite reason. While Cather's work seemed too simple in form and too sentimental in theme to qualify as modernist, Stein quickly moved beyond modernism (as seen in "Melanctha") to avant-garde experimentalism and its attendant incomprehensibility (*Rich* 68). Like Cather, Larsen was regarded by some as rearguard because her themes and subject matter did not coincide with critical expectations: "black women novelists, for example, whose settings are the urban North and whose subjects are middle-class black women are not only dismissed in the name of the vernacular; they are condemned . . . for 'historical conservativism'" and considered "less than authentically black" (DuCille 195, 198). In this way, Larsen's status as a Harlem Renaissance writer kept her work from being studied under the rubric of modernism, while her choice of cities as settings and middle-class women as characters pushed her out of some definitions of New Negro writing, as well.[17] Like Cather, who came to be considered rearguard, and Stein, who seemed postmodern before her time, Larsen had trouble fitting into pre-ordained literary critical categories.

All three writers faced resistance to their work because of gender as well as formal issues, and in this area they seemed more willing to appear to conform to expectations as a means of gaining critical acceptance. In response to high modernism's denigration of women's work, Cather, Stein, and Larsen deemed themselves exceptional women and sought approval from male arbiters of art and culture, acceding to male standards. Indeed, Frances Kaye argues that Cather was not alone in "scorning 'ordinary' women and seeing them as 'other' and inferior" and in seeing herself as "qualitatively different from other women" (186). Butler mitigates the sting of Kaye's indictment: "if Cather's texts often appear to idealize masculine authorship through a displaced identification, it may be that the displacement of identification is the very condition for the possibility of her fiction" (*Bodies* 148–9). Deborah Carlin similarly acknowledges "Cather's subversive feminism," which she identifies as "elements of female power that function as red herrings" in Cather's works (40). Stein's and Larsen's texts contain powerful female characters as well, though Stein "often emerges as male-identified," a stance which helped her "enter the male world of culture and genius" (Chessman 7). Although Larsen did not divide the artistic world into "geniuses" and "wives"

as Stein did, she identified artistic success with men and considered women
rivals more than friends: "seeking approval from male power-brokers as an exceptional female, she saw herself as being in competition with other women
for finite rewards" (Davis 14). Hence all three writers needed to selectively
emphasize and consciously construct aspects of their identities in order to
achieve their professional and personal aims. It is worth noting, however, that
Cather, at least, never lost track of what she was doing: "the construction of
any identity—sexual, cultural, authorial—requires the forging and sustaining
of numerous illusions. Cather makes us perceive how perilous and fragile this
process is, for those who do not feel they have a cultural identity ready-made,
or are not at home with the one on offer" (Lee, "Bridge" 54).

     Cather, Stein and Larsen were each, in at least one way, outside of the
ready-made identities available to them. As women artists—a lesbian, a Jew,
a woman of color—these writers were fully aware that identity formation and
perpetuation is a continual process. Furthermore, "identity is necessarily unstable," as Dollimore remarks of Freud's great contribution to the understanding of the human psyche (183). Appiah elaborates: "identities . . . grow out of
a history of changing responses to economic, political and cultural forces, almost always in opposition to other identities. . . . They flourish despite . . .
their roots in myths and in lies. . . . There is . . . no large place for reason in
the construction of [identities]" (110). Emphasizing both fluidity and perfor-
mativity, Butler asks: "to what extent is 'identity' a normative ideal rather than
a descriptive feature of experience?" (*Gender* 16). Speaking of a postmodern
theory of identification, Rattansi argues that "terms are permanently in between, caught in the impossibility of fixity and essentialization," and proposes
a view of "*ethnicity* as part of a *cultural politics of representation,* involving
processes of 'self-identification' as well as formation by disciplinary agencies"
(253, 257). Perhaps by necessity as much as precocity, all three writers seem
to have been ahead of their time in terms of offering innovative conceptualizations of identity.

     As writers, Cather, Stein and Larsen used the medium of language to es-
tablish identities and as a means of identification.[18] The idea that language actually constitutes, and not merely expresses, the subject is a key
post-structuralist tenet, and these women certainly demonstrated it in their
texts. Furthermore, Gillian Bottomley comments that "language is obviously
crucial to the process of identity formation. . . . Many of the struggles over ad-
justment in a new society are struggles over language, sometimes for basic understanding, sometimes for recognition" (124–5). Although she speaks mainly
about immigrants who need to learn a new language, her words also apply to
writers who are trying to find an audience and to achieve critical attention.

Benedict Anderson and Horace Kallen similarly emphasize the cohesive quality of language. Anderson notes that "from the start the nation was conceived in language, not in blood" (145), while Kallen states: "of the linkages [that bond people together], the most pervasive and important is, of course, language. Language . . . functions both as a shaper and sustainer of a culture; embodies indeed its traditions regarding the human enterprise in the modes that the group whose language it is images the enterprise and transmits the image from generation to generation" (28). The relationship between language and identity has also been considered a particularly American issue. Thus John Commons proposed in 1920 that American unity derives from having a single dominant language: "this is essential, for it is not physical amalgamation that unites mankind; it is mental community" (20). Nearly seventy-five years later, Ann Massa and Alistair Stead argue that American identity has been historically more dependent on language than the forging of identity for residents of England (4). As American writers, Cather, Stein and Larsen all used language to create, interweave, sustain, and exchange identities.

SURVIVING THE CROSSING

For the women in this study, writing was a crucial strategy for identification and survival.[19] Stein's assessment of the relationship between writing and identity could easily be applied to Cather and Larsen, as well:

> And I was not writing. I began to worry about identity. I had always been I because I had words that had to be written inside me and now any word I had inside could be spoken it did not need to be written. . . . But was I I when I had no written word inside me. It was very bothersome. I sometimes thought I would try but to try is to die and so I did not really try. I was not doing any writing. (*EA* 66)

Reality, as Derrida and others would later argue, is "constructed by our discourse rather than reflected by it" (Eagleton 143–44). Language constitutes experience, and so the absence of language produces an aporia of identity. While not writing could be "very bothersome," the act of writing was a powerful tool: it allowed these women to break free of the discourse that treats identity as singular, consistent, and unchanging, assuming "that partial ancestry may have the power to become totally defining" (Sollors, *Neither* 249). Cather could be both Godfrey St. Peter and Louie Marsellus; Stein could be herself and Alice simultaneously; Larsen could be both Irene Redfield and Clare Kendry. At the same time, the characters they created were always both more and less than the authors themselves.

The creation, re-creation and representation of reality, identity, and experience produce a pattern that is more a cross-hatch than a circle or a line.
In offering fictional representation of possible selves, these writers go over the
same ground repeatedly, but always to a different end. For example, Cather
writes a novel about a successful artist (Thea Kronberg of *Song of the Lark*)
twenty years before she writes about an avatar of herself who fails to become
great and dies young (the eponymous *Lucy Gayheart*). Along similar lines,
Stein's *Q.E.D.*, "Melanctha," and *The Autobiography of Alice B. Toklas* have all
been read as aiming towards resolving the problematic relationship between
Stein and May Bookstaver (Will 220). In their representations of individual
characters and in the shape of their respective oeuvres as well, Cather, Stein
and Larsen employ fluid identity categories. For this reason, the motif of
crossing more accurately reflects how these writers perceived identity than
"being," since the former term connotes adaptability, movement, and the possibility of having to retrace one's steps.[20] Indeed, the title of this study deliberately invokes the rhetoric of specific significant crossings in American
history—from the voyage of the Mayflower to the Middle Passage, from the
western-bound settlers' crossing of the Great Divide to the largely steerage-
rate ship passages taken by European immigrants and the steamer trips which
carried American expatriates back to Europe, to name a few. "Surviving the
crossing" (as opposed to "making the crossing") calls particular attention to
the machinations and compromises required for pilgrims to achieve both
physical and psychological/emotional success on such journeys; it also emphasizes that crossing is an ongoing process as opposed to a single defining
moment. Lee observes that Cather was "always writing about cultural con-
frontations and *crossovers*" ("Bridge" 39; emphasis added), while Paul Gilroy
includes Larsen in his list of "black intellectuals" whose lives "*crisscrossed* the
Atlantic Ocean" (6; emphasis added). Crossing also brings up other issues important to my work, including rebellion/subversion, gender crossing (cross-
dressing, male pseudonyms and narrators, etc.), ethnic hybridity, and crossing
the color line. Dollimore enumerates several other important connotations:
"we might also usefully recall that to cross is not only to traverse, but to mix
(as in cross-breed) and to contradict (as in to cross someone); also that cross-
dressing involves both inversion and displacement of gender binaries" (288).
Cather, Stein and Larsen moved back and forth across continents and oceans,
employing identities fluidly—national, ethnic, and gender; personal and professional—both in their lives and in the worlds they created.

Furthermore, crossing is closely linked to passing, a discourse entrenched
in binaristic, totalitarian models: to pass for something one's *not* implies that
one *is* something else (Ginsberg 3).[21] Although the term "passing" had at one

point referred "to the crossing of any line that divides social groups," by the 1920s it was used mainly "as if it were short for 'passing for white'" (Sollors, *Neither* 247). Recent theorists have contended that "passing" can apply to "class, ethnicity, and sexuality, as well as gender," in addition to race (Ginsberg 3), and it would seem that this was equally true seventy years ago. Indeed, Cather, Stein and Larsen all depicted and lived out different types of passing. Butler makes this connection between Cather's life, texts, and time period: "considering the historical importance of 'crossing' or 'passing' for lesbians at the turn of the century—and Cather's own early penchant for pseudononymous writing—it may be that what we find in Cather is a narrative specification of that social practice, an authorial 'passing' that succeeds only by producing the final indecipherability or irreducibility of the fictional directions that it mobilizes and sustains" (*Bodies* 163). Lauren Berlant offers the term "paper transvestitism" to describe the phenomenon whereby some female writers (like Cather and Larsen) published texts under male pseudonyms ("National" 119). If pseudonymy can be taken as a form of cross-dressing, then the decision to remain closeted might also be taken as an attempt at passing (Edelman 4). From Godfrey St. Peter, who declares that "more than anything else, I like my closets" (Cather, *PH* 34), to "Alice Toklas," who, at the end of her "autobiography," is unveiled as Gertrude Stein, to Clare Kendry, whose "color [is] 'outed'" when her white husband sees her at a Harlem party (Butler, *Bodies* 170), instances of crossing, passing, being closeted, and coming out abound.

   None of the writers under consideration passed for white, and yet all engaged in some form of passing themselves.[22] Recent critics have taken steps towards problematizing and reconstructing the notion of passing. For example, Mary Helen Washington emphasizes the metaphorical quality of passing (163–64), while Marren employs Peter Rabinowitz's distinction between social and rhetorical strategy in racial passing (114–17). Sollors analyzes the moral condemnation our society places on racial passing and begins to make connections between different kinds of passing by noting that racial passing is sometimes accompanied by sexual cross-dressing (*Neither* 247–50). Cross-dressing is one manifestation of gender passing, which, according to Sherri Helvie, can provoke as much murderous rage as racial passing. Instead of seeing passing as basically conservative (i.e. assimilationist, attempting to move from one firmly established category to another), Helvie suggests that passing can be an attempt to transcend categories entirely or at least a representation of slippage between absolutes (39). Cather, Stein and Larsen provide examples of different kinds of passing in both their lives and their creative work. Taking a broad approach to crossing and passing is crucial to understanding the role these concepts play in modernist representations of identity.

PASSING FOR MODERNISM

Perhaps because of the slippery quality of their affiliations, Cather, Stein and Larsen all wrote multivalent and provocative texts that have traditionally been read as coded.[23] The discourse which insists on reading "polysemous" texts (to borrow Lisa Ruddick's term [*Reading* 7]) as coded represents a retreat into the strict binarisms that belie the texts and biographies of the writers under consideration. Julie Abraham has already suggested the tenuousness of viewing works by homosexual authors, or those containing homosexual subtexts, as coded (25). Furthermore, terms such as "passing," "masking," and "coding" assert a hierarchical relationship between different aspects of a character's personality, different layers of meaning, or different levels of textual interpretation. In other words, coded texts are ones that lend themselves to binary readings of surface vs. depth. This model for reading brings with it a set of power relations which subvert the more complex representations across categories that allow for mobile deployments of versions of identity. Instead of using a discourse that opposes surface and depth, it is possible to affirm a cubist play of surfaces, privileging no single meaning above any other.[24] For example, instead of saying that ethnicity is a mask for homosexuality in Cather (Irving, qtd. in Pers 29), we can say that ethnicity and homosexuality are both key concerns of the text; instead of saying that *Passing* is about race, or about gender, or about repression, we can validate the multiplicity of readings the text sustains.

Close readings that avoid binary approaches to identity and authorship facilitate a breaking down of oppositions in literary classifications: realism vs. romance/nostalgia (Cather), experimental vs. money-making writing (Stein) and radical vs. rearguard (Larsen). Indeed, it is unnecessary to have to choose between such terms as pioneer literature, modernism, and Harlem Renaissance in examining these writers and their art. Boundaries between non-fiction, autobiographical writing and fictional, or wholly created writing become more fluid as well. Cather, Stein and Larsen all blur the line in their texts (and in some instances, in their lives) between autobiography and fiction. Genre studies have examined autobiography and moved towards a genderized theory (see, for example, Janice Morgan), but modernist autobiographies constitute their own category. Furthermore, personal experience plays a key role in the work of ethnic writers (Burch 58), and so the rubric of ethnic autobiography also facilitates an understanding of what these writers attempted and achieved.

While the texts under consideration defy literary categories such as fiction/non-fiction and realism/romance, they also resist neat identification as novels. *My Antonia* and *The Autobiography of Alice B. Toklas,* for example, might be more fruitfully conceived of as stories in Walter Benjamin's sense.

Identifying storytelling as a pre-war (i.e., pre-1914) phenomenon, Benjamin credits the storyteller with providing people with "the ability to exchange experiences," emphasizing that stories—even written stories—are interactive and social, whereas novels are predicated on book form and are ultimately bound up with death (83, 87, 101). *My Antonia* and *The Autobiography of Alice B. Toklas* both elide time (and thereby elide death?) in what is perhaps an authorial attempt to reconcile a need for tradition with a recognition of change. It is also problematic to consider Larsen's works as uncomplicated realist novels because her endings are poor, puzzling, or complex by such standards; we either need to apply a different paradigm or accept that Larsen was not a very good writer (cf. Kaplan 159–60).

Narrative form provides a further illustration of how these writers use language to unhinge fixed conceptions of identity. While Stein is known for her narrative experimentalism, Cather and Larsen also use innovative narrative forms despite seeming to be classic and simple. For example, Lilienfeld argues that "Cather . . . craft[s] her own female modernism which encodes women's complicated economic, social, and sexual relations by subverting that most traditional of genres, seemingly realistic American fiction" (52). Suggesting that Cather's work not only subverts but combines genres, John Swift identifies *My Antonia* as "simultaneously bildungsroman and social history" (115). With regard to narrators and narrative style, Carlin points out that Cather manages to present several conflicting viewpoints simultaneously and sympathetically in "Old Mrs. Harris" (101). Like Cather, Larsen manipulates point of view, as Sollors's analysis of "the eroticized gaze" between the two mixed-race protagonists in *Passing* suggests (*Neither* 276). Beth McCoy's reading of *Passing* identifies the narrative form of the novel's second half as a "roman a clef" (78), while Yves Clemmen argues that *Quicksand* possesses a "multidirectional plot" (459) and notes that "instead of a bildungsroman that feeds on experience, we have . . . a narrative that feeds on difference" (460). Clearly all the writers in this study manipulate language, narrative form, and genre in their attempts to represent more fluid conceptualizations of identity.

TRANS-NATIONAL AMERICA REVISITED

My project is, in part, an attempt to take up the challenge implied in Ammons's description of her broad study of late nineteenth- and early twentieth-century women writers as "suggestive, a beginning" (19). I provide closer readings of three of Ammons's subjects, accepting both her contention that these women were not a coherent group and her belief that it is worthwhile to study them together. Thus, although I am not positing that Cather, Stein and Larsen were members of a close-knit community, the preponderance of real-life contacts and mutual friends suggests that they can profitably be examined in light of one another. Tuzyline Jita Allan provides a model by offering a comparative analysis of Larsen and Virginia Woolf, who has been included in studies of Cather and Stein, as well.[25] The existence of a personal relationship between Larsen and Stein is documented in Larsen's praise of "Melanctha" (Larsen, Gallup 216), while Stein's agreement with Carl Van Vechten that the innovative writing coming out of post-war America comes from the Harlem Renaissance suggests that the awareness—if not the influence—went in both directions (Simon 39). Van Vechten provides another important link between the three. Stein's literary agent and Larsen's foremost promoter, Van Vechten also knew (and photographed) Cather. If Walter White, one of Larsen's most outspoken advocates, compared her to Cather on several occasions (Davis 217, 295), it seems logical that Larsen would have read Cather's work, as well as Stein's. Europe provides another commonality of experience. Larsen's interest in Europe was deep and abiding, Stein lived in France for most of her adult life, and Cather visited numerous times and demonstrated a sustained interest in modern European art. Both Stein and Cather have been compared to Cezanne. Further, Cather and Stein were both influenced by William James, and all three writers possessed eclectic knowledge that extended well beyond literature. Stein was well-versed in art, music, and philosophy; Cather had a strong background in art, music, religion, and history; Larsen was familiar with the intricacies of modern science, particularly of physics. Given three voracious and eclectic readers—all of whom were popular during each other's lifetime—we can only conclude that they were aware of each other.

Similarities in biography are marked, as well. Both Cather and Larsen persistently moved forward their date of birth, and both changed their names, wrote under pseudonyms, and claimed questionable heritages; Stein's various "autobiographies" call into continuous question the concept of the authorial self. All three women experienced a long apprenticeship before achieving critical and popular acclaim for their writing—Cather was thirty-nine and forty when she wrote her two "first novels," forty-five when she wrote the one many consider her best (*My Antonia*); Stein was thirty-five at the publication of "Melanctha," fifty-nine before she achieved popular success with *The Autobiography of Alice B. Toklas;* Larsen's first novel was published when she was thirty-seven. As children, all three experienced displacement and maintained a complicated relationship to places. Stein's assessment of East Oakland—"'there is no there there'" (*EA* 298)—echoes Cather's reflections on first moving to Nebraska (spoken through the voice of Jim Burden): "there was nothing but land: not a country at all, but the material out of which countries are made. No, there was nothing but land" (*MA* 7–8). All were influenced by Europeans and their culture, and throughout their lives all evidenced a desire to set themselves apart, continually inventing and reinventing themselves.

In chapter two, the analysis of Cather's use of multiple subject positions as a technique for finding and adequately representing fluid fictional and personal selves concentrates on representations of identity categories such as gender, nationality, and ethnicity in three texts: *My Antonia, The Professor's House,* and "Old Mrs. Harris." *My Antonia,* an early, prototypical pioneer text, provides a means of framing some of the significant issues throughout Cather's career. This novel provides an essential foundation for any study exploring issues of ethnicity, identity and narrative in Cather, and it was also enormously popular, influencing her career track, other writers, and her later work. Next, I focus on *The Professor's House,* a classic text from Cather's middle period (after the world had broken in two but before disillusion and reclusiveness had taken a firm hold). More reflective and philosophical than the stories of heroic pioneers which made Cather famous, this novel uses the medium of ideas and contrasts to address "the hardest human questions" (Skaggs 64), many of which involve issues of identity and identification. Finally, "Old Mrs. Harris" constitutes a return to fictionalized autobiography, female identification, and early roots. Coming near the end of Cather's career, it demonstrates both the consistency of her views over time and her ability to offer new insights into old stories as she reaches a different place in her life.

My third chapter explores how Stein enacted transitivity, the loosening of inherited forms and definitions, and the blurring and blending of boundaries in her writings. In her literary representations of group affiliations, Stein unhinged words from their meanings (see Jackson 248), but she also used her fiction to promote the dispersal of fixed identity—personal identity (her status as woman, lesbian, and Jew), professional identity ("becoming the man that being a genius required her to be" [Pierpont 84] and simultaneously serving as the "grandmother of the modernist movement" [qtd. in Wagner-Martin, *Favored* 154]) and national identity (living out expatriation while espousing American pride). "Melanctha," which came out in 1909 as part of Stein's first published collection (*Three Lives*), provides a baseline for how Stein will employ multiple subject positions across time and categories. In this text, which she considered the dawn of the twentieth century, Stein explores the nature of the self, both in relationships and on its own. In *The Autobiography of Alice B. Toklas,* which came after more than twenty years of immersion in avant-garde experimentalism, Stein returns to narrative, following up the bifurcation she uses in "Melanctha" with projection and identification. Using the voice of Alice, Stein speaks for both her beloved and herself simultaneously in a triumph of communication, a recognition of the limitations of mimesis within so-called non-fictional texts, and a reworking of spiritual autobiography. *Everybody's Autobiography* takes the notion of identification one step further, proposing that Stein's experiences in America qualify as everyone's life story. Whereas Stein's first autobiography was filled with tales of artists, their successes and their scandals, her second autobiography offers much more prosaic details, such as menus and travel schedules. If *The Autobiography of Alice B. Toklas* was about the world of art, *Everybody's Autobiography* tries to integrate art (the spirit) with life (money). Stein's awareness that she will not be able to churn out another *Autobiography of Alice B. Toklas* extends to an acknowledgment of the impossibility of repetition, a prominent theme in both *Everybody's Autobiography* and *The Geographical History of America*. The latter is an abstract philosophical work that nevertheless returns to some early preoccupations. Tracing Stein's literary and philosophical movements through these texts, it is also possible to see the convergence of national identity, sexual orientation, ethnic identity in each. Furthermore, the migrations and crossings which marked Stein's art and life are replicated in her texts as well: Baltimore ("Melanctha"), to Paris (*The Autobiography of Alice B. Toklas*), to America (*Everybody's Autobiography*), and finally, back to France (*The Geographical History of America*).

Chapter four looks at how Larsen, a "woman writer during the male-dominated Harlem Renaissance" (McDowell xii), struggled with issues of gender, as well as race. Thadious Davis observes that "in a field dominated by men, she was a woman who had the courage and the conviction not only to pursue her writing but to bring attention to it as well" (8). Her competitive streak and lack of friendliness with other women echo Stein's position as self-appointed queen of a kingdom of male geniuses (and disdain for women's groups), along with Cather's adoption of male modes (epic, pastoral, etc.) and seemingly misogynistic tendencies (Ammons 127). Arguably Larsen's behavior has its roots in generational conflict, complicated by racial issues. Ammons observes that the subjects of her study "were full members neither of their mothers' world, at the one extreme, nor of that of the privileged white male artist, at the other" (10). Furthermore, like other women and particularly like other women of color, Larsen felt constrained to deny key components of her identity (Ammons 11). Larsen wanted to be considered a novelist—not a black novelist, and certainly not a black woman novelist. She clearly tried to use fiction in the way that many of her contemporaries in Ammons's study did: "to create a public image of themselves as independent, self-directed creators emphatically not bound by historical assumptions based on gender and, for women of color, on race as well" (123). This striving is also peculiarly American, according to Hugo

Munsterberg, who identifies the key aspect of the American character as "yearning . . . after self-direction" (3). *Quicksand* provides an in-depth character study of a mixed-race, mixed-nationality protagonist (much like Larsen), while *Passing* projects the internal bifurcation of *Quicksand's* Helga Crane onto two separate people, examining how identities form in relationships. Taken together, they provide an incisive look at how race, class, geography, and nationality interact in the imposition and adoption of identities.

In my final chapter, I look briefly at how the salient issues continue to play out in today's society. This project addresses the cultural moment at which Willa Cather, Gertrude Stein, and Nella Larsen were conceiving literary explorations of identity in a trans-national context (1909–1937). It complicates binary paradigms of national, ethnic, and gender identities by showing how these writers bring language to bear on the fixity of identity, thereby loosening categorical boundaries and creating a uniquely modernist self. Accepting that Cather, Stein and Larsen all had a lifelong involvement with the culture of Europe and yet retained a sense of American identity, this study asks the timely question (then and now) of how the experience of trans-nationalism facilitates the possibilities for an American subjectivity.

Chapter Two
"The Peculiar Combination of Elements Long Familiar": Willa Cather

"If there is anything unique in American literature, it is perhaps the peculiar combination of elements long familiar" (Munsterberg 458). Hugo Munsterberg made this pronouncement in 1904; Cather independently came to the same conclusion and made it one of her guiding principles in art. Cather did not publish her "first novels" until she was thirty-nine and forty, respectively, and *My Antonia,* the novel she later called "the best thing I've done[, my] . . . contribution to American letters" (qtd. in Bennett 203), did not appear until she was forty-five. In light of her oft-quoted pronouncement that an author's most important material is gathered before the age of fifteen (Woodress, *Literary* 40), we can conclude that Cather's material had (and required) plenty of time to incubate before emerging in mature art.[1] In addition to working with stories and experiences gleaned from her early days, Cather combined and recombined these components in distinctive and experimental ways. She both practiced and preached fidelity to using traditional materials as the basis for modern literature. In her essay on Thomas Mann, Cather expresses disdain for the "reckless improviser," arguing instead that "what we most love is not bizarre invention, but to have the old story brought home to us closer than ever before, enriched by all that the right man could draw from it and, by sympathetic insight, put into it" (*NUF* 119). Cather's own work consists largely of the reworking of "the old story," and each new configuration thereof brings a different angle to light.

Cather includes autobiographical elements—her old story—in most of her fiction, and provides an example of what Morgan observes of twentieth-century women writers who wrote autobiographical fiction, namely that they "retain a sense of the self as plural . . . [and of] roles/identities as multiple" (8). In the process of trying to make sense of herself and her experiences through

her art, Cather continually re-envisions herself, often putting seemingly mutually exclusive terms into simultaneous play. She is both Jim Burden, who
moved from Virginia to Nebraska as a child, and Antonia, who wears men's
clothing; she is both Thea Kronborg, the successful artist, and Lucy Gayheart,
the mediocre one who fails; she is both Godfrey St. Peter, the professional historian, and Lesley Ferguesson, the underage schoolteacher. Like the subjects
of Gambrell's study of women modernist insider/outsiders, Cather "refused
ever to let a subject go" (184). Continually re-envisioning herself throughout
her career, Cather showed an attitude towards identity which can only be described as modern. Her characters are multi-faceted and complex, and we
never see a case in which "partial ancestry . . . [has] the power to become totally defining" (Sollors, *Neither* 249). Many of them, like their creator, have
cosmopolitan aspects. In exploring and evaluating cosmopolitanism in
Cather, I find it useful to think of the term's adjectival and noun forms separately. For example, we can say that someone has a cosmopolitan outlook
without arguing that he or she is a cosmopolitan. This distinction is important in part because of a tendency to conflate the cosmopolite with metropolitan man.[2] Certainly the "crucible of the [early twentieth-century]
metropolis" (R. Williams 46), to which many immigrants and intellectuals
alike were drawn, played a key role in the emergence of a modernist sensibility. Even while discussing the importance of the metropolis, however,
Williams warns of "the metropolitan interpretation of its own processes as
universals . . . not only in history but as it were above and beyond it" (R.
Williams 47). Cather provides a good illustration of the need for such skepti-
cism. In spite of a lifetime spent crossing the country and the Atlantic and
years with a New York City address, she retained "her sense of being a
Nebraskan rather than a New Yorker" (Lindemann, "Fear" 30). Further,
Cather's cosmopolitanism does not translate to the political liberalism which
Michael Novak seems to assume in his contention that "the true liberal spirit
is *cosmopolitan* rather than *universalist*. The connotations of these two words
suggest the difference between a liberalism that expects, and desires, a certain
homogenization and a liberalism that expects, and delights in, variety.
Cosmopolitan liberalism is surely closer to the heart of the authentic liberal
spirit" (39). Novak sees "cosmopolitan liberalism" as a single term, but Cather
would not fit so neatly into such a paradigm. Cather disdained assimilationist calls for immigrants to forget their native tongues and traditions, and yet
while she has been connected with cosmopolitanism by many sources, she
is never considered a liberal. Thus, Nelson sees Cather as "a woman artist
with a cosmopolitan outlook" but concludes that her status is fundamentally "ambiguous" (21), while Carlin characterizes her as "a cosmopolitan

Midwesterner [and] a conservative Republican" (6) in the same breath. Cather's representations of cosmopolitan characters show a similarly complicated and fluid positionality.

It is difficult to fit Cather into neat social or political categories in part because her sense of herself changed throughout her lifetime. Cather's many fictional cosmopolitan avatars are indicative of the fact that her pronounced revisionist streak had both creative and ambivalent facets, extending from textual representations of herself to basic attitudes towards her life, letters and legacy. She extensively revised her collections and works before they underwent subsequent publications, actually seeming to harbor real regret for works and passages she later came to be ashamed of. In fact, the phrase that recurs most often in E.K. Brown's passages describing Cather's assessments of her work is "in later years" (*Critical Biography* 145, 160, 189). This phrase usually introduces a change of positions and a wish that things had been otherwise. "Later" is, of course, opposed to "earlier," suggesting a binary view of Cather's life. Her own comment that "the world broke in two in 1922 or thereabout" (*NUF* v) is a binarism that has led scholars to discuss her novels within a distinct two-phase paradigm. Morton Zabel considers Cather's statement both preposterous and conceited: "the space of seventy years is too short in human history, even in modern history, to permit anyone to claim that he saw the world break in two during it" (226). Taking a less literal approach, Merrill Skaggs characterizes Cather as a writer who "formulated her ideas through oppositions" and explains that 1922 "became Cather's personal symbol for a time of disruption, discontinuity, fragmentation, and loss" (183–84). While the phase theory is useful for the purposes of literary criticism (and some excellent work has been done on the differences between early and late Cather texts), it does not adequately account for the complexities and the ambiguities inherent in Cather's individual texts. The phase theory also overlooks the fact that many themes and methods recur throughout her oeuvre, independent of period.[3] Willa Cather was a perfectionist who never rested on her laurels or claimed to have found ultimate answers, and so her works tend to defy categories rather than to fall into neat groupings.

Cather's penchant for revision might well have been related to her equally salient desire to keep the upper hand in all relations between herself and the world. In both her work and her personal relations, Cather seemed almost "neurotically controlling and self-conscious" (Skaggs 187). She cared deeply about the kind of print selected for each of her novels, and one of the reasons that she wanted Knopf to publish her works was her dissatisfaction with the drab bindings provided by Houghton Mifflin (E. Lewis 108–112). Following a disastrous screen rendition of *A Lost Lady,* Cather denied

Hollywood further right to adapt her works. Wanting to keep her personal life equally under wraps, even after her death, Cather burned most of her correspondence and forbade verbatim quotation from any of her remaining letters. In light of this history of care and control, it is not surprising that possession is a key theme in her novels and stories. While Cather became more reclusive and less giving of herself in many ways as she aged,[4] her texts move towards a gradual acknowledgment of the ultimate impossibility and undesirability of complete possession. Certainly Cather had to come to terms with relinquishment—through marriage (Isabel McClung's 1916 marriage to Jan Hambourg) and through death (her father in 1928, her mother in 1931, her brother Douglass and McClung in 1938, her brother Roscoe in 1944). It is equally viable to read Cather's evolving attitude toward possession as an expansion in definitional possibilities.

Like so many terms important in Cather, possession has multiple meanings, including ownership, domination, self-control, and the psychological state of having one's personality replaced by another. These terms encompass a full range of valences, and Cather manipulates them in sometimes surprising ways. In *My Antonia,* for example, the self-possessed businesswoman (in the figure of Lena Lingard, Lincoln dressmaker) appeals to Jim. Middle-aged Tiny, on the other hand, receives a harsh judgment and an unflattering portrayal from Jim for many of the same qualities. Along similar lines, Jim considers it a terrible waste for Antonia to join the rest of her family in deferring to her older brother ("Antonia often quoted his opinions to me, and she let me see that she admired him" [82]), but the prospect of losing one's personal identity and being absorbed into a larger unit has its place in his universe as well: "that is happiness; to be dissolved into something complete and great" (14). In the latter case, the narrative voice of a retrospective Jim, or perhaps even an authorial intrusion, declares the ultimate desirability of an erasure of personality.

Historically and theoretically, the concept of possession interacts with representations of ethnicity and gender in complex ways; it also plays an important role in rootedness, a key concern of (im)migrants. Social scientists, African-American scholars, feminists, and queer theorists alike have understood that possession has ramifications for identity and have taken up this question of how to formulate the relationship, participating in an ongoing debate about whether identity categories such as ethnicity, race, gender and sexual orientation represent something that a person *has* or what a person *is.* Roughly speaking, the *has* perspective generally falls along social constructivist lines, while the *is* view represents a more essentialist approach. Bottomley argues for the advisability of adopting a constructivist view of ethnicity as "'a consciousness of kind,' . . . constructed and reconstituted in relation to specific political and economic circumstances" (57). David Salvaterra agrees that "ethnicity is now understood to be a multifaceted, dynamic phenomenon. It emerges under certain circumstances and recedes or virtually disappears under others" (39). And yet when we speak of identity, most of us would concur with Gleason's baseline assertion that "identity is what a thing is" (*Speaking* 124). Novak sees both the constructivist and the essentialist side of the coin: on the one hand, "each of us is responsible for creating his or her own identity" (54), but "each person is also influenced by social factors over which he or she has had no control. . . . We do not choose (entirely) how others will regard us or what, even despite our best intentions, they may ascribe to us" (41). Sollors sees this tension between chosen and imposed identities as crucial to the American experience. His study "takes the conflict between contractual and hereditary, self-made and ancestral, definitions of American identity—between *consent* and *descent*—as the central drama in American culture" (*Beyond* 5–6).

Applying the terms of this debate to specific groups, other scholars have shown how different American sub-populations have tried to deal with the concept of identity. Writing of Asian-American experiences, Lisa Lowe calls attention to the potential fluidity of identity, and she suggests that "rather than considering . . . ['ethnic] identity' as a fixed, established 'given,' perhaps we can consider instead . . . ['ethnic] cultural practices' that produce identity" (64). Similarly, Appiah, a multi-racial person "who grew up in both Ghana and Britain and who now lives in the United States" (Nicholson and Seidman 14), argues that "identities are complex and multiple and grow out of a history of changing responses to economic, political and cultural forces, almost always in opposition to other identities" (110). In the realm of gender theory, Butler urges us to think of gender as performative (*Gender* 25) and to consider how identity might be prescriptive rather than descriptive (16). Taking the "ultimate unknowability of sexuality" (xv) as axiomatic, Edelman opposes his work to earlier gay and lesbian studies, which looked for qualitative "'homosexual difference'" rather than seeing variations as relative and fluctuating, depending on context (3). These writers agree in their desire to suspend essentializing concepts of identity, and yet they all recognize that the notion of identity is not one that we cannot discard entirely. Thus we see that the attempt to pinpoint how identity devolves or is attributed has not yielded any conclusive information. Furthermore the polarization of essentialism and anti-essentialism has become value laden in a way that might not be useful or even accurate, as Fuss has pointed out: "in and of itself, essentialism is neither good nor bad, progressive nor reactionary, beneficial nor dangerous" (xi). For this reason, I would like to displace the constructivist/essentialist debate by refiguring these categories in terms of possessing identity (having identity) versus being possessed by identity (being identified). Such a displacement is particularly useful for examinations of Cather because she herself takes a both/and approach to almost every binary she encounters or portrays. Rather than coming down on one side or the other of the constructivist/essentialist debate, Cather puts the terms in motion and lets them land where they will.

PRECIOUS BUT INCOMMUNICABLE: *MY ANTONIA*

The motif of possession provides a useful approach to the larger issues of identity in *My Antonia*. In this text, the weight of possession or ownership falls with the preface, when Jim affixes the possessive "my" to the manuscript he has brought. Butler points out that Lawyer Jim's act of bringing Antonia's story in legal cover gives him "the weight of legitimation" (*Bodies* 148). Rather than seeing Jim's "my" as a mark of possession, however, Harold Bloom contends that "we say 'my' precisely where we have lost what we could never hope to have possessed, so that 'my' in such a context is a metaphor or fiction, a verbal figure substituting for a desired but unlikely possession" (1). Viewing Jim more in the vein of a Niel Herbert peephole as opposed to the Cather stand-in Bloom posits, Susan Rosowski observes that Jim "writes possessively about *his* Antonia as the archetypal woman who provides an anchorage for his travels and a muse for his imagination. . . . [H]owever, Cather contradicts these assumptions by creating a woman who works out her individual destiny in defiance of her narrator's expectations" (88). In context, Jim's addition of "my" to the title of his manuscript has multiple meanings. On the one hand, Jim's act could be seen as a patriarchal attempt at ownership; by the same token, "my" could be an acknowledgment that this version is only one of many possible ones. Since Mr. Shimerda's "te-e-ach, te-e-ach my An-tonia" (20) stays with Jim for years afterwards, he could be honoring the older man's memory by using his term, or he could be trying to put himself in a paternal relation to Antonia (who is actually four years his senior). Finally, Jim could be applying "teach my Antonia" not as "give lessons to my daughter, Antonia," but rather as "tell other people about the Antonia I know and love."[5] At any rate, the Cather/author figure makes no interpretation, noting only that the addition "seemed to satisfy" Jim (2).

The text thus paves the way for a hands-off approach to Jim's material. Indeed, by the end of the text we hardly recall that the Cather/author figure ever made an appearance. When the introduction concludes and the novel begins a second time (with the first actual body chapter), we are taken back to Jim's boyhood. The first section of *My Antonia*, "The Shimerdas," relates the (im)migration experiences of Jim Burden and his Bohemian neighbors. Set in the country during Jim's and Antonia's childhood, this section could well have been called "The Wild Land" along with the first book of *O Pioneers!*. In Cather's earlier novel, however, Alexandra Bergson considers the land her benefactress and retains a sense of herself as custodian of the land rather than landowner. She "belong[s] to the land" (229) and looks across her productive acres only to affirm that "the land belongs to the future" (229). Conversely, *My Antonia* offers talk of "your country" and "my country," the "Old Country" and "my old country." Physical land and abstract nation alike are staked and claimed, and possession is continually foregrounded—Lena Lingard's insistent, "I can't order [Ole Benson] off. It ain't my prairie" (109), not withstanding. The Shimerdas, for example, face real poverty and difficulties, but they own their land and recognize that working it will bring them what they want. The entire family participates in the farm work (even the developmentally disabled brother, Marek), and Antonia and Ambrosch compete over who can break more sod each day. Although the Burdens are of a higher socio-economic class than their European neighbors, they also seem to recognize the importance of possessing land. When Grandfather Burden decides to move the family to Black Hawk, he chooses to retain ownership of the old homestead, renting it to the Widow Steavens and her brother. While Rosowski sees the setting of Book I as "a pastoral, Edenic world" in which "nature ministers to the child" (77, 81), the land requires human attention to have meaning. Riding out to his grandfather's farm on that first night, Jim remarks, "there seemed to be nothing to see; no fences, no creeks or tree, no hills or fields. . . . There was nothing but land: not a country at all, but the material out of which countries are made" (7). The settlers possess the land by making it into a country—planting fields, building roads, watering trees. By the same process, they become a part of the country they create.

In the second section, the eponymous hired girls play out the sociological transition from an agricultural system to a money-exchange economy. Antonia, Lena, Tiny, the three Bohemian Marys, and the Danish laundry girls sell their labor (and sometimes their love) for the money that will help their parents and their younger siblings to get ahead. These young women are not mere cogs in a great mechanical wheel because their individuality is honored, or at least recognized, but they have certainly left behind the direct and tangible relationship between work and product. The Harling family essentially embraces Antonia, while Tiny enjoys the social perks of working at the hotel and Lena is apprenticed to learn a valuable skill. Nevertheless, the mobility provided by town life (Antonia can leave and find another job when Mr. Harling's rules become too constraining) suggests that possession has been modified to mean ownership of one's labor alone as opposed to the more concrete ownership of land and farm implements, the means of production.

Antonia has nothing to rely on for sustenance except the services she can render. She "take[s] her good times when she can" (133), dancing, wearing pretty clothes, and dating whom she pleases, but Cather seems to suggest that Antonia did better as "a ward of the Harlings than as one of the 'hired girls'" (131). As a hired girl, Antonia becomes "'the Harlings' Tony' . . . [like] 'the Marshalls' Anna' or 'the Gardeners' Tiny'" (131). As much as she possesses freedom, Antonia is also owned. Antonia's eventual return to relative poverty as a land-owner suggests that Cather believes advancement should not necessarily be evaluated in terms of income alone.

The tension between freedom and compromise plays a major role in Book II. While the first section chronicles Jim's and Antonia's experience of the country itself and the Shimerdas's fight to tame "The Wild Land," the second section might analogously be considered Black Hawk's attempt to domesticate "The Wild Girls." The young women who come to town from their various European enclaves in the country have a "freedom of movement" (127) and a freedom from inhibition which the town-dwellers find distasteful and even potentially threatening. While "the daughters of Black Hawk merchants had a confident, unenquiring belief that they were 'refined,' and that the country girls, who 'worked out,' were not" (128), their elders tended to view the hired girls with less equanimity. As John Murphy points out, the hired girls represent a threat "to the social order maintained by Pennsylvanians, Virginians, and other established settlers" (Bloom 50). These young women serve the families they "belong" to, and they are also seemingly for hire. Cather was aware of this double entendre and refused to clarify it, perhaps because she found both connotations viable.[6] At any rate, the girls' wildness is in some ways contained by the men who harness or otherwise take advantage of it. Wick Cutter, for example, demands sexual favors of at least two of the Swedish girls he employs and then serves as a pimp: "one of them he had taken to Omaha and established in the business for which he had fitted her. He still visited her" (135). While they are not treated like prostitutes, the "scandalous" (130) three Bohemian Marys run into trouble as well, having to "retire from the world for a short time" (130) every so often, and yet they never lack for a job. They "were considered as dangerous as high explosives to have about the kitchen, yet they were such good cooks and such admirable housekeepers that they never had to look for a place" (130). These women have skills and a vitality which are always in demand. Even the seemingly asexual Jim reacts to the sexual energy of the hired girls, having a recurrent dream of being possessed by Lena, a pronounced instance of gender inversion. In this dream, Jim imagines that Lena meets him in a harvest field and "with a soft sigh . . . [says], 'Now they are all gone, and I can kiss you as much as I like'" (144). Jim kisses Lena and has tried unsuccessfully to kiss Antonia; he accepts her rebuff good-naturedly. He wishes that Antonia would want to possess him, but he never has "this flattering dream about Antonia" (144).

Jim's fantasies about Antonia are seemingly suspended in Book III, in which the other hired girls are gone and Lena can kiss Jim all she likes. Most notably, Antonia has no place in Jim's college life in Lincoln, and it is Lena Lingard who gives the section its name. Further, the transition from town to city represents a yet another remove from the secure sense of place that marked Jim's childhood days in "nature's womb" (Rosowski 77). Cather's caricature of boarding house life shows the discomfort and lack of privacy inherent in such situations. Jim's rooms are small, cold, and "inconveniently situated for students" (166), while Lena is continuously interrupted by her landlord and her neighbor offering their assistance. As three men (Jim, the college student; Ordinsky, the Polish violin teacher; and Colonel Raleigh, Lena's transported Southern landlord) vie for the right to offer paternal and chivalric protection to Lena, it becomes increasingly clear that this independent businesswoman is the most self-possessed of the group. In spite of her mock courtship with Jim, Lena already knows that she will not marry. She expresses surprise at Jim's naiveté, exclaiming, "Why, I'm not going to marry anybody. Didn't you know that?" (186). Jim's platitudes about future loneliness do not swerve Lena's steadfastness: "You can't tell me anything about family life. I've had plenty to last me. . . . It's all being under somebody's thumb" (187). Lena does eventually form some semblance of a family life, but it is one based on independence and equality. When Lena agrees to move to San Francisco with Tiny Soderball, she does so as a self-sufficient professional. For his part, Jim's heart belongs to Virgil and his representative on earth, Gaston Cleric. When Cleric and Harvard beckon, Jim gives up his flirtation for academic immersion. Jim's years at Harvard are not eventful in retrospect, and he leaves them out of his narrative entirely. Jim picks up his story again two years later, when he returns to Black Hawk for the summer vacation before law school and learns what Antonia has been doing. At this point, the novel takes a step back to tell "The Pioneer Woman's Story," Book IV. Antonia's story is narrated even less directly than Jim's reminiscences in the first two books, as it is the Widow Steavens who tells the story of Antonia's seduction and abandonment. Antonia has learned the hard way that she cannot hold a dishonest man simply by being a good housekeeper. After giving birth to Larry Donovan's child, she nearly loses her maternal rights as well as her fiancé, but for the Widow Steavens's timely intercession with Ambrosch, who wanted "'it put out in the rain-barrel'" (204). Importantly, "poor" (201)

Antonia refuses to become the lost lady that Jim and the Widow Steavens try
to construct her as.[7] It is true enough that Antonia is meek with the townspeople, who therefore extend pity in place of condemnation: "folks respected
her industry and tried to treat her as if nothing had happened. . . . She was
so crushed and quiet that nobody seemed to want to humble her" (202). But
although she is disappointed and ashamed, Antonia needs neither sympathy
nor hand-outs. She continues with her masculine farm work, wearing "a
man's long overcoat and boots, and a man's felt hat with a wide brim" (203)
and herding cattle right up until the time she gives birth. Antonia has returned to her family in shame and presumably to become "Ambrosch's
drudge" (191), yet she does not become the proverbial doormat. She treasures her child and indulges in all of the rites of pride of first-time mother-
hood, as the Widow Steavens tells Jim: "she loved [her baby] from the first
as dearly as if she'd had a ring on her finger, and was never ashamed of it . .
. no baby was ever better cared-for" (204). As long as the farm remains in the
family, Antonia will not be rootless or without a place, and it is the country
that gives Antonia a sense of herself: "I'd always be miserable in a city. I'd die
of lonesomeness. I like to be where I know every stack and tree, and where
all the ground is friendly" (206).

In Book V, Jim returns to the Shimerda farm twenty years later to find
a "battered but not diminished" Antonia (214). Once again, issues of ownership play a prominent role in Jim's conceptualization of his childhood friend.
Mrs. Cuzak (significantly not Jim's Antonia) lives what Tiny considers a miserable life but one that Lena concedes suits her. At any rate, Antonia's current
lifestyle is far removed from Jim's experience, cosmopolitan though it has
been. And yet as Mrs. Cuzak, Antonia has the legal legitimation that arguably
places her on the same plane as Lawyer Jim. Although she lives in relative
poverty, we see her as immeasurably richer than Jim, who has pursued a re-
munerative career and married an heiress. Surrounded by her children and her
productive fields—"big and little, tow heads and gold heads and brown, and
flashing little naked legs; a veritable explosion of life" (218)—Antonia has
clearly "dissolved into something complete and great" (14). Jim, on the other
hand, has only his memories and his plans, a past and a future vitiated by the
complete absence of a viable present.

Perhaps part of Jim's failure derives from the fact that by the end of the
novel he has no place he can call home. Whereas Antonia and her husband
own their homestead, a crucial aspect of the American Dream, Jim lives in a
rented apartment in New York City. Arguably he has nothing to hold onto except the past as epitomized by his (version of) Antonia. Further, Jim spends
most of his time traveling back and forth across the country. Although he

travels on important and respectable business, the frequency of his trips suggests not progress but circularity. While circularity can create the beautiful closure of seeing Antonia again, "the sense of coming home to [oneself], and of having found out what a little circle man's experience is" (238), it also suggests the kind of meaningless motion of the "successful" Sister Carrie in her rocking chair.[8] Through repetition, Jim's later trips become almost a parody of his first momentous train journey across the country. Whereas on that first trip he and Jake were innocents abroad, "becoming more sticky and grimy with each stage of the journey . . . [, buying] everything the newsboys offered" (5), the mature Jim has become a jaded cosmopolitan. Sitting in the isolated comfort of his own stateroom, Jim tries to "amuse" (2) himself by remembering his childhood with Antonia. It is important that Jim maintains his sense of identification with the west, "lov[ing] with a personal passion the great country through which his railway runs and branches" (2), but his capacity for rootedness is limited by changes (he recognizes no one in Black Hawk) and fear (he avoids Antonia for years to shield himself from the sight of diminishment). Still, in spite of having experienced "disappointments," he retains the "romantic disposition" (2) that characterized him as a child and seems to us to have remained a Nebraska boy at heart. In any case, Jim clings to his identity as a country boy and as Antonia's friend. The final image Jim offers in his narrative is one of possession, a shared stake in "the precious, the incommunicable past" (238).

This ending is curious in part because Cather denies her novel a symmetrical frame. Instead of calling attention to the fact that this is Jim's memoir by having a return to the "author" and Jim in New York, Cather leaves Jim's words as the novel's final ones. His words raise questions about the ramifications of telling a story that ultimately derives its force from the incommunicable. Is *My Antonia*, like Toni Morrison's *Beloved*, "not a story to pass on" (Morrison 274)? If it is not meant to be passed on, why tell it? If it is meant to be passed on, to whom? Jim has no children and Antonia's children live the story—they do not need to read about it. The "author" of the introduction accepts Jim's manuscript with interest but has her own memories; her conspicuous absence from the ending suggests that the story was not told for her benefit either. Further, the last line, "whatever we had missed, we possessed together the precious, the incommunicable past" (238), does not pose the expected binary pair: it should read, "whatever we had *lost,* we possessed together the precious, the incommunicable past." Cather chooses every word with care, particularly the words which comprise her beginnings and endings, and so the diction here—"whatever we had missed"—demands interrogation. "Missed" could be interpreted in the sense of "missed out on" together, and yet there is no feeling that the many things that Antonia and Jim were not (siblings, sweethearts, parent and child, etc.) were ever really attainable. Here Bloom's contention that the "my" in the preface is not really about actual possession could be useful. Indeed I might extrapolate from his analysis by proposing that we say *missed* "where we have lost what we could never hope to have possessed" (Bloom 1). In this light, Cather's ending would seem to suggest that the winning vs. losing (or having/possessing vs. losing/relinquishing) paradigm is not the appropriate one here. Given that Cather's writing seems to indicate that complete possession is neither possible nor desirable, this unexpected pairing successfully displaces the win/lose (or have/lose) binarism to affirm the impossibility of resolving the ownership issue. So we see that the framework of possession, while related intricately to identity, does not produce an uncomplicated reading of *My Antonia*. The subject matter and form of *My Antonia* also raise several important questions about the relationship between Cather's sense of herself and the characters she portrays, many of which have already been addressed by critics (Rosowski 76). First of all, why is Cather, who comes from old Virginian stock, writing about European immigrants? Pers offers several hypotheses: those were her childhood friends, and she is merely writing out of her own experience; Cather wanted to be a European so she writes about them as the next best thing; Cather is really writing about herself as a migrant (or a lesbian) and using European immigrants as a mask (29). Given that Cather is going to write a story in which European immigrants play a central role, why does Cather introduce Jim? (Why the preface? Why the 1926 revisions of the preface? Why is Jim male? Is this Jim's story, Antonia's story, or Jim's story about Antonia?) Finally, what does Cather want us to take from the story? Is this a circular exercise in nostalgia or does it have some transcendent and lasting meaning? Any attempt to answer this array of questions must accept what seem to be contradictions in Cather's work. Sharon O'Brien's observation that "at times Jim is Cather's mask and spokesman, whereas at others she is ironically detached from him" (Bloom 53) hints that Cather will not allow any character who shares so many biographical details with her own younger self to be a simple or straightforward one. Along similar lines, Cather's espoused goal in writing the novel was to present a single object from multiple views (Sergeant 13), a strategy that recurs in later works. Thus from the beginning, Cather intended to utilize a unitary subject that is fragmented into a multiplicity of faces or aspects. Images of doubleness permeate the text, but instead of reinforcing a world that is completely black and white, they paradoxically facilitate the representation of gradations, loosening up the categories the text ostensibly poses. Gender roles, for example, are continually inverted and blended, as Helvie has observed:

"Antonia's identity, like Cather's, is not explainable in terms of our traditional categories of 'masculine' and 'feminine,' 'male' and 'female'; our binary categories begin to collapse" (36). Antonia has manly aspects, while Jim has effeminate ones, but other characters also participate in this gender-crossing. Russian Peter, for instance, keeps a house that is unusually "comfortable for two men who were 'batching'" (25). When Antonia and Jim first come to visit, Peter takes a break from doing laundry to show them his cow, of which he "was very fond" (25). Peter particularly likes having the cow because the milk is good for Pavel, "his companion" (24).[9] While Peter and Pavel are described in terms that might well refer to a gay couple, Otto Fuchs displays a different form of gender complexity or deviance. "[O]ne of those drifting, case-hardened labourers who never marry or have children of their own," Otto invariably treats Jim with gentleness. "[H]e was so fond of children!" (55), Jim observes. Along with nurturing men, the novel presents independent women like Frances Harling who would talk with her father "about grain-cars and cattle, like two men" (97); Tiny Soderball similarly becomes a shrewd manager in the economic world. Cather herself showed enough androgynous traits for critics to surmise that she puts parts of herself into both Jim and Antonia. Patrick Shaw, for example, argues that "in the Jim-Antonia juxtaposition we see the twin selves that were suppressed within Cather" ("*MA:* Emergence" 127), while Clara Cooper adds to the picture by identifying Jim and Antonia as "a woman-in-man narrator" and a "man-in-woman heroine" (32), respectively. Taken as two parts of Willa Cather—or at least as two parts of a larger unit—Antonia and Jim also fulfill the roles of both types of storytellers delineated by Benjamin, namely the man "who has come from afar . . . [and] the man who has stayed at home, making an honest living, and who knows the local tales and traditions" (84). Evelyn Hively makes a similar observation, but without relating it to Benjamin, as she notes, "the woman remains rooted in her country, while the man travels; the woman is content with things of the earth, while the man seeks intellectual activity; the woman finds spiritual fulfillment, while the man fails spiritually" (73). In her binary conceptualization, however, Hively neglects to take into account that Antonia too has "come from afar." She knows both the local Nebraskan tales and the local Bohemian tales, and she maintains traditions from both places. Antonia keeps one foot in the Old World, remembering it in all its details and keeping these memories alive for the next generation; her children will not even learn English until they go to school, and she will come to forget much of what Jim taught her. For his part, Jim has remained connected to his Nebraskan home—his heart "remains rooted in [his] country," and he tries to sustain his connection to "things of the earth" by planning a hunting trip with Antonia's older

boys. Even in middle age, Jim is romantic and idealistic, and he seems successful in convincing himself, at least, that "the precious, the incommunicable
past" (238) serves as a well from which he can draw spiritual strength.

Cather's use of Jim and Antonia as essentially co-protagonists signals a
broader attempt on her part to move beyond the classic realist novel. Another
formal strategy that Cather employs towards this end is the use of an un-story,
what she herself called "the other side of the rug" (*IP* 77), punctuated with
numerous side-stories. "Un-story" is not meant to suggest encoding (subtext)
or subversion (anti-story), but rather a departure from expectations about
what a novel should include. Mildred Bennett explains some anomalies in
Cather's style by noting that "her method of writing was to suspend the immediate thread of a narrative and insert a colorful, if unrelated, tale of the
past. Critics have said that she used this device to give her stories depth, but
it is more likely that she wrote her material in the way in which she had acquired it [i.e. through oral storytelling]" (109). Certainly for Cather the stories heard in rural Nebraskan kitchens "tease[d] the mind over and over again
for years," but they underwent conscious and meticulous transformations before they got "put down rightly on paper" in Cather's mature work (*NUF* 76).
Therefore I would contend that Cather is trying to replicate neither the oral
tales passed down to her nor the traditional realistic novel. Rather she is using
narrative to accomplish something qualitatively different. Indeed, Brown
states that Cather "always showed impatience at the complaint that *My
Antonia* is not precisely a novel. Why should it be?" (*Critical Biography* 199).
If we want to accept Cather's defensive stance that *My Antonia* was not intended to be a novel, we might classify it as a story. This is certainly what
Brown seems to be suggesting when he continues: "in this book she was gath-
ering her memories of some persons and places very dear to her, and as she
was a writer of stories, the memories had taken a narrative form" (*Critical
Biography* 199). Brown uses the term "story" loosely to denote narrative, but
Benjamin offers a more specific definition and one which can usefully be applied to Cather's techniques and goals in *My Antonia*. Hannah Arendt suggests that in Benjamin's conceptualization, "insofar as the past has been
transmitted as tradition, it possesses authority; insofar as authority presents itself historically, it becomes tradition" (38). Memory, a key motif in *My
Antonia,* is also central to identity. Jim faithfully records everything that
Antonia's name recalls to him, and Antonia passes on the tales of their child-
ish exploits to her own children. If Jim's narrative and Cather's novel share
some characteristics with the traditional story (as Benjamin conceptualizes it),
they are a far cry from the realistic novels many of Cather's contemporaries
were writing. By dispensing with some of the conventions of realism (such as

linear organization, meticulous recitation of detail, and a story with a well-developed plot), Cather signals that her goal is not mimesis. Rather, Cather and Jim repeatedly excuse *My Antonia* for its lack of story-ness, reminding us that it has not been organized properly and that nothing much really happens, in order to direct our attention beyond the paradigm of the classic realist novel.

Cather's decision to show "the pattern that is supposed not to count in a story" (*IP* 77) links her to other modernists who employed palimpsest, including H.D., Gertrude Stein, and Nella Larsen. As Shari Benstock explains, "the palimpsest simultaneously documents and destroys its own history, preserving earlier forms in the remnants of imperfectly erased portions of its continuous text while 'writing over'—rewriting—the earlier record. . . . Indeed, a palimpsest possesses no single, identifiable source but rather raises various, often conflicting—images that present themselves as origins of the meanings the text provides" (350).[10] In *My Antonia* "there is no love affair, no courtship, no marriage, no broken heart, no struggle for success" (*IP* 77). Rather, Cather presents us with "a series of dramatic or elegiac episodes" (Grumbach xxiv), which lend themselves to multiple interpretations. Further, Benstock's observations on women's uses of the palimpsest suggest that the emphasis of recent Cather scholarship on coding may be misplaced: "the creation of a palimpsest that would counter predominant male myths is not produced by 'encod[ing] revisions of male myths' [Gubar 197]. Rather the palimpsest exposes through the layers of its compositions the feminine countersign of the male myth *already present* in the culture" (350). In this light we can argue that the other side of the rug is not necessarily a code; we do not need to see Jim as merely as mask for a lesbian author or as a peephole through which to show another character.[11] In writing *My Antonia,* Cather certainly uses male forms like the epic and the pastoral, but she adapts and appropriates these forms to tell stories which would not have been considered suitable subjects for these classical forms by their earlier practitioners.

Another important appropriation Cather performs is a re-writing of the ethnic novel. Although Cather, like Jim, carries the legitimating force of white Anglo-Saxon Protestant upbringing, we might remember that WASP is an ethnicity (Sollors, *Beyond* 25), as is, Cather might argue "southern." (This possibility will be explored further in the section about "Old Mrs. Harris.") Indeed, Betty Ann Burch includes *My Antonia* in her study of women's ethnic novels, although she notes that Cather's text is an anomaly. While most immigrant literature is told by the ethnic writer through the immigrant's viewpoint, *My Antonia* "portrays the vitality of Antonia through the eyes of Jim, a boy of colonial Virginian ancestry" (60). Regardless of his place of origin, Jim has many of the characteristics of the typical ethnic hero, who "carries the burden of identity: what does it mean to be an American? Am I an American? Where do I fit in American society?" (Burch 56). Jim's closest friends and associates are immigrants and he is himself a migrant from an "old country" (54) to a "new world" (5).[12] Thomas Ferraro also offers a definition of ethnic group that would include Jim Burden, arguing that such "include[s] not only socially marginal peoples but any group that uses symbols of common descent and tradition to create or maintain power" (21). In this light, Jim's legal-bound manuscript, his "incommunicable past," can be read as a manipulation of common experience for power. Gleason finds further substantiation for the immigrant/migrant comparison in the work of early twentieth century anthropologists: "For Mead and Gorer, then, the 'ethnic'—that is, the immigrant or person of immigrant derivation—is a prototypically American figure, *not* because of any distinctiveness of cultural heritage but for exactly the opposite reason, namely, because he or she exhibits in extreme degree the 'character structure' produced by the *American* experience of change, mobility, and loss of contact with the past" (*Speaking* 169). Surely the Shimerdas cannot feel any further from civilization than Jim does on that first wagon ride out to their respective homesteads. And yet Jim has the legitimating forces of white, male, middle-class respectability behind him. Although Burch sees Jim's portrayal of his European neighbors as basically sympathetic, it is worth noting that on multiple occasions, both implicitly and explicitly, Jim asks the quintessential question of native-born Americans: "'why can't they be more like us?'" (Burch 61). The novel begins before the turn of the century, but Cather writes it from the context of the World War I backlash, during which time "the goal of the education of immigrants was not to teach them about America but to teach them to behave as Americans" (Dearborn 85). Jim even loses patience with Mr. Shimerda, for whom he usually has only respect bordering on reverence. When Antonia tells Jim of her father's unhappiness, he lashes out, "'People who don't like this country ought to stay at home. . . . We don't make them come here'" (59). Jim, like his creator, vacillates between an acceptance of diversity and a more reactionary nativism.

A social conservative, Cather is sometimes considered an anti-modern writer who uses simple (even simplistic) vocabulary and techniques, when compared to her avant-garde contemporaries.[13] Modern physics, however, appears to have freed up space for Cather's use of time in non-linear ways (Shaw, "*MA:* Emergence" 130). This attitude towards time also marks *My Antonia* as less novelistic. As Benjamin explains, "according to Lukacs [in *Theory of the Novel*], the novel is . . . the only art form which includes time among its constitutive principles. . . . [O]ne can almost say that the whole inner action of a novel is nothing else but a struggle against the power of time"

(99). Cather's text neither tries to mimic the deployment of time found in realistic novels nor shares modernism's attempt to capture each fleeting moment as it happens. Cather acknowledges the past as well as the present, but the past never exerts a controlling influence on the present. Thus, although Cather avoided stream of consciousness and the avant-garde search for a continuous present which so occupied Stein, she did not accept the "sins of the fathers" view of the past's influence on the present as espoused by contemporaries like Porter and Fitzgerald: "she could not readily conceive of the 'me' of the present forever fleeing some 'me' of the past down an inescapable tract of time" (Shaw, "*MA: Emergence*" 130). Time is both less important and more fluid in Cather's work than in that of many of her literary peers. Cather might not have agreed with William Faulkner's insistence that "the past is never dead; it's not even past" (*Requiem* 80), but she certainly saw her characters as shaped by their heritage. Heritage, moreover, is sometimes conveyed by names. Although "symbolic or meaning-full names" (Skaggs 14) are a trademark in Cather, few critics have explored the ramifications of names in *My Antonia*. The Burdens, for example, call up images of the white man's burden, consistent with the family's caretaking of and sometimes condescending attitude towards their Bohemian neighbors. White/black relations play a submerged, but significant role in the text, as well. Grotesque and racist though the caricature of Blind D'Arnault might seem, the mulatto pianist is depicted as typically American, at least according to Munsterberg's criterion: "the American is supposed to be quite destitute of any sense for form or measure, and to be in every way inartistic; and if any true poet were to be granted to the New World, he would be expected to be noisy like Niagara" (458). Further, Ammons suggests that Blind D'Arnault shares his status as non-western/non-white artist figure with Mr. Shimerda (132). Although the seemingly tangential episode of Blind D'Arnault constitutes the only appearance of African-Americans in the text, race is present from its earliest pages. Some of the dynamics between "native" Black Hawk citizens and their immigrant neighbors do in fact parallel certain aspects of traditional representations of black/white relations. Young women such as Antonia, Lena, Tiny and the three Marys hire themselves out as domestic servants, something that the girls in even the poorest white families will not consider. If Black Hawk boys marry not Black Hawk girls but hired girls, the danger of mongrelization becomes immediately present.[14] Judith Fetterley picks up racial overtones in Cather's satirical portrait of town life as well: "the anemia, paralysis and unlived lives of the 'white,' middle-class town girls must also be laid in part at the door of a sexuality which requires 'purity' in wives and mothers and vents its lust on the bodies of servants" (138). The would-be rape of Antonia by the nefarious

Wick Cutter also suggests the sexual violence imposed on female slaves by the men who owned them, while the offspring of hired girls and their American employers (in the case of the Bohemian Marys) or boyfriends (in the case of Larry Donovan and Antonia) constitute the beginnings of an indigenous mulatto population.

Cather's characterizations immediately force us to see beyond black and white, however, as Otto Fuchs states early in the novel that "Bohemians has a natural distrust of Austrians. . . . [I]t's politics. It would take me a long while to explain" (16). While mainstream Black Hawk applies the totalizing term "foreigner" to anyone from another country, Cather repeatedly underscores racial/national difference among the various European immigrant groups. It is amusing to read Cather in light of Professor William Graham Sumner's comment about the impossibility of nationhood in America: "Sumner used to tell his students at Yale that the United States had no claim to the name of nation because of the presence of so large a negro population, the implication being that between the white and colored races there exist such lively recognitions of dissimilarity that they can never establish the degree of common feeling necessary to true nationality" (Fairchild 54). Cather would seem to be saying that if people from two central European countries have grudges against each other, then it is not the white/black division alone that will stand in the way of nationhood for the United States—Austrians and Bohemians (among others) will not be melted in the same pot. Yet all the Black Hawk citizens can see is foreigners, or maybe Europeans. Jim explains the town's view that "all foreigners were ignorant people who couldn't speak English," clarifying that "There was not a man in Black Hawk who had the intelligence or cultivation, much less the personal distinction, of Antonia's father. Yet people saw no difference between her and the three Marys; they were all Bohemians, all 'hired girls'" (129). At least one critic makes the same mistake as the townspeople: writing in a 1924 collection on contemporary authors, Percy H. Boynton identifies Antonia as "a Bohemian immigrant child of less than mediocre parentage" (7).

The Burdens get to see the enduring strength of Old World national prejudices firsthand when the problem of burying Mr. Shimerda's body arises. Upon learning that "the Norwegian graveyard could not extend its hospitality to Mr. Shimerda," Grandmother Burden indignantly replies, "'If these foreigners are so clannish . . . we'll have to have an American graveyard that will be more liberal-minded'" (73). The irony, of course, is that the nativists with backgrounds like the Burdens are the most clannish. Grandmother Burden tries to emphasize the similarities between herself and her "foreign" neighbors, but through an elision of differences which Cather herself does not seem to support. Time and again Grandmother Burden compares her own experience to the Shimerdas,' as if to say "I worked my way up and you can too, if you'll be diligent" (or plucky, lucky, and hard-working). Further, she pushes everything painful or difficult from her mind. Visiting the Shimerdas during their first starving winter, Grandmother Burden responds to Mrs. Shimerda's scornful laugh and vindictive looks by "talking in her polite Virginia way, not admitting their stark need or her own remissness" (49). Her interactions with her foreign neighbors, to whom "she always spoke in a very loud tone . . . as if they were deaf" (17) sometimes takes the form of translation, as she "mirrors" back a completely different message from the one she has received. Thus when Mrs. Shimerda informs the Burdens, "house no good, house no good!" Grandmother replies, "you'll get fixed up comfortable after while, Mrs. Shimerda; make good house" (17). Linda Wagner-Martin notices the same tendency in Jim, who "has never worked that countryside" and tells "happy-ending placebos" (Bloom 62); Rosowski concurs that "Jim's allegiance is consistently to ideas; when they conflict with reality, he denies the reality" (89).

Cather is not Jim, however, and while she creates characters who represent a range of social and political positions, she does not validate any single view. Along these lines, it is also interesting to note that the tramp who commits suicide by jumping into the threshing machine leaves a nativist eulogy for America as his last words: "'My God! . . . [S]o it's Norwegians now, is it? I thought this was Americy'" (114). Cather could not state any more definitively that this version of "Americy" has met its end. If we view the tramp as symbolic—and there is no reason to insist that this inset is a meaningless tangent in such a deeply symbolic novel—he represents the "race suicide" theory of American identity. Foreign vs. native-born, assimilationist vs. nativist, clannishness vs. liberalism—none of these binarisms withstands Cather's scrutiny. In this way, she provides an insider/outsider paradigm that is consciously refigured and blended to the point where any dichotomy is impossible to sustain. Thus we can argue the doubleness that pervades Cather—and this novel in particular—is not binaristic. Or, more accurately, Cather transforms binary categories by refusing to endorse one totalizing category over its mutually exclusive counterpart. The sun and the moon face each other, and, at least for a moment, neither gives way: "for five, perhaps ten minutes, the two luminaries confronted each other across the level land, resting on opposite edges of the world" (206).

Cather endorsed neither nativism nor melting pot ideology (Pers 40; Lee, "Bridge" 40), and yet she was very much aware of the preoccupations and controversies of her time. Fuchs identifies 1880–1920 (roughly the period between Cather's coming to Nebraska and her writing *My Antonia*) as a time in which "concerns about class, culture, and race" (56–7) were everywhere manifest. Throughout these years, the Americanization of immigrants was a major concern. One index of Americanization which Cather highlights in her novel is language.[15] For example, Jim's relationship with the Shimerdas is at first predicated on his ability to speak English and his willingness to transmit this knowledge to Antonia (and later to Yulka). In acting as a teacher of language, Jim occupies a powerful position, as Arendt explains, "for Benjamin to quote is to name, and naming rather than speaking, the word rather than the sentence, brings truth to light. . . . Benjamin regarded truth as an exclusively acoustical phenomenon: 'Not Plato but Adam,' who gave things their names, was to him the 'father of philosophy'" (49). Jim truly is Adam, the name-giver, as he teaches Antonia the keys to the world around her: "blue sky, blue eyes" (19). The need to learn the language is essential on a practical level (e.g., to prevent opportunist like Kraijiek from profiting from one's ignorance), but it is also important symbolically. Anderson argues that language creates and enables the solidarity of a nation (154, 145), while Cather's contemporary, Commons, similarly contends that a single dominant language is a prerequisite for true nationhood (20), anticipating Anderson's "imagined communities" thesis by seventy years. When the Shimerdas first arrive, only Antonia can speak any English at all, as the train conductor informs Jim: "'They can't any of them speak English, except one little girl, and all she can say is "We go Black Hawk, Nebraska"'" (6). Antonia's father wishes her to learn English, illustrating what Mary Dearborn has observed throughout ethnic novels, namely that education is the path to Americanization and success for the ethnic heroine (80). We immediately see that she is an intelligent, motivated pupil and yet her skills never progress very far. While Tiny and Lena eventually come to travel widely, speak with the local idiom, and become polished American citizens, Antonia raises children who do not even learn English until they go to school, and she forgets almost all of what she learned. As a young woman, Antonia claims that she has become too busy to continue with her lessons, as she explains: "'I ain't got time to learn. I can work like mans now. . . . School is all right for little boys. I help make this land one good farm'" (80). However, she immediately asks Jim to "tell [her] all the nice things [he] learn[s] at the school" (80). Functional fluency is a necessity, but learning for its own sake is a luxury.

While Jim's family can afford for him to spend his days in school, Antonia's requires her assistance. The rubric of the family acts as a crucial framing device in all of Cather's novels, and particularly in *My Antonia*. The Shimerdas arrive not only in a family group (in contrast to immigrant groups in which the man usually preceded the women and children) but as a Family of Man: a suicide (Mr. Shimerda), a complaining old woman (Mrs. Shimerda), a shrewd and ruthless older brother (Ambrosch), an attractive and sexually charged sister (Antonia), and a "crazy boy" (51, 67).[16] They arrive as a unit and their Americanization (or lack thereof) will take place as a unit. As Priscilla Wald explains, during the time period that saw the arrival of large numbers of European immigrants, "assimilation efforts used the traditional American family as both metaphor and medium to Americanize immigrants" (246). In Cather's own experience of migration, an enterprising father dragged a reluctant mother and heartbroken children (along with a resigned grandmother) from Virginia to Nebraska, but in Cather's novel Mrs. Shimerda provides the impetus for her family's relocation. Mr. Shimerda will not Americanize—he does not want to be an American, and, as Fairchild insisted, the immigrant "must devoutly wish to be Americanized" (222) for the process to take place. Grandmother Burden observes to Mrs. Harling that "things would have been very different with poor Antonia if her father had lived" (100), but the nature of that difference is never explored. If Mr. Shimerda had lived, Antonia would have kept her nice ways, and then what? She would not have been Jim's Antonia. In order for this ethnic heroine to move forward, she has to lose her only real parent, "find[ing] herself alone" (Dearborn 76). Antonia must separate from her Old World biological father in order to adopt the American Founding Fathers as her own (Dearborn 89). While the suicide of Mr. Shimerda has a prominent place in the text, the death of both of Jim's parents predates the first chapter and receives only a passing reference. Jim expresses no homesickness, no sadness for his loss. It is interesting to note that the recent movie version of *My Antonia* adds a scene in which Jim attends his parents' burial.[17] Apparently the screenwriters found this omission odd, as well. The second sentence of Cather's text's second beginning introduces Jim as an orphan, a key figure in both the *bildungsroman*—especially the female *bildungsroman*—and in the novel of the American dream. Not only has Jim lost his parents, but, and perhaps equally devastating in Cather, he has lost his place. For reasons the text never explains, Jim's "Virginia relatives were sending [him] . . . to [his] grandparents, who lived in Nebraska" (5). Thus we see Jim as bereft of his heritage and, presumably, his inheritance. In both the preface and the text's end, we are reminded that Jim has no family. His wife is a relative in name only: "she has her own fortune and lives her own life. For some reason she wishes to remain Mrs. James Burden" (2). Jim has no children, and, if the "author" is any indication, few close friends whom he sees regularly.

At the end of the novel, Antonia has seemingly left the Founding Fathers behind to marry a fellow countryman, Anton Cuzak. Cuzak is not unlike Mr. Shimerda, a "philosopher" (229) and "a city man" (235), not cut out for a farmer's life. But whereas Mrs. Shimerda drives her husband to an early grave, Antonia offers her husband support, freedom, and companionship. As much as Jim would like to become part of this family unit, his plans to play "Uncle Jim" to Cuzak's boys ring hollow; we don't believe that the hunting trip will ever come to pass. Further, Jim's slightly condescending intention "to tramp along a few miles of lighted streets with Cuzak" (237) seems equally far-fetched. Why should Cuzak want to go tramping with Jim? This imagined family is an add-on, not something organic, and therefore it remains shallow and implausible. Here again we see possibilities for reading Jim as a gay man or a lesbian. Like Otto Fuchs and Roddy Blake, Jim deserves boys of his own. His section heading completely elides Antonia's girls in favor of Cuzak's boys, and the result is that his "plans seem curiously empty, irrelevant to the center of life represented by the female world of Antonia" (Rosowski 91).

We also find out by the end of the book that, unlike Jim, Lena and Tiny have successfully formed a family unit of a sort: "Tiny lives in a house of her own, and Lena's shop is an apartment house just around the corner. . . . Tiny audits Lena's accounts occasionally, and invests her money for her; and Lena, apparently, takes care that Tiny doesn't grow too miserly" (212). The women are comfortable with their differences and have a joking, but respectful manner with each other. I will not insist that Tiny and Lena constitute a lesbian couple, since Cather portrays Lena as radiating heterosexual energy and Tiny as increasingly asexual.[18] The qualities of the relationship, however, certainly suggest the mutuality and liberating aspects of some lesbian partnerships. It is also worth noting a remarkable similarity between the description of Jim's wife offered by the "author" and the characterization Jim provides of middle-aged Tiny Soderball. The "author" does not care for Mrs. Burden: "she is handsome, energetic, executive, but to me she seems unimpressionable and temperamentally incapable of enthusiasm" (1). When Jim runs into Tiny in Salt Lake City in 1908, he observes that "she was a thin, hard-faced woman, very well-dressed, very reserved in manner. . . . She was like someone in whom the faculty of becoming interested is worn out" (194). His description is neither sympathetic with Tiny's basic loneliness nor admiring of her accomplishments. It would seem that Jim is hurt or puzzled by a woman who is not matronly, expressive, and easily impressed. Or perhaps he faults Tiny for not Americanizing by becoming part of a normative heterosexual family. For Jim, married life is unpleasant and relatively unimportant—nothing to dwell upon. Antonia eventually creates a good marriage, but only after she falls and then accepts the necessary compromises. Whatever the nature of their arrangements, Lena and Tiny clearly participate in a feminine friendship that is not condemned as unnatural.[19]

Bound up with discussions of attitudes towards immigrants and ethnicity is the larger notion of difference. Critics have discussed ethnicity and gender at length, but the difference Marek brings into the text has been largely overlooked.[20] Marek provides an overt example of abnormality, a motif that recurs more subtly across the novel. On a physical level, Marek stands out because of his fingers, "which were webbed to the first knuckle, like a duck's foot" (18), and because of his resistance to the cold and to other hardships: "he's terrible strong and can stand anything" (47). Marek is an object of pity ("poor Marek!" [67, 202]) and potentially one of fear ("he won't hurt nobody" [18]). He makes animal noises, "crow[ing] . . . like a rooster" (18), "bark[ing] like a dog [and] whinny[ing] like a horse" (51), and he embarrasses his family. Mrs. Shimerda rushes to assure her new neighbors that Marek "was born like that," immediately adding, "the others are smart" (18). Marek's difference is something to be explained away and pushed to the side.

Without reading too deeply into his characterization, it is easy to dismiss Marek as a minor player, the token idiot in a Family of Man. We learn a few things about him during the course of the first book, none of which is particularly incriminating: "he was always coveting distinction" (67); "Marek was always trying to be agreeable" (51); and "he could never . . . [learn] to cultivate corn . . . [because] he always bore down on the handles of the cultivator and drove the blades so deep into the earth that the horses were soon exhausted" (85). Throughout Books II and III, we hear nothing of Marek, until in the course of telling Antonia's story, the Widow Steavens mentions off-hand to Jim that "Poor Marek had got violent and been sent away to an institution a good while back" (202). This is particularly surprising because we see no prior indication of Marek's aggressive tendencies. According to Shaw, Marek's attributes suggest a genetic disorder called syndactyly, and people with this condition rarely behave violently ("Marek" 30–31).[21] His unexpected fate, which Cather bothers to make known to us, suggests that it would be a mistake to consider him merely a token idiot, and yet the text leaves a disturbing explanatory gap regarding his sudden turn to violence and his family's subsequent disposal of him. Cather does not tell us of Yulka's future and it would have been just as easy for her to omit Marek's as well, but instead she teases us with enough information to make us curious but provides no further insights.[22]

In trying to untangle this half-told tale, I would like to start by pointing out that Marek is unnatural, not-quite-human, as perhaps is everyone who does not conform to societal standards. He defies categories—part human, part animal. His brute strength, resistance to cold, and seeming inability to learn finer skills makes him a caricature, the barbarian foreigner carried to the extreme. While Cather was always interested in the maimed and the monstrous, beginning with her teenager experiments in vivisection (O'Brien, *EV* 89), it would seem that Marek represents a fear as well as an avocation. Cather felt herself unnatural, an anxiety-producing state, and Lindemann notes a "tension in Cather's letters of the 1890s between fears of looking and feeling queer and her protests against the supposed unnaturalness of female same-sex love" (*Queering* 65). Nevertheless, Shaw has concluded that Cather basically agreed with the Victorian condemnation of lesbianism and its insistence that sex was dangerous ("Victorian" 25). Thus we could argue that Marek is an externalization of a fear of legibility, of having one's difference recognized and of being punished for it without cause. As Ralph Waldo Emerson famously said, "For nonconformity the world whips you with its displeasure" (1516). Marek is born like that, treated like that, and excised for that. He is different, and he is doomed.

Whether or not we wish to read Marek as the projection of a part of Cather, we should remember that Cather was considered a bohemian by the time she arrived in Pittsburgh (Brown, *Critical Biography* 77), suggesting a provocative link between herself and her Bohemian characters. *My Antonia* has its basis in the historical experiences of Annie Sadilek Pavelka, so I will not argue that Cather's Bohemians are a mask for her bohemianism. Given that Cather always picks her words carefully, however, it can be no coincidence that the Shimerdas are Bohemians, a term loaded with double meanings. It is true enough that the Shimerdas are from Bohemia, but had Cather only aimed to identify their country of origin, the term Czechs would have worked just as well. Otto Fuchs refers to the Shimerdas as Czechs on one occasion, but to the Burdens, the Shimerdas remain "Bohemian" (15). They are wanderers and vagabonds, people who seem in many ways strange and unconventional to their American neighbors. Jim's first glimpse of the Shimerdas suggests that he does in fact perceive them as gypsies of some sort: "the woman wore a fringed shawl tied over her head, and she carried a little tin trunk in her arms. . . . Two half-grown boys and a girl stood holding oilcloth bundles, and a little girl clung to her mother's skirts" (6–7). Similarly, Jim immediately notices the difference between his grandfather's house—"the only wooden house west of Black Hawk" (11)—and the Shimerdas' "ugly cave" (43), while his grandmother "drew back" (50) in shock upon learning that Antonia and Yulka slept in "a round hole, not much bigger than an oil barrel, scooped out in the black earth" (50).

The Bohemians also have strange customs, manners, and behaviors, in the eyes of the Burdens (though the Shimerdas consider themselves perfectly normal, if not superior). Although Jim and Antonia have a "wonderfully pleasant" (19) time playing together during his first visit to her family's farm, the mood changes abruptly when Antonia tries to give Jim her ring. Jim explains: "I felt there was something reckless and extravagant about her wishing to give it away to a boy she had never seen before" (19–20). He later notes that "there never were such people as the Shimerdas for wanting to give away everything they had" (29), a propensity that makes Jim feel uncomfortable. In addition, Jim and his family are "horrified . . . at the sour, ashy-grey bread [Mrs. Shimerda] gave her family to eat," (22) though Mrs. Shimerda seems to think her own culinary techniques superior. She boasts: "You got many things for cook. If I got all things like you, I make much better" (58). Because of certain "untranslatable[s]" (Lee, "Road" 163), the most generous gift Mrs. Shimerda ever bestows on the Burdens, the packet of mushrooms, goes to waste— uncomprehended and unappreciated. Furthermore, Antonia's refusal to admit that Jim's family's way is better causes him much chagrin. William J. Stuckey notes that, "as Jim gets to know Antonia better, his difficulty with her reduces to the unpleasant fact that she prefers to be more like her family than like his" (100). And yet this same quality appears in Vickie Templeton (OMH 275), the closest portrait of her teenage self that Cather would ever provide in her fiction (Woodress, *Life and Art* 39).

In spite of obstacles, Jim and Antonia largely transcend their difference to form a close and lifelong friendship, albeit a limited one. They eventually learn to respect each other and to appreciate each other's strengths, but their own identities remain distinct. This possibility is prefigured by a scene at the end of the first section in which Jim and Antonia are lying together in perfect companionship, just on the verge of entering a new phase of their lives (i.e., adolescence), a scene that clearly echoes their first meeting. When Jim first visited the Shimerdas' farm, he recalls: "we were so deep in the grass that we could see nothing but the blue sky over us and the gold tree in front of us" (19). Similarly, in these closing images of Book I, Jim reports: "Antonia and I climbed up on the slanting roof of the chicken-house to watch the clouds. The thunder was loud and metallic . . . and the lightning broke in great zigzags across the heavens, making everything stand out and come close to us for a moment" (89). In both cases Jim and Antonia feel a close camaraderie with each other and with nature, yet just as Jim feels distanced by Antonia's desire to give away her ring in the beginning of Book I, so in the end Antonia explains why the two of them will always be different: "'If I live here, like you, that is different. Things will be easy for you. But they will be hard for us'" (90). Antonia cannot explain why this should be so, but Jim can make no response to the contrary. Sometimes language cannot fill the gap. Some things are incommunicable.

"A DIMINISHED THING": *THE PROFESSOR'S HOUSE*

After "the world broke in two" (*NUF* v), Cather moved from novels about pioneer heroines to more philosophical and reflective texts. Granville Hicks considers this shift the beginning of the end for Cather's art, contending that because she fails "to see contemporary life as it is . . . she has been barred from the task that has occupied most of the world's greatest artists, the expression of what is central and fundamental in her own age" (144). Although critical opinion has moved since Hicks, Cather is still largely known by her early Nebraska novels (e.g., *O Pioneers!* and *My Antonia*). As Carlin noted in 1992, only Cather's early novels are unanimously considered cannonical (7). Cather has in some ways perpetuated the assumption that she is more interested in an idealized past than in "contemporary life as it is" (Hicks 144), affirming her membership among "the backward" (*NUF* v). At the same time, however, she was very much aware of what was happening in the world around her and what her contemporaries and peers were producing. She did not try to hide from the present or to deny its existence, but sought to engage it on different levels and through different experiments. While form and time period are among the most obvious of these manipulations,[23] representations of otherness also play an important role in Cather's later novels.

One such example is Cather's use of the Jewish cosmopolitan as a more prominent character in her fiction. Cather lived and wrote in a time in which Jews were marginal yet ubiquitous, demonized yet responsible for major innovations and positive changes.[24] Thus it is not surprising that Cather's literary treatment of Jews is both ambivalent and inconsistent. On the one hand, it is true enough that "the Jews Willa Cather . . . represent[s] in her fiction are not viewed from the same angle as her Bohemians, Scandinavians, Germans, and French" (Schroeter 365), but nor does she offer a monolithically negative image of Jews. Indeed, Cather's German Jews are among her most sympathetic characters (Pers 80). Absent from her early prairie novels or occupying only minor roles,[25] Jews nevertheless had a formative impact on Cather's life—both positive (the Weiners and their library) and negative (the loss of Isabel McClung to Jan Hambourg). Cather's inscription of Jewish identity evolves from the unsavory (and stereotype-laden) portrayals she offers in her early stories to a more rounded look at the Jewish cosmopolitan, a figure who is remembered and reworked in Louie Marsellus in *The Professor's House* and Mr. and Mrs. David Rosen in "Old Mrs. Harris." Aside from any biographical ties, these Jewish cosmopolitans offer Cather another way to explore multiple subject positions. In exploring these figures, Cather does not depart completely from her earlier preoccupations and techniques. Rather, boundaries which seem firmly laid and impermeable loosen up to offer greater possibilities for representation.[26]

My Antonia was one of Cather's most successful and renowned novels, and it seems to epitomize her earlier writings in many ways. *The Professor's House,* which is also sometimes called Cather's finest text, clearly belongs to her later period. Diminishment, diminution and disillusion abound, and the novel's protagonist is an "immensely complex and tired male autobiographical figure" who "ask[s] Cather's distressed questions and illustrate[s] her knotted concerns" (Skaggs 185). And yet seven years and a world removed from *My Antonia,* there are a surprising number of holdovers in theme, structure, and characterization. To begin with, *My Antonia*'s "*Optima dies. . . . prima fugit*" could serve as the epigraph for *The Professor's House* as well, given the amount of time the Professor spends reminiscing about the past and feeling dissatisfied with the present. Although he now has both honor and money as a result of his scholarly series, *The Spanish Adventurers in North America,* the Professor wishes that he could write his life's work over again and return to "those golden days" when he felt "simple, natural, and happy" (32). He similarly believes that his protégé, Tom Outland, did well to die in the Great War. Indeed, St. Peter feels almost envious of Tom for honorably exiting the scene before he would "have had to 'manage' a great deal of money, to be the instrument of a woman who would grow always more exacting. He had escaped all that. He had made something new in the world—and the rewards, the meaningless conventional gestures, he had left to others" (261). Furthermore, St. Peter hearkens all the way back to Tom's student days as his best, reflecting "that those first years, before Outland had done anything remarkable, were really the best of all" (125).

St. Peter longs for earlier days not only professionally but in his personal life. "[H]e was very much in love" (31) when he married his wife, but he now believes "he could not live with his family again—not even with Lillian. Especially not with Lillian!" (274). Thinking back to when his children were young, the Professor asks rhetorically, "when a man had lovely children in his house, fragrant and happy, full of pretty fancies and generous impulses, why couldn't he keep them?" (126). The follow-up St. Peter offers, "was there no way but Medea's?" (126), actually prefigures the direction that he is headed—towards death. Throughout the book, the enervated Professor drifts closer to death himself, and yet the final section of the novel includes a paradoxical yearning for a return to youth. While Harvard-bound Jim Burden "wishe[s] [he] could be a little boy again" (*MA* 207), the depressed Professor is actually reunited with an earlier avatar, the "Kansas boy," who returns to him as "a primitive" (*PH* 265). Instead of seeing his life over again as he approaches death, the Professor negates his life: "he had never married, never been a father" (265). Clearly the Professor envisions disruption as opposed to continuity between his boyhood and his mature life.

Along with the abrupt break between childhood and adulthood which *The Professor's House* posits, the novel shares *My Antonia*'s saturation with images of doubleness. Hively suggests several: Tom is the Professor's second self (120); the Professor lives two lives and has two daughters and two romances (124); and Scott McGregor observes that the country is split in two socially (124). Further, Cather suggests another underpinning of doubleness in her discussions of the novel's structure, explaining that she tried "two experiments in form[,] . . . inserting the *Nouvelle* into the *Roman*" (*OW* 30) and using the framing technique of "old and modern Dutch paintings" (*OW* 31). This seems to be a very different approach from Cather's "set[ing] an old Sicilian apothecary jar[,] . . . filled with orange-brown flowers of scented stock, in the middle of a bare, round, antique table" (Sergeant 13) to serve as a framing image for *My Antonia*. Nevertheless, we might recall that the middle section of *My Antonia* bore another character's name (Lena Lingard) just as *The Professor's House* includes "Tom Outland's Story." "Lena Lingard" does not have the autonomy of "Tom Outland's Story" (which was in fact published separately) and the absence of Antonia in that section does not carry the same disruptive force as the "'massive dislocation' achieved by Cather in introducing [Tom's Story] . . . into the professor's" (Murphy, "Modernist" 59). Still, it is worth noting that Tom's story requires mediation in order to reach fruition. Although the first-person narrative is ostensibly written by Tom, the task falls to the Professor to edit it, to frame it with an introduction, and to make it public. Skaggs indirectly questions the Professor's fitness for this task. When St. Peter prefaces Tom's story with the remark, "it was nothing very incriminating, nothing very remarkable; a story of youthful defeat, the sort of thing a boy is sensitive about—until he grows older" (176), Skaggs concludes "that we cannot entirely or naively trust *any* sentence from the narrator who largely speaks from the professor's point of view" (67). Just as we come to distrust Jim's reliability as narrator, we see that the Professor's assessments are not necessarily safe to accept at face value. Skaggs also points out that "both [the Professor and Scott McGregor] make [Tom] into an abstraction" (79), much like Jim does to Antonia. Thus doubleness, mediation, and issues of representation are stylistic and thematic holdovers from *My Antonia* to *The Professor's House*.

Also like Jim, St. Peter experiences a childhood dislocation from a lush landscape to a monotonous one: "when he was eight years old, his parents sold the lakeside farm and dragged him and his brothers and sisters out to the wheat lands of central Kansas" (30). Like Willa Cather, "St. Peter nearly died of it" (30). Seemingly a born cosmopolitan, the Professor feels claustrophobic away from the changeable water. Indeed, St. Peter considers Lake Michigan itself to be his real family of origin, "the great fact in life, the always possible escape from dullness" (30).[27] This landscape finds no analog in any of his many travels to beautiful and exotic countries, and St. Peter feels inadequate to describe it in terms of any other. When the French boys for whom St. Peter serves as a tutor ask about *"le Michigan,"* he responds, "It is a sea, and yet it is not salt. It is blue, but quite another blue. Yes, there are clouds and mists and sea-gulls, but—I don't know, *il est toujours plus naif*" (31). The fact that he finishes up in French suggests that Cather wants us to share in the experience of the untranslatable. Not logic but feeling guides the Professor in his decision to return to Lake Michigan when the opportunity arises. He accepts a teaching position in Hamilton, "not because it was the best, but because it seemed to him that any place near the lake was a place where one could live" (31). Like Virgil and Jim Burden, St. Peter strives to bring the muse to his patria, his little corner of land. But while Jim can return to the scenes of his youth, even finding the original road out to his grandfather's homestead, St. Peter's world changes rapidly and irreversibly. For Jim "memories are realities" (*MA* 211), and he dwells in a world with no present and little future, taking comfort only in his version of the past. The dilemma of *The Professor's House,* on the other hand, is how to "go on living" (*PH* 94), even with the knowledge that one's life will henceforth be "without delight" (282).

While the adult Jim finds Antonia "battered but not diminished" (*MA* 214), St. Peter feels a "diminution of ardour" (*PH* 13) from the first pages of the book. Within this context, the task of Cather's novel becomes to offer its own answer to the question posed by Robert Frost's 1916 poem, "The Oven Bird," namely, "what to make of a diminished thing" (l. 14). Bennett hypothesizes that Cather purposefully avoided having to grapple with this question firsthand by never marrying. If Cather had married, Bennett reasons, she would have run the risk of falling out of love the way that her Professor does: "could it be that she avoided reaching out to grasp anything that might conceivably have vanished for her in the grasping?" (221). More recent biographers, however, have contended that Cather knew diminishment and renunciation well, particularly in the guise of losing Isabel McClung to Jan Hambourg. Critics vary in their assessment of Cather's relationship to Hambourg, some seeing the dedication of *The Professor's House* as a mark of reconciliation or friendship (Woodress *Literary,* 284–85) and some seeing it as ironic and incisive (Schroeter 376). Similarly, enough critics have conflated Louie with Jan to trigger a backlash (Murphy, "Modernist" 72). At any rate, the Professor shares many characteristics with Cather. What Lillian observes of her husband might well be said of Cather at the same age: "you're naturally warm and affectionate; all at once you begin shutting yourself away from everybody" (162). Further, Skaggs contends that "both the Professor and his creator would prefer to be back in preadolescent youth" (76). Both long for a less complicated time, when roles and personas were more unitary and responsibilities to other people were fewer. Whether or not McClung and Cather were lovers (or whether Cather wished for that to be the case), McClung was an old friend and one whose father's house was Cather's home away from home. Losing the home in 1915 and the exclusive relationship with a "lover whose love and company were always available" in 1916 brought about "irrevocable" changes and constituted an "overwhelming" loss (O'Brien, *EV* 239). Cather's ambivalence towards Hambourg and her sense of loss in her personal relationship with McClung peaked again during a "disastrous 1923 visit" (O'Brien, *EV* 240) to the Hambourgs's home in France; O'Brien contends that, among other things, "the emotional impact the visit had on Cather can be glimpsed in . . . the profound spiritual and emotional crisis reflected in *The Professor's House*" (*EV* 240). It is clear that Cather was struggling with the issue of knowing oneself when the supporting structures which have sustained that self (both physical and human) are no longer available. Without jumping into the critical fray, I would like to suggest that whatever the personal relations behind the novel, *The Professor's House* is, perhaps above all, a novel about identity.

In what scholars have called her most modernist novel in both form and subject matter, Cather approaches identity issues via a profoundly anti-modernist motif, history. Cantor argues that modernism "emphasized ahistorical . . . ways of thinking" (6) and that the movement was characterized by "antihistoricism" (35). Cather's historian provides a different approach to modernism. While Abraham identifies the central histories explored in *The Professor's House* as "the European-oriented history of great men[,] . . . a native history of cliff-dwelling people . . . [and an] international, contemporary, political history" (47), provocative aspects of the personal history of the Professor himself are especially relevant to questions of cosmopolitanism. St. Peter presents an interesting paradigm of ethnic identity: "though he was born on Lake Michigan, of mixed stock (Canadian French on one side, and American farmers on the other), St. Peter was commonly said to look like a Spaniard" (12). Apparently the experiences and the scholarship have become conflated with the man, as this Spanish identity has been attributed to him because "he had been in Spain a good deal, and was an authority on certain phases of Spanish history" (13). Furthermore, while Professor St. Peter's name sounds Catholic, his mother's staunch Methodist people are the religious ones in his family. Taking Commons's 1920 pronouncement that "religious differences in America are not so much theological as racial in character" (186), we see that St. Peter is very much the product of a "mixed marriage" (100). Thus we could argue that the Professor himself embodies the melting pot, and that he is a product of both amalgamation, "a blending of races," and assimilation, "a blending of civilizations" (Commons 209). St. Peter's family will only become more complex, as his older daughter's marriage to a Jew culminates in the imminent arrival of "a young Marsellus" (273). This child will not be Jewish by orthodox law, which holds that the child follows the status of the mother, and yet it will clearly be considered of Jewish descent by its non-Jewish relatives.

To add to the ethnic mix present within the Professor himself, St. Peter's greatest non-professional achievement is arguably the fact that he "had succeeded in making a French garden in Hamilton" (14)—on land owned by his German landlord, no less.[28] The French garden plays a crucial role in St. Peter's sense of himself. Indeed, "his walled-in garden had been the comfort of his life" (14), providing a space in which he might keep himself together by rigidly controlling his surroundings. Compared to heroic pioneers like Alexandra Bergson and Antonia who struggled to make unbroken soil into productive farmland, however, St. Peter's efforts seem meager or pitiful: "St. Peter had tended this bit of ground for over twenty years, and had got the upper hand of it" (15). His victory does not make him seem like a robust American, but rather an effeminate aesthete. Along similar lines, only a few pages later we see the Professor having a panic attack over the impending removal of the family sewing lady's forms. With perhaps the greatest fervor we ever see him muster, the Professor insists, "they shan't be wheeled. They stay right there in their own place. You shan't take away my ladies. . . . you can't have my women. That's final" (21–22). What better indication of diminution than the Professor's passionate speech on behalf of his ladies? St. Peter is clearly not a pioneer or a hero. He sounds like a cross between a fashion designer and a pimp.

The Professor wants to control his surroundings and the "women" in his life to maintain a past that is no longer viable. While *My Antonia* traces Jim's attempt to connect with a classical past (Swift 111), *The Professor's House* starts from the premise that the past is irrecoverable and takes a caustic look at what the world has become. Thus possession reappears in the later novel, but in a different guise. The title could refer to any of several literal and figurative edifices, including the house St. Peter raised his children in, the new house his wife has bought with the book award money, Rosamund's and Louie's "Outland," the womb, and the grave. Further, the Professor repeatedly bemoans the problems of wealth and offers an indictment of modern materialism. Many critics have dealt at length with the symbolism and significance of houses along with the problems of money, and so I am more interested in looking at the ways in which the characters in the novel are possessed as opposed to dwelling on their problematic possessions.

The Professor, for one, is thoroughly possessed. He does not feel like himself anymore, and he no longer believes that he ever really had control over his life. For example, the Professor retrospectively observes that "all the most important things in his life . . . had been determined by chance. His education in France had been an accident. His married life had been happy largely through a circumstance with which neither he nor his wife had anything to do. . . . Tom Outland had been a stroke of chance he couldn't possibly have imagined" (257). We do not know if Rosamund and Kathleen had been planned pregnancies, but St. Peter certainly does not seem to think that any of his plans panned out. He reflects that "all the years between [childhood and the present] had been accidental and ordered from the outside. His career, his wife, his family, were not his life at all, but a chain of events which had happened to him" (264). The Professor is possessed because he is manipulated by forces beyond his control; he is also the Devil. Godfrey St. Peter is "God-free[,] . . . as arbitrary as God *or* Devil" (Skaggs 76–77). His "wicked-looking eyebrows" and his fiery eyes lead his students to nickname him Mephistopheles (13), and he plays the part with evident pleasure. His nemeses, Crane and Langtry, the one who wants financial rewards and the other who craves status, have the character of Faustian strivers, and St. Peter all but tells them, "this is Hell, and nor am I out of it."

The Professor's double (Kaye 146) and protégé, Tom Outland, is possessed, as well. Although he might not recognize it to the same extent that St. Peter does, Tom also exercises little control over his formative experiences, as Skaggs notes: "Tom's whole life seems shaped by random luck and accident" (68). Tom's story also shares the motif of possession with his mentor's. Money and the question of ownership taint Cliff City and precipitate Tom's break with Roddy Blake. And like Jim Burden in his grandmother's garden, Tom reaches a pinnacle when he relinquishes control and becomes one with something outside himself. Spending a night alone on the mesa for the first time, Tom feels "a great happiness. It was possession. . . . a religious emotion. . . . happiness unalloyed" (251). Here Skaggs points out that Tom both "possessed and was possessed by this object of his desire, the Blue Mesa" (70).

Tom's account of his days in New Mexico, "Tom Outland's Story," is itself engulfed or possessed by a larger body—namely *The Professor's House*. On a literal level, the manuscript sits in the attic study of St. Peter's house awaiting annotation and introduction. The Professor considers Tom's story a fairly typical boy's tale, "nothing very remarkable" (176), and the narrative is certainly tangential compared to the main plot line in the novel. At the same time, "Tom Outland's Story" is literally central. Comprising the middle book of the novel, it comes between "The Professor" and "[His] Family." Tom precipitated the Professor's alienation from his wife and daughters, and even after Tom's death the manuscript exerts an almost hypnotic power over St. Peter, who stays back from a family trip to Europe to "pleasantly trifle . . . away nearly two months at a task which should have taken little more than a week" (263). Situated between the two parts of the Professor's narrative, Tom's story is also the "turquoise set in dull silver" of the novel's epigraph, as Schroeter explains: "the point is that Book II is the 'turquoise' and Books I and III are the 'dull silver'" (370). However, the turquoise does not sit neatly in its dull silver, since it is both the epigraph and the text itself. Furthermore, the turquoise and the silver interact, melting into one another as opposed to remaining discrete entities. Silver is malleable—a "turquoise set in dull silver" is not set in stone.

As an alternative to readings that consider the insertion of Tom's narrative into the Professor's a bold but ultimately unsuccessful experiment,[29] I would point out that the inclusion of Tom's story, while atypical in the novel genre, makes more sense if one considers St. Peter and Tom co-storytellers in Benjamin's sense. Just as Jim and Antonia jointly fulfilled the role of "The Storyteller" as Benjamin conceptualizes it, St. Peter and Tom together, sometimes through cooperation and sometimes through tension, give Cather's text a greater fullness and complexity than either's tale would provide alone. St. Peter provides an introductory "presentation of the circumstances in which . . . [he has] learned what is to follow" (Benjamin 92), adding credibility to Tom's narrative. The story receives further validation from the fact that Tom has been dead for ten years by the time we hear his story: "death is the sanction of everything that the storyteller can tell" (Benjamin 94). However, Tom, a former call-boy and cow hand, makes a better storyteller. "Rooted in the people" (Benjamin 101) in a way that the Professor never was, Tom has also mastered the "art of . . . keep[ing] a story free from explanation as one reproduces it" (Benjamin 89).[30] Furthermore, untrustworthy though St. Peter's dismissal of Tom's story might be, it does signal to us that plot or transference of information is not the most important part of the narrative. Clearly Tom's story retains its value and its power over time, unlike "information [which] does not survive the moment in which it was new" (Benjamin 90). St. Peter's ability to live again through Tom's manuscript also demonstrates Benjamin's contention that "a man listening to a story is in the company of the storyteller; even a man reading one shares this companionship" (92). Working on Tom's manuscript brings back many memories of Tom, but it also reincarnates "the original, unmodified Godfrey St. Peter" (*PH* 263).

Tom, like Benjamin's storyteller, is gone. Contemporary society has lost its storyteller (Benjamin 83), and St. Peter has lost his protégé, his youth, and his second self. In spite of the unmistakable doubling that occurs in Cather's characterization of Tom and the Professor (Hively points out that "Thomas" means "twin" [120]), Tom represents something quintessentially American, but St. Peter is only nominally so. It is interesting to note that while St. Peter seems to offer unmitigated, even mythologizing approval for Tom, he displays varying attitudes towards Americans and the United States in general. For example, Lillian achieves only limited success by appealing to St. Peter's sense of patriotism or national pride in arguing for installing an attractive bathroom in the new house: "'If *your* country has contributed one thing, at least, to civilization, why not have it'" (12, emphasis added). Lillian's use of "your" to refer to both her husband's country and her own is curious. It would almost seem as if Lillian is trying to remind her cosmopolitan husband that he does, in fact, have a country—that he is, in fact, an American. The Professor's relationship to the American landscape is also complex. Although being torn from Lake Michigan as a child was traumatic for St. Peter, he subsequently identifies his truest self as the "Kansas boy" (265). Further, St. Peter considers the southwest "Outland's country" (270) and plans to visit because it epitomizes Americanness. He does not really believe that he will live to see the fall term, but he decides that if he travels the following summer, he will go "to look off at those long, rugged, untamed vistas dear to the American heart. Dear to all hearts, probably—at least calling to all" (270). At this point the Professor makes an unlikely leap: "Else why had his grandfather's grandfather, who had tramped so many miles across Europe into Russia with the Grande Armee, come out to the Canadian wilderness to forget the chagrin of his Emperor's defeat?" (270). Although St. Peter's ruminations on his great-great-grandfather's trans-Atlantic journey seem out of place here, they signify the importance of journeys and crossings within the novel.

Crossing recurs as a motif throughout. In terms of geography, we hear about many crossings of the Atlantic ocean: the original immigrant St. Peter comes from France to Canada; Sir Edgar, "the English scholar . . . come[s] all the way to Hamilton . . . to enquire about some of Doctor St. Peter's 'sources'" (36); Lillian and Godfrey meet while both are overseas; St. Peter plans to travel to Paris with Tom, but the war interferes; and the Marselluses take Lillian on a European vacation. On a more metaphorical level, the Catholic overtones of the novel, as embodied by Augusta, also call up images of the cross and of crossing oneself. Further, mixed marriages suggest cross-breeding and hybridization. In the realm of gender, several critics have noted that Louie, marginal for his ethnic identity, also has many characteristics of a gay man. As Abraham observes, "Louie is sensitive, emotional, and flamboyant, knowledgeable about aesthetics, objects, and women's clothes" (51; see also 188, n. 15). Louie is a married man and a father-to-be, so these characteristics and predilections suggest a certain gender transitivity. He continually crosses the line between masculinity and femininity. Tom, Louie's predecessor, is ruggedly masculine, but he stands out for his apparent lack of interest in women (his engagement to Rosamund notwithstanding). Indeed, Cather leaves plenty of room for us to conclude that Tom was gay, or at least bisexual. Tom's primary emotional attachments were to other men, and he and Roddy might well have been lovers. It is also doubtful that the Professor's romance with Tom was strictly platonic, "of the mind—of the imagination" (258). Tom's questionable sexual orientation—like Louie's gender transitivity, Augusta's religious fervor, and St. Peter's trans-continental travels—serves to remind us of the importance of crossing within Cather's novel.[31]

Crossing plays a prominent role in class and racial issues in the text, as well, although African-Americans are curiously absent from this novel in which American identity is so central. In fact, the only people of color who receive any mention are the dead native-Americans, the Cliff Dwellers. Cather's use and representations of the Cliff Dwellers has garnered her charges of ethnocentrism (Ammons 133–36). Nevertheless, I would argue that Cather does more than perpetuate and reproduce "inherited, conventional, white western narrative tradition" (Ammons 134). The ways in which ethnic and racial issues suffuse *The Professor's House* show that Cather had an awareness of the complicated interactions between, for example, class and ethnicity. For instance, Augusta, the St. Peter family's German seamstress is presented sympathetically, even when such a portrayal places St. Peter in an unfavorable light. The Professor teases Augusta about religion, which is no joking matter to a devout Catholic, and it is clear that his words are tinged with a not completely good-natured irony. Augusta tries to meet him in his bantering, but the two do not stand on equal intellectual footing. The passage in which Augusta makes a rare reference to her own hopes and goals is representative of the way in which St. Peter views her. Augusta confides to St. Peter: "'When I first came to sew for Mrs. St. Peter, I never thought I should grow grey in her service.' [St. Peter] started. What other future could Augusta possibly have expected? This disclosure amazed him" (23). Even after Augusta has saved him from asphyxiation, the greatest praise St. Peter can heap on her character is that she is "kind and loyal" (281), typical servant material. His "sense of obligation to her" (281) suggests no more than paternalism, certainly not admiration, humility, or a recognition of Augusta's individual humanity. In this way, the Professor's epiphany that he will henceforth live in "a world full of Augustas, with whom one was outward bound" (281) does not differ greatly from his early characterization of her as "the sewing-woman, niece of his old landlord, a reliable, methodical spinster, a German Catholic and very devout" (16). The future life he envisions will be "without delight" (282), a death-in-life in which St. Peter will be surrounded by zombie-like Augustas and dead Mother Eves. In this case, Cather is not glorifying her protagonist, but showing his weaknesses. She does not become a Jim Burden or a Niel Herbert, as Ammons argued (136), but rather, she shows that she is not, despite similarities, Godfrey St. Peter.

The character who most clearly embodies racial/ethnic difference is not at all devout. Louie Marsellus, an assimilated Jewish electrical engineer, has entered the Professor's family by marrying Rosamund, St. Peter's older daughter and Tom Outland's "virtual widow" (45). Some critics see Cather's portrayals of Jewish characters as virulently anti-Semitic (Schroeter 365–68), while others contend that Cather merely reflects the conventions of her time: "no [contemporary] reviewer saw anything objectionable in the characterization of Louis Marsellus" (Woodress, *Literary* 377). Finally, other critics say that positive aspects in Cather's portrayals outweigh any negatives. Nelson, for example, counters charges that Cather employs negative stereotypes of Jews by offering a positive stereotype of his own, arguing that unsavory images of Jews are "relegated to the point of irrelevancy in the face of the erotic energy of Jews and their capacity, generally, to appreciate in others the lost language" (90). At any rate, Louie's difference is certainly racialized and essentialized. Louie is unlike the St. Peters, unlike Scott McGregor, unlike Tom Outland because Louie is a Jew. If Cather had difficulty conceptualizing Jewish identity, she shares that challenge with contemporaries, later social scientists, and statisticians in other countries. In underscoring the distinction between race and nationality, even Cather's conservative contemporary, Fairchild, finds the place of Jews ambiguous: "to just what extent the Hebrews are to be considered a race it is impossible to say" (111). Gleason similarly explains that "Judaism is an 'ethnic religion' in a way quite different from the manner in which Catholicism was an ethnic religion for Irish, or Polish, or Italian immigrants . . . [because] the theoretical distinction between being Catholic and being Irish—or Polish, or Italian, or whatever—could always be clearly drawn" (*Speaking* 242). Anderson further notes as "census categories became more exclusively racial" (164), Asian "census-makers [became] visibly uneasy about where to place those they marked as 'Jews'" (165, n. 3). Although Louie's difference is difficult to pinpoint, it is palpable throughout the novel. Whatever the implications, Cather, like Kathleen St. Peter, "calls [Louie] a Jew" (85). Even with the difficulty in defining Jews ethnically and racially, the term calls up stereotypes and carries political overtones which Cather manipulates strategically. Louie is different, foreign, and yet familiar.

Cather gives us no reason to believe that the Marsellus family has not lived in the United States for generations, but Louie remains marginal when compared to old-timers like the St. Peters. American-born or not, the Jewish Marsellus incontrovertibly constitutes what Fairchild derogatorily terms "new immigration" (112). Further, the historian's son-in-law stands out for being almost completely without a history. We do not know where Louie is from, whether his parents are still alive, where he went to college, or how he and Rosamund met. He has a brother living in China, "engaged in the silk trade" (36), but otherwise Louie seems to have neither roots nor relations. He is the perennial outsider, but he is also excellent raw material for shaping into whatever Rosamund and Lillian wish to make of him. The Professor expresses surprise at the ease with which Lillian integrates Louie into the family, as he reflects: "He would have said that she would feel about Louie just as he did; would have cultivated him as a stranger in the town, because he was so unusual and exotic, but without in the least wishing to adopt anyone so foreign into the family circle" (78).

Louie seems "foreign" to the Professor but not wholly so. He is American-educated, he uses American idioms and presumably speaks without an accent, and his appearance is for the most part nondescript. Indeed, Louie might be fruitfully conceptualized as a person of mixed ancestry, as Commons explains, "it should not be inferred the Jews are a race of pure descent. . . . In the course of centuries, their physical characteristics have departed from those of their Semitic cousins in the East, and they have become assimilated in blood with their European neighbors" (93). Thinking of Louie this way, we might observe that St. Peter expects his wife to see Louie just as Larsen's Scandinavian Axel Olsen sees the American mulatta, Helga Crane— exotic, foreign, and not for formal marital relationships. Instead, Louie is the stimulus for Lillian's beginning "the game of being a woman all over again" (79). Louie fills the gap created "when husbands ceased to be lovers . . . [by] never forg[etting] one of the hundred foolish attentions that Lillian loved" (160). The comparison of Louie to Helga highlights the crucial role the mixed-race or ambiguous-race figure plays in *The Professor's House*. When Judith Berzon observes that "the mulatto has been the central character in the works of some of America's most influential white writers[, including] . . . . Gertrude Stein . . . and Willa Cather" (14), she is probably thinking of Melanctha (Stein) and Nancy Till (Cather). But the identity politics of the mulatto apply to other Cather characters of mixed or ambiguous race as well, including the Professor and Louie.[32]

Although not centrally about race, *The Professor's House* can be considered a passing novel, particularly if we draw on older definitions of the term which more broadly encompass any type of social boundary crossings (Sollors, *Neither* 247). The Professor's socio-economic status is assured and his racial heritage is never called into question, but he passes in other ways. Wall contends that the use of a pseudonym constitutes "a form of passing" (120), and while St. Peter does not give himself a new name, he does deny a part of his name: "Godfrey had abbreviated his name in Kansas, and even his daughters didn't know what it had been originally" (163). Since he has no sons to burden with the tradition, it seems likely that the secret will die with him. By dropping the "Napoleon," St. Peter severs himself from his roots, as "there had always been a Napoleon in the family, since a remote grandfather got his discharge from the Grande Armee" (163); Berzon defines passing as "reject[ing] . . . roots" (6). Furthermore, Washington points out that the term passing "can also connote death" (164), a direction that Cather's protagonist moves towards, while Brown summarizes *The Professor's House* as "a study of the *passing*, prematurely, from middle to old age" (*Critical Biography* 239, emphasis added). Finally, the professor's attachment to his mannequin "ladies" and his obsession with closets should set off a warning bell, to say the least.

Cather plays with the concept of the closet by employing multiple levels of figurative significance. The professor likes his closets at the new house, but he cannot relinquish his sewing room closet at the old house. He treasures his privacy, his ability to closet himself, and the art he creates in his private cell takes on the form of a religious emotion/devotion. St. Peter has skeletons in his closets, things that not even the people closest to him know, and he has also spent an adulthood closeted and trying to pass—for husband, for father, for professor, for American citizen.[33] Along these lines Doris Grumbach sees the Professor's mid-life crisis as "his late and blinding realization that the life he has been leading, the life of father and husband is no longer bearable and that death is preferable to living any longer in the stifling, elaborately furnished and *false* (for him) house of women and marriage" (qtd. in Woodress, *Literary* 371). Further, disillusioned as he has become with teaching, it would seem that the role of professor does not sit well with St. Peter either. Sedgwick's assessment of James's Marcher might also serve to explain St. Peter's situation: "the secret of having a secret . . . functions . . . precisely as *the closet*" (205, emphasis in original). In the opening pages of the novel, St. Peter struggles to "evade the unpleasant effects of change" (15). "[H]e had burned his candle at both ends to some purpose—he had got what he wanted"

(28–29), but the Professor finds the goal less satisfying than the striving. When he finally visits the family doctor, he does not reveal "the real reason for his asking for a medical examination. One doesn't mention such things. The feeling that he was near the conclusion of his life was an instinctive conviction, such as we have when we waken in the dark and know at once that it is near morning; or when we are walking across the country and suddenly know that we are near the sea" (269). St. Peter's secret could be conceptualized in any number of ways: he is clinically depressed, he fell in love with his male student, he no longer shares his family's preoccupations or interests, or he just considers himself generally misunderstood. Even at the very end of the novel, and after surviving a near brush with death, the Professor remains closeted. He is not the person his loved ones believe him to be: "he doubted whether his family would ever realize that he was not the same man they had said good-bye to" (282–83).[34]

The Professor has passed successfully for years and will, in all likelihood, continue to do so, but Louie Marsellus cannot stake a similar claim. Louie tries both to cross social lines (by applying to the Arts and Letters) and to achieve WASP status (by marrying Rosamund), but his Jewishness keeps him from the ranks of "those who can pass for members of the core society" (Berlant, *Queen* 192). Although intermarriage has typically provided a fast-track to Americanization (Dearborn 100), the more typical case is that in which a white man marries an ethnic woman (Dearborn 99). Indeed American immigration policy operated on a double standard that structurally underscored such a process. As Virginia Sapiro notes, between the 1880s and the 1930s the laws were such that "if a foreign woman married an American citizen, she automatically became an American. If an American woman married a foreign man, she automatically lost her citizenship and became an alien, even if no other country in the world claimed her as a citizen" (289–90). In Louie's and Rosamund's case, it is the man who marries above his own social class and seeks entrance into his wife's milieu.[35] Berlant observes that "when a human morphs himself . . . through interracial marriage to a more racially and class-privileged person, that identification and that passing makes him more likely to be a member of the core national culture" (*Queen* 217), but Louie cannot seem to blend into the St. Peter family. A negative reading of Louie's difference might say that he is flamboyant and showy, that he parasitically gets rich off the genius and hard work of others, that he monopolizes conversations and charges ahead without giving a moment's thought to the effect his words might have on his listeners. There is some truth behind such accusations, but at the same time, Cather does not seem to suggest that Louie should change. Cather's opposition to melting pot ideology (Pers 40) manifests itself in a tacit support for Louie's refusal or inability to be melted. Ultimately, the Professor can only accept Louie's difference and thereby accept defeat: "'Louie, you are magnanimous and magnificent!' murmured his vanquished father-in-law" (170). As Skaggs explains it, "one of the bad guys . . . turns into a good guy" (78).

Although James Woodress declares that "the Professor . . . is a self-portrait of Willa Cather" (Slote 59), there is also a good bit of Cather in Louie. For one thing, Cather knew the feeling of being new immigration herself compared to blue bloods like Annie Fields (O'Brien, *EV* 117). Furthermore, Louie's status as a Jew provides a close analog to Cather's as a woman whose primary emotional relationships were with other women, even more so than would be the case if Louie were black. Sedgwick lays the groundwork for such a comparison when she notes that "racism . . . is based on a stigma that is visible in all but exceptional cases . . . [while] ethnic/cultural/religious oppressions such as anti-Semitism are more analogous" to homophobia (75). Growing up in a southern, Christian, Victorian household in a small town filled with "stupid faces" (*SL* 215), Cather felt her difference acutely. Taking Wald's contention the traditional American family (especially as related to marriage) constitutes a key site of Americanization (246, 279), we can argue that Cather has occupied a similar place to Louie's—an outsider, an inassimilable foreigner. The "young Marsellus" (273) will be the product of a mixed marriage, and "miscegenation disrupt[s] the *idea* of family" (Dearborn 139, emphasis in the original), but, I might add, so does homosexuality. If Cather sometimes judges Louie harshly, she is certainly no harder on him than she is on herself.[36] We clearly need to move beyond the "Willa Cather equals Godfrey St. Peter/ Jan Hambourg equals Louie Marsellus" binarism in order to do this text justice. Indeed, instead of identifying St. Peter with Cather and seeing Louie as an outsider or enemy, we might fruitfully conceive of St. Peter and Louie as vessels for different parts of Cather's psyche. Things have changed, and instead of wallowing in nostalgia and bemoaning her losses as some critics suggest, Cather moves beyond one-to-one correspondences to try to conceptualize and place herself in a new world.

From the past-heavy and possessive story of Jim's Antonia, we approach the before/after paradigm of *The Professor's House*. Ultimately Cather's answer to the question of what to make of a diminished thing is much like Frost's— to go on living, albeit without song. St. Peter's epiphany is that mediocrity is liveable, as he realizes "that life is possible, may be even pleasant without joy, without passionate griefs" (282). He is past middle age, but he too can learn new tricks: "he had never learned to live without delight. And he would have to learn to, just as, in a Prohibition country, he supposed he would have to learn to live without sherry" (282). As the Professor ceases in his role of Mephistopheles and returns to the religion of his fathers, "outward bound . . . [with] a world full of Augustas" (281), he also makes a transition from binary paradigms (heaven/hell, childhood/adulthood, passion/death) to a tertiary one (faith).[37] Death and rebirth, a prominent motif in the novel (Hively 130), makes way for life with a difference. Where *My Antonia* ends with Jim's sense of possession, the Professor returns to himself with the knowledge that "he had let something go—and it was gone: something very precious, that he could not consciously have relinquished, probably" (282). And although this is not the triumphant feeling of a man coming home to himself, "[St. Peter] felt the ground under his feet. He thought he knew where he was, and that he could face with fortitude the *Berengaria* and the future" (283). The many transitions in this novel do not reach resolution; Cather leaves us with an open-ended state of affairs. St. Peter thinks he is stable and ready to go on with life, but he is not certain. Still, the Professor has realized that a diminished life is nevertheless a life worth living.

(CATHER'S) THREE LIVES: "OLD MRS. HARRIS"

In examining the ending of *The Professor's House,* Skaggs suggests, "Cather acknowledges the miracles possible in youth, but also in age" (83). This realization forms the crux of "Old Mrs. Harris," as well. While Brown sees in this novella Cather's "vision of the aged, defeated, lonely, and unhappy" (Schroeter 84), Woodress's assessment that "Old Mrs. Harris" ultimately "affirm[s] life" is more compelling (*Literary* 444). Although the title character works hard her entire life and then dies, and the narrator predicts that neither Mrs. Harris's daughter nor her granddaughter will do much better, the story does not seem like a depressing narrative about drudgery and death. Woodress points out that Cather, herself nearing sixty, realized at this time that along with physical degeneration, "something rather nice happens in the mind as one grows older. A kind of golden light comes as a compensation for many losses" (*Literary* 444). This is the backdrop for "Old Mrs. Harris," a story about generations and also about regeneration. Although family relations play a significant role in *My Antonia* and *The Professor's House,* these issues take center stage in "Old Mrs. Harris," which posits both "'vertical generational model[s]'" and "'horizontal relationship[s]'" (Lowe 63). Lowe employs these terms as an alternative to "a traditional anthropological model of 'culture'" (64), which views transmission as "exclusively hierarchical and familial" (63). Cather portrays vertical relations in the three generations of women in the Harris/Templeton family—plus assorted male accessories—but she also explores the more horizontal relationships that these women have with other significant people. These relationships form an intricate web in which it is sometimes not altogether clear exactly how the various players are related to one another. For example, although Mrs. Rosen is Victoria's age, she might be mistaken for an older woman, Mrs. Harris's contemporary, because her primary relationship seems to be with Mrs. Harris and she seems so much more sophisticated than Victoria. And yet Mrs. Rosen consistently calls Mrs. Harris "Grandma" (263–67, 271, 285, 295, 304) thereby aligning herself more with Vickie. Mr. Rosen's courtliness and predilection for reading philosophy also make him seem older than he is.

Significantly, the story was originally titled, "Three Women." Not only have we moved from the binaries with which *The Professor's House* begins to the tertiaries with which it ends, but the most prominent threesome is itself ambiguous. The title could refer to the three generations of Templeton women—Grandmother Harris, Victoria and Vickie—but it could also include Mrs. Rosen. Other critics have suggested that Mrs. Rosen might be substituted for Vickie (leaving us with an elderly mother and two "daughters" with competing notions of filial piety), but I think she could also stand in for Mrs. Harris (a daughter and two "mothers") or for Victoria (two women who respect the third's desire to escape the path of her mother). Woodress has noted that the story "might have been subtitled 'Portrait of the Artist as a Teen-ager'" (*Life and Art* 39), suggesting that Cather's sympathies should naturally rest with Vickie. Yet in writing this story, an older Cather seems to put herself in her mother's and her grandmother's place as well—by age sixty, she has crossed over to the side of those who "know" (314). The web of relations that the story puts into play finds an analog in the narrative style, in which "to posit one line of sight . . . necessitates an intersecting line that either crosses, doubles, or double-crosses it" (Carlin 92). "Old Mrs. Harris" does not privilege a single voice the way *My Antonia* privileges Jim's and *The Professor's House* privileges the Professor's. Nor does it include interpolated narratives which do "not [seem to be] a part of [the novel's] organic structure" (Brown, *Critical Biography* 259), such as the wedding party in *My Antonia* or Tom's story in *The Professor's House*. Instead we have a narrative that moves fluidly across time, employing flashback while maintaining several threads of ongoing action, including Mrs. Rosen's friendship with Mrs. Harris, Victoria's social and domestic difficulties, and Vickie's desire to go to college.

Within this tertiary paradigm, possession as ownership fades from view. The Templetons are not well-off, living in "a little rented house [that] was much too small for the family" (272), but neither is anyone else. Even Mr. Rosen, who seems relatively wealthy in comparison to his neighbors, is described as "the only unsuccessful member of a large, rich Jewish family" (274).

As a result of the Templetons's move from Mrs. Harris's "comfortable rambling old house in Tennessee" (271) to reduced and cramped circumstances, "Mrs. Harris and her 'things' were almost required to be invisible" (272). These "'things'" are of the meagerest sort: a comb, night clothes, soap and a towel, and "her little comforter[,] . . . the dearest of [her] few possessions" (270–71), which is no more than a torn sweater left behind by one of Mrs. Rosen's nephews. As ownership decreases in importance, the value of "be[ing] dissolved into something complete and great" (*MA* 14) receives greater emphasis. All of the main characters are possessed by the Templeton family, or stitched into it, to use the primary metaphor of this story.[38] Grandma Harris sometimes feels "a little low" (289) in the predawn hours, but her depression never continues past her grandchildren's wake-up time: "the moment she heard the children running down the uncarpeted back stairs, she forgot to be low. Indeed, she ceased to be an individual, an old woman with aching feet; she became part of a group, became a relationship" (290). Victoria greets her children with "a real smile, she was glad to see them" (267), and even self-absorbed Vickie is "right good about minding" (267) the baby and obliging about reading to the little boys. Mrs. Rosen is stitched into the web of the family as well—sometimes willingly, sometimes less so.

David Stouck sees Cather's last works, including "Old Mrs. Harris," as a radical departure from her earlier preoccupations and themes: "the subject matter of her fiction now changed; it was important to her to write about human relationships and about life and death, rather than art" (208).[39] However, I disagree with his binary approach to Cather's themes. Although *My Ántonia* is a pioneer novel and *The Professor's House* is a novel about intellect, both are also about people—*My Ántonia* is about what Ántonia means to Jim, *The Professor's House* is most certainly about life and death, and family is always important. Furthermore, Stouck's reading of "Old Mrs. Harris," while valuable, entirely omits Mrs. Rosen. He usefully observes that "the effectiveness of the story derives from the subtlety with which point of view is managed. . . . The story is narrated so that the three women in the family, while not understanding each other, emerge nonetheless as sympathetic individuals to the reader" (209), but he does not even consider that Mrs. Rosen might be one of the three women in question. Similarly, he observes that "the interweaving of multiple viewpoints renders movingly the imaginative tension at the heart of the story: while the memories of hidden longings and isolation are powerfully recreated through Vickie's viewpoint, the narrative overview creates the mother and grandmother with sympathy and compassion" (211). It does not seem like a dramatic leap to go from "interweaving" to "cross-stitch," but Stouck leaves out the master cross-stitcher herself. Thus it seems particularly important to demonstrate how Cather's evolving views on ethnicity and identity can be seen through a close reading of the Rosens.

Mr. and Mrs. David Rosen stand in a paradoxical relation to mainstream Skyline. These genteel immigrants have managed to make a good life for themselves in a small Western town, but while they function comfortably within its society, they remain noticeably above it—economically, educationally, and therefore socially. Still, they do not antagonize their less privileged neighbors, as Marilyn Arnold notes: "Mrs. Rosen holds a superior position among the local women, but she never pushes her advantage" (142). Further, the Rosens do not seem to encounter anti-Semitism, perhaps in part because they are not stereotypically pushy Jews and because they do not call attention to the fact that they are Jewish. Indeed, Mrs. Rosen's "slight accent—it affected only her *th*'s and, occasionally, the letter *v*" (262), constitutes the only flaw her neighbors can discern: "people in Skyline thought this unfortunate, in a woman whose superiority they recognized" (262). Her husband, while considered an underachieving black sheep by his relatives, is nevertheless one of the more well-to-do businessmen in the town. In fact, the Rosens's relatively high standard of living might serve to counterbalance the potentially negative ramifications of their minority status as Jews. In discussing what she terms the "politics of ethnicity" (63), Bottomley explains that financial achievements can bring societal acceptance for marginalized groups: "ethnics are devalued minorities, not a central part of the nation. Those who are accorded centrality . . . are the economically successful" (63). The Rosens have enough money and class to place them in the upper echelons of Skyline society, but without the showiness of a Louie Marsellus or the physical and social unattractiveness of a Miletus Poppas.[40]

Thus Cather presents the Rosens as reasonable and admirable people. They retain traditional Jewish values, such as respect for the elderly and love of children, but they dismiss the letter of the law and fit comfortably into their adoptive society. Using their outsider status as a way to transcend provincial divisions (and their money to ensure not just acceptance but appreciation), the Rosens "belon[g] to no church, [and] contribut[e] to the support of all[, attending] . . . the church suppers in winter and the socials in summer" (282). These are upper-class, educated German Jews, not kerchief- and sidelock-wearing Russian shetl-dwellers.[41] Germany, traditionally considered a cultural and educational center, served as the birthplace of the Jewish enlightenment and the Reform movement, a shift towards cultural assimilation and secular education which began in the late nineteenth century. As exemplars of these trends, the Rosens are learned and culturally refined. Further, the Rosens employ their liminality, demonstrating the permeable and continually shifting boundaries that Kallen describes: "individuals keep disregarding boundaries, whether geographical or cultural. They keep passing into some other group they are out of. Actually, the more 'culture' any of them has acquired, the more liberal or general his education has been, the fuller is his awareness of the values of the *Out-groups,* the freer are his powers to avail himself of them, and the more abundant are his means wherewith to comprehend and enjoy them" (53). The Rosens are everyone's rose garden, the thorn in no one's side.

In spite of their assimilationist tendencies, the Rosens remain noticeably Jewish and even Biblical in their basic affinities. Many Biblical foremothers (e.g., Sarah, Rebecca, Rachel, and Hannah) experience an extended period of childlessness, and Mrs. Rosen similarly grieves over her barrenness: "it was a bitter sorrow to Mrs. Rosen that she had no children. There was nothing else in the world she wanted so much" (273). Mr. Rosen patiently listens to his wife's running commentary about the comings and goings of the Templetons because he realizes that this house full of children serves at least on some level as a surrogate family for his wife, who compares them favorably to their own thankless and self-centered nieces and nephews. At the same time, Mrs. Rosen's interest in the seemingly overlooked Grandma Harris reflects the respect for older people which marks Biblical stories from Noah to Moses.[42] Without preaching or even articulating her beliefs outright, Mrs. Rosen communicates a reverence for the elderly which is a hallmark of Jewish culture. Although Mrs. Harris accepts her position as an old woman as one of relative powerlessness, she deduces that "Jewish people had an altogether different attitude toward their old folks" (272). The Rosens are assimilated Jews, but Jewishness remains an integral part of their identity.

Otherness can easily be cause for condemnation in a small town, but not for the Rosens, whose distinctly Jewish name is also a tag for a central image in the medieval symbol system of courtly love.[43] Medieval romance places the rose image beyond the confines of time and natural decay, creating a world in which "roses do not die, [and] dreams become reality" (Kelly 178). As perhaps the only Jews in Skyline, the Rosens represent an ancient nation still alive today; as the friends and neighbors of the Templetons, the Rosens introduce new and limitless possibilities, a world in which "if you want [something] without any purpose at all, you will not be disappointed" (299). The Rosens show Vickie an alternative to her family's example—a father "too delicate to collect his just debts" (279) who cannot keep his family comfortable, a mother who "had had babies enough" (308) and yet gets pregnant again, a grandmother who receives visitors in "a hideous, cluttered room, furnished with a rocking-horse, a sewing-machine, an empty baby-buggy" (264). Although the hours spent reading in "the deep shadow and quiet" of the Rosens's well-stocked library "never made her dissatisfied with her own" house (275), Vickie's future success is predicated on this kind of exposure to another way of life. In this way, the Rosens model both tradition and modernity. Furthermore, Douglas Kelly explains that the rose derives figurative significance from the contrast "between its appearance and the configuration in which it is placed" (93). The Rosens, whose house provides "the nearest thing to an art gallery and a museum that the Templetons had ever seen" (274), join the symbolism of medieval Europe to that of Jewish mysticism: "like a [rose] among thorns, so is my love among the daughters" (*Jerusalem Bible,* Song of Songs 2.1).[44] Jewish tradition interprets this verse in Solomon's "Song of Songs" as an allegory in which the rose symbolizes the Jewish people, while the thorns represent the other nations of the world. Mr. and Mrs. David Rosen, whose name also invokes that of King David, shine out from their surroundings. Their name is regal, and their neighbors seem to appreciate their worth.

If the Rosens use the otherness of their ethnicity towards positive ends, they also benefit from a cosmopolitan and international background, which once again differentiates them from their fellow residents. Accepting Bruce Robbins's contention that the cosmopolitan or international position tends to be considered as core in our culture (172), we then see that the Rosens occupy yet another privileged position. Even though they have presumably resided in Skyline for some time, the Rosens retain a metropolitan ethos, corroborating sociologist and urban theorist Park's claim that the city is "a state of mind, a body of customs and traditions, and of the organized attitudes and sentiments that inhere in these customs and are transmitted with this tradition" (91). The Rosens can be taken out of the city, but the city cannot be taken out of the Rosens. Park also points out that this ethos is often found in Jews, who "are, before all else, a city folk" (106). Jews are always cosmopolitans with a difference, however. They are free from provincial paradigms, but their position is not necessarily one arrived at wholly by free will. For the Jewish Rosens, the line between mobility and homelessness is a thin one. Thus it is no surprise that Rosens' insider/outsider status in Skyline also suggests the prototype of the Wandering Jew, a figure who retains a detachment from people and places which promotes transcendence of petty preoccupations. Mr. Rosen is a paragon of this type: "all countries were beautiful to Mr. Rosen. He carried a country of his own in his mind, and was able to unfold it like a tent in any wilderness" (282–3). As Park would say, he has clearly "acquire[d] [the] abstract terms with which to describe the various scenes he visits" (106). For her part, Mrs. Rosen has all the sensibilities and tendencies required of metropolitan life, as delineated by Park's mentor, Georg Simmel: "punctuality, calculability, [and] exactness" (51). From her "symmetrically plaited coffee-cake, beautifully browned, delicately peppered over with poppy seeds, with sugary margins about the twists" (262) to "her kitchen [left] in a state of such perfection as the Templetons were unable to sense or admire" (275), Mrs. Rosen is clearly a person who values "order and comeliness" (264). The Rosens's ability to transplant themselves and thrive in a very different cultural climate from that of European capitals and fine opera suggests that they possess "cosmopolitan mobility" (Robbins 172).

Although we are never actually told where the Rosens lived before Skyline, we can infer that they have connections to New York. First of all, we have the popular myth that all American Jews are former New Yorkers (and Brooklyners, to be specific).[45] Beyond this folk wisdom, Cather's text provides more tangible evidence through Mrs. Rosen's associations. The moon in Skyline prompts Mrs. Rosen to think about "the Adirondacks, for which she was always secretly homesick in summer" (282), allowing us to reasonably conclude that she and her husband had spent the winters in New York City and the summers upstate. In any case, it is a combination of the Rosens' different identities—Jewish, European, and cosmopolitan—that makes them so important to the Templetons and to the text. These cultured immigrants serve as a counterpoint or foil to the equally displaced and in many ways equally foreign Templetons. In this position, they can serve as validators, bridge-builders, and enablers.

Mrs. Rosen's traditional Jewish enjoyment of children, respect for the elderly, and belief in education forge a bond between herself and all three generations of Templeton women. Yet not one of these relationships is uncomplicated, a truth embodied by the cross-stitch, Mrs. Rosen's avocation and her method of relating to those she values. In Cather's always-significant opening line (Arnold 141), "Mrs. David Rosen, cross-stitch in hand, [sits] looking out of the window across her own green lawn to the sunburned yard of her neighbours on the right" (262), crossly waiting for an opportune time to run "across the alley-way" (270) to see Mrs. Harris. This scene provides an early intimation of the cross-purposes which will characterize neighborly relations, as Mrs. Rosen continually crosses or criticizes Grandma Harris, Victoria, and Vickie.

Watching baby Hughie nurse on her first visit to her neighbor's house, Mrs. Rosen "could not help admiring him and his mother. They were so comfortable and complete" (280). This Madonna-like depiction constitutes perhaps the most powerfully positive image of Victoria in the story, and Cather accomplishes several aims by including this imagery. First of all, the fact that Mrs. Rosen, a Jew, can appreciate the mother and child suggests the potential for bridging the gaps created by ethnicity and religion. Secondly, Mrs. Rosen's aesthetic appreciation for an image which has so frequently been the subject of art testifies to her cosmopolitan cultivation. Finally, Mrs. Rosen is a person who "gave credit where credit was due" (295); her own disappointing child-lessness does not keep her from admiring a mother of many beautiful chil-dren. Thus Mrs. Rosen's first impression of Victoria serves to somewhat counterbalance her clear disapproval of her neighbor's mothering techniques: "'dat woman takes no more responsibility for her children than a cat takes for her kittens'" (273). As she gets to know the family better, Mrs. Rosen finds herself wanting desperately to "for once . . . get past the others to the real grandmother" (265) and pays court to Mrs. Harris with coffee cakes, cookies, and sweaters. Always "on her guard" (265), Mrs. Harris exasperates Mrs. Rosen with her continual deference to her daughter and grandchildren and her willingness to carry their burdens. Mrs. Harris claims not to mind work-ing for the younger generations, but Mrs. Rosen resists "the chain of respon-sibility . . . the irritating sense of being somehow responsible for Vickie" (277). Nevertheless, although she "hated the girl's bringing-up so much that she sometimes almost hated the girl" (274), Mrs. Rosen's appreciation for scholarship makes her a patient listener to Vickie's Latin translations and a fer-vent advocate for Vickie's ambitions to attend college.

The Rosens encounter a culture clash when they encourage Vickie to try for a college scholarship, however. When Mrs. Rosen reminds Mr. Templeton that his daughter "'has finished de school here, and she should be getting training of some sort'" (277), he merely laughs. Later, the dogged Mrs. Rosen brings up Vickie's studying over tea with Victoria and Mrs. Harris and is politely informed that "none of our people, or Mr. Templeton's either, ever went to college" (295)—the implication here being, "you are for-eign and other, and we do things our way." Education may be second nature to these multilingual Europeans Jews, but their country neighbors do not share their enthusiasm or ambition.

Thus the Rosens bring a different set of ethnically based values to their relationship with the Templetons, creating both bonds and tensions. Another element that the Rosens bring into this cultural cross-stitch is demography. The Rosens have internalized the standards of their more urban and northern background, while the Templetons reflect their rural southern roots (Arnold 152). Like most women of her age and class, Mrs. Harris "believe[s] that somebody ought to be in the parlour, and somebody in the kitchen" (288). Conversely, Mrs. Rosen feels that Mrs. Harris should be accorded more re-spect in her household. It becomes crucial for Mrs. Harris to show Mrs. Rosen that she is not "'put upon' [for] . . . to be pitied was the deepest hurt anybody could know" (272). A stalwart Yankee, Mrs. Rosen feels no affection for typ-ically "willowy or languishing" (279) Southern ladies and refuses on principle to acknowledge "a silly, Southern name" (278) like Adelbert.[46] The Templetons are equally mystified by the way Mrs. Rosen "wasted so much pains and good meat" (298) on her clear soups. Nevertheless, it is interesting that despite Mrs. Rosen's northern affiliations, Mrs. Harris does not classify her with Skyline's "meddlesome 'Northerners' [who] said things that made Victoria suspicious and unlike herself" (288). Furthermore, although Mrs. Rosen worries that old Mrs. Harris is inadequately honored in the Templeton household, she takes pains to work within the system, limiting her response to muttered expressions of indignation and affronted complaints to Mr. Rosen. Mrs. Harris knows that Mrs. Rosen "understood how it was" (271) and appreciates her efforts to avoid alienating Victoria.

This knowledge of how things are and the attendant willingness to play along allow the Rosens to validate the Templetons in important ways. Having the benefit of a wider experience, the Rosens can affirm some of the Templeton norms which seem so foreign to the Main Street denizens of a "snappy little Western Democracy" (288). The transplanted Templetons try without success to recreate a courtly code right out of the Arthurian legend. For example, Victoria, "who had been a belle in . . . Tennessee" (286) where she was "admired and envied" (288), acts the part of the Lady of a courtly romance. Her "tall figure and good carriage" (295), along with her "training . . . to the end that you must give a guest everything you have" (285) suggests noblesse oblige. Her lover and husband—"people usually called him 'young Mr. Templeton'" (278–9)—"came of a superior family" (287), if not wholesale aristocracy. He has a "boyish, eager-to-please manner[,] . . . [a] fair complexion and blue eyes" (279) and chivalrous, "lovely manners" (300), much like Fair Welcome in Guillaume De Lorris' "The Romance of the Rose."[47]

Also like a traditional knight-errant, Hillary Templeton spends a significant amount of time away from home, allowing the Rosens to step in and effectively pay obeisance to the ladies of his house. As if living out the symbolic roots of their name, the Rosens validate the rules of the "feudal society" (288) to which the Templetons still adhere, injecting elements of courtly love into their interactions with the family. Mr. Rosen, perhaps the only non-family member in all of Skyline who truly appreciates Victoria, is essential to her self esteem. Observing and enjoying that Victoria is still a "handsome woman" (262), Mr. Rosen displays his regard by closing "his store half an hour earlier than usual for the pleasure of walking home with her" (267). At the Methodist ice cream social, Victoria's children are proud and happy to notice "how nicely he placed a chair for her and insisted upon putting a scarf about her shoulders" (284). Although he is not a man of many words, he "in his quiet way ma[kes] Mrs. Templeton feel his real friendliness and admiration" (284). When this elicits a negative response from the malicious Mrs. Jackson, Mr. Rosen, albeit unsuccessfully, tries to distract Victoria and protect her from hurt.

Mrs. Rosen is the similarly self-appointed champion of Mrs. Harris. Although Mrs. Harris' "friendship with this kind of neighbor was almost as disturbing as it was pleasant" (272), Arnold goes so far as to suggest that "it is partly Mrs. Rosen's appreciative point of view that accords Grandma dignity and personal worth" (143). Mrs. Rosen considers Mrs. Harris "impressive" (264), and seeks to enjoy her company alone whenever possible. Like the Lover in "The Romance of the Rose," Mrs. Rosen finds her "advances . . . alternatively welcomed . . . and discouraged"(Horgan xii-xiii), as when Mrs. Harris first accepts the gift of the nephew's forgotten sweater and then guardedly parries Mrs. Rosen's questions while barely nibbling her coffee cake. In the end of both De Lorris' poem and Cather's story, however, "love is stronger than reason . . . in spite of the obstacles that separate" (Horgan, xiii). This kind of love and validation leads Arnold to conceptualize the Rosens's role as the "healer" (152).

Thus while other townspeople laugh at Mr. Templeton, scorn Victoria, and pity Mrs. Harris, the Rosens behave in a manner the Templetons can understand for the most part. At times, however, the habits and capabilities of the Rosens exceed even Mrs. Harris's capacity for psychological assimilation, and in these instances she accommodates their idiosyncracies through the rubric of "foreign-ness." For example, Mrs. Harris concludes "that Mrs. Rosen managed to be mistress of any situation, either in kitchen or parlour . . . because she was 'foreign.' Grandmother . . . knew well enough that their own ways of cooking and cleaning were primitive beside Mrs. Rosen's" (289). In this way, Mrs. Harris both explains Mrs. Rosen's capabilities and excuses herself from trying to emulate them. Mrs. Harris' conception of herself as "primitive" further invokes the insurmountable gaps in sensibility between a pioneer community in Colorado and the civilized background of thousands of years in Europe. On another occasion, Mrs. Rosen's effusiveness leaves Mrs. Harris "looking down at her hand [and thinking] how easy it was for these foreigners to say what they felt!" (304). Just as the Rosens's awareness of their own otherness provides them a certain measure of distance from the people around them, Mrs. Harris uses this otherness as a means of achieving detachment from a personal relationship that might become threatening.

The irony, of course, is that the southern-born Templetons are at least as foreign as the European-born Rosens. Both are outsiders, though they seem to be on opposite ends of the spectrum: the people of Skyline consider the Rosens above themselves and the Templetons beneath them. Mrs. Harris, however, sees her family's southern heritage as placing them a cut above, and she thinks "with modest pride that with people like the Rosens she had always 'got along nicely.' It was only with the ill-bred and unclassified, like this Mrs. Jackson next door, that she had disagreeable experiences. Such folks, she told herself, had come out of nothing and knew no better" (306). In Mrs. Harris's own home in Tennessee, "there had been plenty of helpers . . . glad to render service to the more fortunate" (287–88). Her daughter was a belle, and her son-in-law had good breeding, if not inherited wealth. Indeed, in the context of Cather's story, it would seem possible to argue for "southern" as an ethnicity and the Templetons as ethnic (im)migrants.[48] Sollors paves the way for this sort of reading when he points out that White Anglo-Saxon Protestant is an ethnicity, although "it is a widespread practice to define ethnicity as otherness" (*Beyond* 25). Using Sollors's characterization of "ethnic" as denoting difference or even a lack of full citizenship (according to mainstream Americans) (*Beyond* 25), we can insist that the southern Templetons experience the difficulties of their status as a marginalized minority in Skyline. Through their cosmopolitan advantages, the Rosens win a position of acceptance in their Colorado community (and one not usually available to Jews). Instead of reinforcing their own position by pushing the Templetons down further, the Rosens use their liminality to heal, so that the otherness they share cements a bond between them. The complexity of this bond is once again embodied in the cross-stitch.

Although the task of forming innumerable small, meticulous *x*-shapes can seem arduous or meaningless, the resulting gestalt is often beautiful. Mrs. Rosen's impatience with and criticism of the Templetons also eventually gives way to what Arnold identifies as the "rather marvelous friendship" that evolves between Mrs. Rosen and Mrs. Harris (150). Mrs. Rosen transcends and exceeds blood ties when the torn sweater she gives to Mrs. Harris "become[s] the dearest of Grandmother's few possessions. It was kinder to her . . . than any of her own children had been" (271). Further, Mrs. Harris demonstrates a real trust in Mrs. Rosen by turning to her for help when Vickie reveals that her father will not fund her college education. In a rare expression of emotion "Mrs. Harris's red-brown eyes slowly [fill] with tears . . . [and she says] 'Thank you, ma'am. I wouldn't have turned to nobody else'" (304). Mrs. Harris treats Mrs. Rosen like family. Mrs. Rosen's response, "that means I am an old friend already, doesn't it Grandma?" (304), does not receive direct affirmation from Mrs. Harris. On her deathbed, however, Mrs. Harris reflects that "she didn't have to see Mrs. Rosen again to know that Mrs. Rosen thought highly of her and admired her—yes admired her. Those funny little pats and arch pleasantries had meant a great deal" (313).

Although Mrs. Rosen claims to help Vickie solely out of a desire to please Mrs. Harris, Cather indicates that Mrs. Rosen the cross-stitcher might also be stitched into the web of life by others. If Mr. Rosen has adopted Victoria and Mrs. Rosen has adopted Mrs. Harris, it would seem that Vickie has adopted the Rosens. In their relationship with her, they become enablers, and these childless members of an ancient nation forge a link with the future. Vickie, who "never paid compliments, absolutely never" (277), verbally expresses her desire to emulate the Rosens, admitting, "I want to pick up any of these books and just read them, like you and Mr. Rosen do" (277). Similarly, a frustrated Vickie reacts to her family's apparent indifference to her needs with the pouting observation that "nobody but Mr. Rosen seemed to take the least interest" (312). Although "sometimes Vickie Templeton seemed so dense, so utterly unperceptive, that Mrs. Rosen was ready to wash her hands of her" (277), the relationship triumphs, and the Rosens encourage, inspire, and enable Vickie to take the road out of Skyline that "led toward the moon" (282).

When Vickie receives her acceptance letter, she goes first to the Rosens with the good news. Mrs. Rosen, "delighted[,] . . . squeezed the girl's round, good-natured cheeks, as if she could mould them into something definite then and there" (298). For his part, Mr. Rosen looks at Vickie "through his kind, remote smile" (299). Then trying "to distract her and help her to keep back the tears" (299), he gives Vickie her first French lesson: "'*Le but n'est rien; le chemin, c'est tout.*' That means: The end is nothing, the road is all'" (299). This scene shows that the biologically barren Rosens have figuratively created a child in their own image. The Rosens then take the step of putting this new-born creation on its feet, so to speak, by granting Vickie an unsecured loan that will enable her to actually attend the university. Now Vickie "won't just sit on de front porch" (298), but will make something of her life, and through her, the Rosens will help create the future.

It is worth noting that Vickie's future success will also be brought about through migration, and specifically through migration to a city. In facilitating Vickie's move to Ann Arbor, the Rosens point her in the direction of the cosmopolitan and also towards another degree of otherness. As Judith Fetterley and Marjorie Pryse point out, "Vickie . . . move[s] outside the home, beyond female community, and into the larger male-dominated world of the university" (596). Furthermore, this entrance will bring both freedom and conformity, as Mrs. Rosen makes clear. Since Mrs. Rosen comes "from a much wider experience" (296) than the Templetons, she takes it upon herself to teach Vickie the proper etiquette, informing her, "if you are going off into the world, it is quite time you learn to like things that are everywhere accepted" (300). Ironically, Mrs. Rosen prepares Vickie for moving into the world by making her more conformist, but perhaps Mrs. Rosen aims to save Vickie from the future embarrassment of being viewed as a country-bumpkin. In finding her niche in Skyline, Mrs. Rosen has clearly discovered that gaining respect requires a measure of conformity.

The Rosens—Jewish, cosmopolitan, and foreign—comprise a crucial element of this story by virtue of the tension they create, the bonds they form, and the roles they play. Instead of submerging or smoothing over their multiple identities, the Rosens nurture and utilize their otherness as a "ditch to build bridges over" (282). Still, the Rosens can only build bridges to the future—they cannot provide closure. Noting that we do not know what will happen to Victoria and Vickie, David Daiches remarks that "patterns which involve different generations are never complete" (93). Carlin similarly points out that Vickie occupies a particularly ambiguous position, as "her destiny is left open-ended and unsignified, seemingly different from the other women's in the text" (112), and yet Cather does tell us that Vickie's "lot will be more or less like" Grandma Harris's (314). In this story, the narrative voice allows the reader to sympathize at various times with all the major characters (Brown, *Critical Biography* 259). Furthermore, this sympathy reflects Cather's identification with (or at least her willingness to adopt the view of) three people at once—teenager Willie Cather, middle-aged Mary Virginia Cather, and old Rachel Boak. But she is also herself nearing sixty. Even in one of the last stories published during her lifetime (and one of her most autobiographical) Cather continues her career-long attempt to represent fluid fictional and personal selves through multiple subject positioning.

Cather continually saw herself and her art anew, experimenting with narration, form, and characterization and relentlessly trying to capture and communicate "the inexplicable presence of the thing not named" (*NUF* 50). In her personal life and in her fiction, Cather persistently defied easy categorization across a broad range of identity categories. Critical models which seek to place her definitively on one side or another of such binarisms as nativist/pluralist, nostalgic/modernist, patriarchal/feminist, prejudiced/open-minded end in quagmires which do not provide insight into Cather's goals or accomplishments. By engaging with some crucial issues of the early twentieth century—personal identity and the nature of the self, national identity and immigration, tradition and change, love and relationships—repeatedly and across her lifetime, Cather created an oeuvre of multi-layered texts with lasting relevance, works which represent both an American subjectivity and a looser conceptualization of identity.

Chapter Three

"Fiction Was Another Way of Telling the Truth": Gertrude Stein

Gertrude Stein had a lot in common with Willa Cather, but their literary lives turned out quite differently. Still they did share some views on the art of writing. Although Cather wrote subtle and often conservative fiction where Stein offered highly experimental and explicitly erotic works (Shaw, "Victorian" 23–24), both knew that journalism and literary art were incompatible. Just as Cather came to see the truth in Jewett's admonition that she would never be a great writer as long as she was working at *McClure's*, Stein told Hemingway, "if you keep on doing newspaper work you will never see things, you will only see words and that will not do, that is of course if you intend to be a writer" (*ABT* 213).[1] While both Cather and Stein needed and wanted to make money at their profession and to secure an appreciative audience, both wrote for reasons other than fortune and fame. Both writers were "trying to do something quite different," in the words of Cather's Godfrey St. Peter, and like St. Peter, both struggled to communicate with a critical readership that "merely thought [they were] . . . trying to do the usual thing, and had not succeeded very well" (*PH* 32). Experimental in her own way, Cather sought to create her own kind of realism and explored different possibilities for the novel demeuble.[2] For her part, Stein showed a career-long interest in the potential of modern narrative, particularly as it related to the virtually concomitant coming of age of modernity and of her own sense of self.

Stein never identified herself as an expatriate, and justifiably so, according to Benjamin Spencer (211). However, subsequent critics have emphasized her outsider status, particularly her position as a Jew, a lesbian, a woman artist/intellectual/genius, and an American whose permanent residence was overseas. Perhaps against what would have been Stein's own self-concept, Dearborn identifies her as an "ethnic expatriate" (173). Ethnicity was not always a salient aspect of Stein's sense of who she was, and Jewishness is not a major preoccupation in her earlier texts. Indeed, *Three Lives* seems to deflect attention from Stein's own ethnic heritage by concentrating on people who seem—on the surface, at any rate—to have little in common with her, although many of these characters are "ethnic" in American terms. In ignoring her own ethnic roots, however, Stein set up a roadblock of sorts to any kind of satisfying sense of self. William Gass's characterization of the young adult Stein as "a faithless Jew, a coupon clipper, exile anyhow, and in addition . . . desperately uncertain of her own sexuality" (16) highlights the connection between these identity categories. Although Gass declares that "the problem of personal identity . . . is triumphantly overcome in *The Geographical History of America*" (16), Stein's coming to terms with her own personal identity, as well as with the concept of personal identity as a whole, actually takes place over a longer period of time. With regard to ethnicity, for example, the transformation from writing about ethnic others to owning one's self as ethnic, from hiding behind the mask of ethnicity to employing it as a strategy, occurs over an extended period, roughly between "Melanctha" (1909) and *Everybody's Autobiography* (1937). "Melanctha" deals mainly with lower-class black characters, and *The Autobiography of Alice B. Toklas* speaks about Jews, but only as objects of disparaging and distancing remarks. By *Everybody's Autobiography*, however, Stein owns herself as Jewish and sees that as a valuable link between herself and other geniuses (Stimpson, "Lie" 160). Stein was a highly autobiographical writer. As Benstock has observed, Stein "tak[es] her own biography as her artistic subject matter," adding that "everything in her adult life became a subject for and was subjected to her art" (14). If biography was Stein's main source of literary inspiration, admitting her heritage and roots and owning her ethnic identity could only add to the fullness of her writing.

On the surface, Stein does not seem like someone intent on loosening up the boundaries between identity categories, in part because she was not outspoken in some of her identifications. She downplayed her Jewishness (i.e., ignored her ethnic identity), preferred to live where no one else spoke English (i.e., submerged her national identity), and set up a remarkably traditional patriarchal household for herself and her "wife," Alice (i.e., reinforced traditional gender categories). Nevertheless, she would eventually find strength in the same aspects of herself which she seemed most intent on suppressing or denying. Stein could not create herself *ex-nihilio*. Rather she needed to learn to accept and to use her roots as an asset, as William Carlos Williams insisted: "no use for Stein to fly to Paris and *forget* it. The thing, the United States, the unmitigated stupidity, the drab tediousness of the democracy, the overwhelming number of the offensively ignorant, the dull of nerve—is *there* in the artist's mind and cannot be escaped by taking a ship. She must resolve it if she can, if she is to *be*" (58). The same could be said of Stein's ethnic heritage and sexual orientation. The tensions that Gass enumerates are resolved in part through Stein's life and in part through her texts—the line between the two is often blurred. A writer of meandering and eclectic works, Stein was also a Wandering Jew and a thoroughgoing cosmopolitan from an early age. As Donald Sutherland notes, "that she was personally disconnected from any native or local context is again partly a Jewish situation and partly the accident of being born in Pennsylvania, traveling in France and Austria, and living in California and Baltimore, all before turning up for college work at Radcliffe, in the deliquescence of New England and the Puritan tradition" (M. Hoffman 93). Thus thinking of Stein as "completely and entirely american" (*ABT* 16) or connecting her exclusively with Paris still leaves out a good bit of the geographical crossing she experienced and chronicles in her texts (e.g. Belley, Spain, England). Stein admits that the habit of picking up roots and moving can create a sense of rootlessness, but qualifies this assertion by pointing out that "'our roots can be anywhere and we can survive, because if you think about it, we take our roots with us'" (Preston 157). Further, she argues that it is not necessary to return to roots; it is only necessary "'to have the feeling that they exist, that they are somewhere'" (Preston 157). As a lifetime traveler and an American, a lesbian and a patriarchal presence, a Jew and an anti-Semite, Stein occupied multiple subject positions. As a writer intent on creating a continuous present and committed to giving birth to the twentieth century, Stein offers visions and re-visions of her own development and that of the world around her.

Over the course of a lifetime of writing and changing, Stein discovered that adaptation and survival in the modern period required transitivity, the loosening of inherited forms and definitions, and the blurring and blending of boundaries. She redefined some genres, such as autobiography, and discarded those which no longer seemed relevant, such as the realistic novel.[3] Binaries like fiction/non-fiction she dismantled beyond recognition.

MELANCTHA HERBERT, NEW TRUE WOMAN

Stein considered the story she placed in the center of her first published collection "the first definite step away from the nineteenth century and into the twentieth century in literature" (*ABT* 54). "Melanctha" does indeed constitute an early prototype of what Cantor would call the expressionist strain of modernism, portraying minds immersed in short, energized bursts of experience (80). As the middle narrative of *Three Lives,* "Melanctha" occupies a symbolic discursive position. The story is a microcosm of the larger work, focusing on three lives in and of itself, namely Melanctha Herbert's, Rose Johnson's, and Jeff Campbell's.[4] Indeed, although Melanctha is the title character, the story itself begins with Rose Johnson, and the first several pages are devoted to Rose's background and Rose's view of Melanctha. The fact that many critics identify Stein with Jeff would also lead us to expect him to take over the story (as, for example, *My Antonia* becomes more about Jim—a Cather-figure—than Antonia), and yet the story remains distinctly Melanctha's.[5]

In addition to serving in a synechdochic capacity, "Melanctha" is framed (flanked, enveloped, enclosed, entrapped) by two stories about working-class German-American (white) women. This placement was clearly intentional because the order of composition was "The Good Anna," "The Gentle Lena," and, lastly, "Melanctha" (Wagner-Martin, *Favored* 77). "Melanctha" both disrupts and elucidates the stories which frame it. In it, Stein details a black world. No white characters of any importance appear within the context of the story, and few are even mentioned (although Melanctha does wander with a few unnamed white men at various points). And yet the white world impinges on Melanctha's from both sides. While we can see Melanctha as hemmed in by a legacy of slavery and by ongoing racism, we might also observe that Stein's collection simultaneously poses a certain de-facto equalization.[6] Implicit in referring to the eponymous three lives as such is a lack of value judgment or distinction. All three women live. All three women have troubled sexual and emotional relationships. All three women die. White and black, smart and dull, the women end up in much the same place. The same conclusion can be reached through Stein's assessment of *Three Lives* as dealing with "'niggers and servant girls and the foreign population generally'" (qtd. in Wald 240). While this quote is racist, totalizing, and as politically incorrect as possible, it nevertheless shows that Stein had some understanding of the marginal status shared by lower-class, immigrant, and black Americans around the turn of the century.

Stein certainly claims to have firsthand knowledge of the kind of people about whom she writes, referring to *Three Lives* as "'a book about different characters, three different people I knew long ago'" (qtd. in Wagner-Martin, *Favored* 87). While we cannot connect the name "Melanctha" with that of a specific person as we can for Cather's Antonia (Annie Sadilek Pavelka) or Stein's Good Anna (Lena Lebender), Wagner-Martin writes that Stein would have had opportunities to gain insight into how people like Melanctha lived: "during [Stein's] teen years in Oakland, California, she had listened to and watched blacks in Fruitvale; during her practical training at medical school, she had known black women as patients in Baltimore" (*Favored* 78).[7] This explanation hardly supports Stein's claim that "no one knew black culture better than she" (Wagner-Martin, *Favored* 78), but it does to some degree legitimate Stein's use of black subjects. Some have seen this text as a racist and classist appropriation, a way to play it safe by deflecting her own difference onto less privileged others.[8] Although this phenomenon plays a role in the text's mode of representation, "Melanctha" should not be reduced to "merely" a code or a set of substitutions. For instance, Stein's Paris present comes into play in the text as well, if we can trust "Alice," who recalls that "the poignant incidents that [Stein] wove into the life of Melanctha were often these she noticed in walking down the hill from the rue Ravignan" (*ABT* 49). Further, both Jeff and Melanctha are comprised of some of the attributes of Stein's younger self.

As Cather would later do in *My Antonia*, Stein projects aspects of herself onto both a male and a female character in "Melanctha." She is Jeff Campbell, steady and reliable man, and Melanctha Herbert, wild and wandering woman. Ruddick sees this "bifurcat[ion]" as a division into "a Jamesian male and a victimized woman," noting that "Stein tends to think of herself as variously male and female" (*Reading* 53). While I agree with Ruddick's general point, I resist the binary implications of a term like "bifurcation." Ruddick sees Melanctha as a repository for the "parts of Stein that Jeff (and William James) did not express" (4), but I would point out that "James" runs in Melanctha's blood, as well. The father whom she both hates and admires (and certainly takes after) is also a James, namely James Herbert. Further, I would hesitate to identify Melanctha purely as a victim, though Wagner-Martin also sees Melanctha as a "victim . . . of prescriptive heterosexual culture" (*Favored* 79). The woman-as-victim paradigm is essentially Victorian, and it is the Victorian sensibility that Stein clearly rejects in her creation of "Melanctha" (Blackmer 34). Stein shows Melanctha from her girlhood as smart, savvy, and able to take care of herself. Her decisions might not always be the best ones, but she is not ignorant, passive, or helpless. This heroine has nothing to do with purity (she sleeps around), piety (she rarely attends church), domesticity (she has no permanent home), or submission (she defies her parents and rarely acknowledges any kind of authority), and yet she wins the reader's sympathy. Melanctha is a new kind of literary heroine, the True Woman of the twentieth century.

In addition to adhering to the tenets of the Cult of True Womanhood, the nineteenth-century True Woman was, by definition, Anglo-Saxon, cultured, polite, and heterosexual. Melanctha, on the other hand, is an American bisexual mulatta, an individualist, a free spirit, and a paragon of mixed blood. Indeed, her story itself invokes an American sensibility which actually stood as a barrier to publication. When Stein submitted the manuscript of *Three Lives* to Grant Richards for possible publication in England, Richards responded that the text would have trouble attracting an English readership, in part due to "the question of scene and atmosphere, both in this case so very American that the ordinary English reader would be a little at a loss" (54). Even more so than the protagonists of the other two stories, Melanctha elides categorization. As if to dramatize this difference, Stein leaves this title character on her own, without adjectives or modifiers. She is not "good" or "gentle," but simply "Melanctha: Each One as She May." This subtitle has several connotations. On the one hand, it invokes a moral hands-off: to each his own. The relativism such a stance implies is characteristic of modernist texts (Cantor 39), and it prefigures the position that Stein will take on such taboo issues as promiscuity and lesbianism in the narrative that follows. Taken from a Darwinian or economic perspective, the statement of non-judgementalism found in the story's subtitle suggests a lack of communal responsibility, a sense that everyone is on her own. The narrator seems to sympathize with Melanctha, but no one can save her or help her escape her predicaments.

Melanctha's name is not typically black American the way that Anna and Lena are common German-American names, but it does give us some indication of what kind of a person she is. Melanctha is melancholy, as we see from the beginning pages of the narrative: "sometimes the thought of how all her world was made, filled the complex, desiring Melanctha with despair. She wondered, often, how she could go on living when she was so blue" (48). And yet she also possesses the capacity for foolish joy. Further, the name Herbert invokes the subtle and "lowly herb" (Skaggs 54) in contrast to Rose Johnson's flamboyant, strong-smelling, love-symbolizing bloom. "Herb" suggests Melanctha's socio-economic status (low), her tendency to display a meek "sweetness" (73), the possibility of a bitter life for her (i.e., bitter herbs), and her potential for varied usefulness (e.g., healing, producing a pleasant taste or smell). Melanctha is thus unlike both the women whose stories frame hers and the other women in her text.

Blackmer identifies Melanctha as "a mulatta suspended between two races and sexualities" (15), but I would argue that she is not so much suspended as passing. She neither passes for white nor engages in cross-dressing, and yet she is ultimately "mysterious" (50, 61) and unknowable. This is true on a physical level as well as on a more symbolic one. Stein underscores the enigmatic quality of race by telling us that Melanctha's mother is a mulatta while her father is very black, and then referring to Melanctha on several occasions as "half white" (48). In this way Stein shows the futility of applying scientific terms to racial composition. Figuratively speaking, Melanctha's mystery might stem from her refusal to adopt and conform to a single, unitary subject position for any sustained period of time. She will not settle down to the exclusionary role of wife, mistress, or midwife. Unlike Larsen's Helga Crane, whose passing is connected to her serial identifications,[9] Melanctha passes by eliding categories altogether. She has no essential self. Helvie speaks to this phenomenon when she attests that "perhaps the word 'passing' is more accurately a reflection of the ability of some people to transcend artificial binaries, representing the slippage which occurs every time we attempt to use an adjective" (39), simultaneously noting society's discomfort with this sort of ambiguity.

Melanctha's fluid sexual orientation is potentially as threatening as her ambiguous racial heritage. Elaine Ginsberg notes that gender ambiguity causes at least as much anxiety and backlash in our society as racial crossing: "it can be argued that gender, in the arbitrariness of its cultural prescriptions, is a trope of difference that shares with race (especially in the context of black/white passing) a similar structure of identity categories whose enactments and boundaries are culturally policed" (13).[10] Thus, I would argue that Melanctha does not hover between categories, as Blackmer's term "suspended" would suggest. Rather, she assumes and discards different identities fluidly. Furthermore, while Melanctha might be viewed as a passing subject, I resist the temptation to view her text as passing for *Q.E.D.*, a blackface version of Stein's earlier work. In agreeing with Blackmer's assertion that "Melanctha" is not just a translation of *Q.E.D.* in which race substitutes for or masks sexuality (55–56), I would further point out that (homo)sexuality is not at all submerged, repressed, masked, or coded in "Melanctha" (or, for that matter, in "The Good Anna"). All of these issues are integrally connected with "Melanctha" as an autonomous text.

As a passing subject, Melanctha is very much a "sel[f] in transit, between narratives as much as between geopolitical locations" (Wald 238). She needs to wander in order to live, like a shark that must move continually in order to keep oxygen pumping through its gills. When she stops to perform a single unitary identity position, she is imminent danger of suffocating or drowning. Thus Melanctha continually role-plays and experiments. From being hoisted onto construction sites (58) to trying "drinking and some of the other habits" (59) of her companions, Melanctha finds out who she is through experiential learning. She has "a strong sense for real experience" (59), and recognizes it in others. For Melanctha, "real experience" is lived experience, as opposed to book learning or story-telling. Her taste for it leads her to "experience[d]," "roughened," and "reckless" people like Jane Harden (59). "Real experience" is inflected with danger and connected with "bad habits" (59). Furthermore, its association with wandering suggests that the path to such wisdom is not direct or predictable. Hence, Melanctha does not settle, but merely passes

through. Melanctha's wandering helps her "to really understand" (59), and
she seems to be well-liked by the people she encounters. In some ways,
though, her passing is unsuccessful. Unlike Clare Kendry, who will pass in
order to get the things she wants (Cutter 84), "Melanctha had not found it
easy with herself to make her wants and what she had, agree. Melanctha
Herbert was always losing what she had in wanting all the things she saw"
(50). After pages and years of wanting, having and losing, Melanctha ultimately passes away.[11]

Although wandering is preferable to stagnation, it is not a comfortable
place to reside. Indeed it is not a place at all, but a no-place. Whereas migration implies a destination, wandering does not have the positive connotations
of directed movement. The quintessential wanderer is, of course, the
Wandering Jew,[12] a figure who has paradoxically been inflected with both the
curse of homeless immortality and the enviable position of complete freedom
coupled with the possession of extraordinary knowledge (Stableford 20–21,
7). Like the Wandering Jew, Melanctha seems to find her "situation carefully
made intolerable by one additional affliction or another" (Stableford 21), but
unlike the prototypical wanderer she is at least released to death by the end of
Stein's text. While the parallels to the symbolic Wandering Jew are limited and
Melanctha does not seem like the stuff of archetype, a provocative type of cosmopolitanism inheres in her wandering. From a young age, Melanctha gives
the appearance of a cosmopolitan, though her worldliness is more social than
geographical. Although she stays in roughly the same location, Melanctha
takes on the demeanor of a world traveler, as the narrator reports, "in these
days, Melanctha talked and stood and walked with many kinds of men. . . .
They all supposed her to have world knowledge and experience" (55). Still,
we might argue that Melanctha's wandering bestows upon her a "cosmopolitan mobility" (Robbins 172). She learns to escape and to keep relationships
from getting too deep, like a true metropolitan man. We might further see
Melanctha's characteristic mysteriousness as a manifestation of metropolitan
reserve (Simmel 53). In order to function in an environment requiring almost
continual interaction, the city-dweller must adopt a protective stance which
includes a detachment from the people around him or her. Melanctha has intimate relationships, but many of her wanderings take her into contact with
only nameless people who do not penetrate her psychic space. Indeed, one
could not imagine Melanctha's story set in the country. As an early or "[al-
most] modernist" text (DeKoven, *Rich* 68), "Melanctha" reflects the convergence of the growth of American cities and the beginnings of the modernist
movement.[13] Melanctha's coming-of-age is tied to that of the twentieth century, literary modernism, and, therefore, the modern metropolis.

Since "Melanctha" deals with multiple comings-of-age, it might seem plausible to consider the text a *bildungsroman*. Indeed, this lens provides a context for the numerous details of Melanctha's childhood and family life that Stein includes in her story. In the course of the text, we see Melanctha grow from girlhood to sexual maturity and womanhood. The ending denies us a successful marriage and instead offers death,[14] but the coming-of-age plot is easy to trace. At the same time, it is problematic to assign a traditional generic category to a text which is structurally underscored by and thematically saturated with images of mobility, wandering, and passing. Furthermore, while a young person's coming of age generally follows a linear and predictable path (like growing older itself), "Melanctha" employs a wandering sense of time. Paradoxically, DeKoven sees "Melanctha" both as utilizing "nineteenth-century narrative forms . . . as structuring frames" and as constituting a "naturalistic antibildungsroman of Melanctha's thwarted life" (*Rich* 67).[15] Although "Melanctha" enters into problematic dialog with the *bildungsroman* tradition, Melanctha's life is not completely "thwarted." Also, if the story does not seem pedantic or moralistic, then neither is it naturalistic. M.H. Abrams defines naturalism in the following way:

> [I]t is distinctively a mode of fiction that was developed by a school of writers in accordance with a particular philosophical thesis. This thesis, a product of post-Darwinian biology in the nineteenth century, held that a human being exists entirely in the order of nature and does not have a soul nor any mode of participating in a religious or spiritual world beyond nature; and therefore, that such a being is merely a higher-order animal whose character and behavior are entirely determined by two kinds of forces, heredity and environment. A person inherits compulsive instincts—especially hunger, the accumulative drive, and sexuality—and then is subject to the social and economic forces in the family, the class, and the milieu into which that person is born. (175)

While Melanctha seems to take after her mother in having an innate drive to wander, her intellectuality is continually underscored. The narrator characterizes Melanctha as "subtle" and "intelligent," while Rose reports that "Melanctha is so bright and learned so much in school" (48). Even Jane Harden, who cheerfully slanders Melanctha whenever given the opportunity, admits that "Melanctha Herbert had a good mind, Jane never denied that to her" (64). Similarly, Jeff Campbell quickly (and to his great satisfaction) determines that Melanctha "had a good mind" (76). Furthermore, naturalism's belief in the power of heredity and environment to totally define stands in stark contrast to the epigraph of *Three Lives,* which is taken from Jules Laforgue:

"*Donc je suis malheureux et ce n'est ni ma faute ni celle de la vie* [Therefore I am unhappy and it is neither my fault nor that of life]" (iv). The source of the speaker's unhappiness is neither inborn nor wholly a function of environment. Perhaps the speaker is cursed like the Wandering Jew, doomed by a miracle (see Stableford 3), or perhaps the notion of blame itself has lost its relevance in the speaker's world. In either case, Melanctha, like Stein, lives at a transitional period in American and world history. Naturalism's adoption of Darwinian theories of evolution and natural selection stands in contrast to modernism's anti-historicist stance, which "did not believe that truth lay in telling an evolutionary story" (Cantor 35). Therefore it would seem that rather than reifying the nineteenth-century's preoccupation with the all-encompassing explanatory power of heredity and environment, Stein is trying to move in a new direction, namely that of the twentieth century. In any case, *bildungsroman* or anti-*bildungsroman, Three Lives* is not a novel and "Melanctha" is not a novella. Stein's response to questions about the book's genre sound almost exactly like the answer Cather will give ten years later about *My Antonia:* "when asked if *Three Lives* was a novel, she replied in her plainspoken way, 'I hate labels. It's just a book . . . '" (Wagner-Martin, *Favored* 87).[16]

Stein's refusal to identify *Three Lives* as a novel suggests that she considered the work she was doing in the peculiarly twentieth-century "Melanctha" a radical departure from nineteenth-century modes and concerns. In fact, "Melanctha" embodies some of the tension between residual nineteenth-century forms and emerging twentieth-century ones. For example, Stein's text shares the *bildungsroman*'s preoccupation with the problematic nature of families, while simultaneously constituting a breaking away from "the characteristic plot of mid-nineteenth-century 'woman's fiction'" (Showalter 362). In this, Stein finds an unlikely ally in Edith Wharton, whose Lily Bart wrestles with finding a functional subject position in a transitional society. Elaine Showalter observes that Lily "is stranded between two worlds of female experience: the intense female friendships and mother-daughter bonds characteristic of nineteenth-century American women's culture . . . and the dissolution of these single-sex relationships in the interests of more intimate friendships between women and men that was part of the gender crisis of the turn of the century" (358). Melanctha, too, finds herself exchanging intense filial relations for more shallow friendships and chance encounters with women and men outside of her family. Thus Stein demythologizes Victorian conceptualizations of families, and thereby enters the turn-of-the-century debate over the nature of family. One example of the way Stein opposes Victorian notions of the family is by offering an alternative to the reigning image of mothers who adore and fathers who protect their children. Melanctha's parents do not like her very much. They "found it very troublesome to have her" (50) and take no pains to hide their disappointment in their daughter, as Rose informs her husband: "one day Melanctha was real little, and she heard her ma say to her pa, it was awful sad to her, Melanctha had not been the one the Lord had took from them stead of the little brother who was dead in the house there from fever" (127). The feeling is mutual, as Melanctha dislikes her father intensely and "had not liked her mother very well" (50) either. Furthermore, she uses her book learning and her "nasty" tongue "to annoy her parents who knew nothing" (51). Melanctha does her filial duty by her dying mother, but there is never any sense of reconciliation: "Melanctha's mother never liked her daughter any better" (65). Early in the text, Melanctha becomes a heroine whose mother, like Lily Bart's, "is dead and unmourned" (Showalter 362). Melanctha's problematic relation to her parents is further complicated by racial issues. In contrast with the stereotypical cases of little girls taking after their mothers and little boys taking after their fathers, the light-skinned Melanctha identifies with the "black coarse father" she "almost always hated" (50), downplaying her ties to her "pale" (ghostly, ineffectual, unexciting) and "yellow" (weak, cowardly) mother.[17] Melanctha looks like her mother, but inside she is filled with her father's venom: she "loved very well the power in herself that came through [her father]" (50). Her inheritance from her "pale yellow, sweet-appearing mother," on the other hand, "never made her feel respect" (50).[18] While Melanctha resembles her mother in physical features, the raw power she longs to wield is modeled by her black and male parent.[19] Like her creator, Melanctha first seeks to become part of a community of men: "in these young days, it was only men that for Melanctha held anything there was of knowledge and power" (54). Although she recognizes that her power derives from her father, she does not necessarily see the extent to which she shares his traits. Jane Harden, albeit an unreliable source, insists that "Melanctha was always abusing her father and yet she was just like him, and really she admired him so much and he never had any sense of what he owed to anybody, and Melanctha was just like him and she was proud of it too" (64). In this way we might read Melanctha's disdain for her father as a form of masochism or self-flagellation. All the same, Melanctha eventually suffers because of her social legacy from her mother. In a patriarchal society which demands fidelity and regularity, "'Mis' Herbert had always been a little wandering and mysterious and uncertain in her ways" (50; see also 52). Her "sweetness, and [her] way of listening with intelligence and sympathetic interest" (59) are also typical female traits, passed on from mother to daughter. Although she does not have any children herself, Melanctha expends all her energy nurturing others until there is no one left to nurture her.[20] She occupies the position of both nurse and mammy when she cares for her mother and for Rose's baby. Ultimately, however, Melanctha finds that the affiliative bonds she has created with men (like Jeff Campbell and Jem Richards) and women (like Jane Harden and Rose Johnson) cannot fulfill one main purpose of family, that of providing care. Melanctha occupies the position of black mammy or domestic servant, but her blackness comes from her father, whose skin color is linked to virility and strength, but also to abandonment and irresponsibility. In this way, race complicates gender identity, and both require a revamping of the traditional nuclear family.

In her first attempts to create a mutually supportive affiliative relationship to take the place of the Victorian family, Melanctha finds Jane Harden. Melanctha initially looks towards Jane as a parent-figure and eventually acts as a caretaker for her, suggesting that Jane provides a microcosmic re-enactment, both idealistic and ironic, of a mother-daughter relationship. Melanctha is sixteen when she meets Jane, a hardened woman of twenty-three, and she feels honored to be accepted by the older woman, "very proud that this Jane would let her know her" (59). For the first year of their relationship, "Jane had been much the stronger" (60). Jane occupies the powerful position of teacher, while Melanctha is "sweet and docile" (60). During her year as a disciple, "Melanctha sat at Jane's feet for many hours . . . and felt Jane's wisdom" (60). Before too long, however, the power dynamic shifts—almost imperceptibly, yet irreversibly: "slowly now between them, it was Melanctha Herbert, who was stronger" (61). Just as Melanctha's book learning gives her power over her parents, her wisdom-learning makes her stronger than Jane. This change spells the end of the relationship, as "slowly now they began to drift apart from one another" (61). The falling out takes place over about a year, just as Melanctha's waxing attraction to Jane does. By the time the relationship peters out, Melanctha is eighteen, a legal adult and a person who was "ready now herself to do teaching" (61). Melanctha does not drop Jane completely, but the relationship loses its fire.

Not long after the relationship with Jane winds down, Melanctha's mother begins to die. And "Mis" Herbert takes a long time getting around to it. Prefiguring *The Autobiography of Alice B. Toklas* in which circular time prevails and events occur and recur out of chronological order, "Melanctha" repeatedly announces "Mis" Herbert's death and brings her back to life again. The plotting of the story line suggests that Stein means to underscore the wandering and mysterious tendencies of Melanctha and her mother by telling about their relations in a wandering, repetitive, indirect manner. The narrator starts by informing us that "during this year . . . Melanctha's pale yellow mother was very sick, and in this year she died" (62). A few paragraphs later, we find out that "Melanctha did everything that any woman could, and at last her mother died, and Melanctha had her buried" (63). In terms of the story, however, "Mis" Herbert is far from buried. At this point, the text backtracks to describe the evolving relationship between Melanctha and Jefferson Campbell, the "serious, earnest, good young joyous doctor" (63), who attended to "Mis" Herbert in her illness. Throughout this flashback, "Mis" Herbert is "always getting sicker" (65) and "it was pretty sure that she would have to die" (72), but she "linger[s] on" (77) for several days in story time and quite a few pages of the text before "slowly and without much pain she died away" (77). Melanctha's mother will not pass away swiftly, completely, or simply. Hence, Melanctha has difficulty separating from her mother and her mother's legacy of meekness and impotence. Melanctha's need to define herself in opposition to her parents (or at least as autonomous from them) has a psychological (and particularly a psychoanalytic) basis, but it also reflects the position of the ethnic or immigrant heroine in America. As Dearborn has pointed out, the typical ethnic heroine separates from her parents in order to establish an independent American identity; distancing herself from her literal father (or mother) enables the heroine to adopt the Founding Fathers as her own (76, 89).[21] Melanctha's goal does not conform to an ideal of Americanization, but her homelessness is emblematic of the American condition. As Joseph Urgo has extrapolated from a James Baldwin essay which discusses Americanism, "an entire nation predicated on the belief in origins *elsewhere* is a homeless nation" (195). Hence Melanctha's position as a homeless member of a homeless nation makes her a particularly apt figure for Stein's explorations of how an American self defines itself and functions in the world. Following her mother's death, Melanctha loses her living quarters and becomes an orphan without a place or a purpose: "she lived now with this colored woman and now with that one, and she sewed, and sometimes she taught a little in a colored school as substitute for some teacher. Melanctha had now no home nor any regular employment" (62). Paradoxically, Melanctha's status as orphan and homeless person allows her to move forward, as the narrator immediately informs us: "life was just commencing for Melanctha" (62).[22] Indeed, her mother's death might well be taken as a commencement ceremony of sorts. Although she receives no formal degree, Melanctha now has "wisdom" (62) and the capacity for independent action. She "did not need help now to know, or to stay longer, or when she wanted, to escape" (62). At this point, Melanctha is ripe for the heterosexual relationship which supposedly takes the place of the mother-daughter bond, according to some models of human development. Drawing on psychoanalytic theory, Nancy Chodorow observes that "because her first love object is a woman, a girl, in order to attain her proper heterosexual orientation, must transfer her primary object choice to her father and men" (192). Melanctha's orientation towards her father is an attraction to the sources of his power as opposed to a desire to take her mother's place. Nevertheless, her eventual ability and willingness to enter into a sustained relationship with a man (namely Jeff Campbell) is linked both textually and symbolically to her mother's death. Furthermore, from the point of view of literary (as opposed to human) development, "Melanctha" moves away from the pattern of nineteenth-century woman's fiction and its emphasis on close mother-daughter relationships by offering a heterosexual friendship which must have seemed quite risqué and ground-breaking at the time.

The literary representation of close friendships between unmarried men and women was new and perhaps even radical, and it was certainly indicative of Stein's plans and desires to be an innovator. Although Jefferson Campbell enters Melanctha's life in a stereotypical and symbolic manner, Stein immediately subverts these conventions. As the fatherless Melanctha prepares to nurse her mother during her final illness, Jeff appears as the powerful and paternal doctor. By the time, "Mis" Herbert dies, Melanctha is ready to affirm Jeff as everything a man or woman could be to a woman for all times: "'you certainly are mother, and father, and brother, and sister, and child and everything, always to me'" (78).[23] Jeff is handsome and successful, an educated professional, and class plays an important role in the text. Although some critics see the entire story as dealing with a monolithic "lower-class" (e.g. Wagner-Martin, *Favored* 77), Jeff is in fact middle-class. While I do not disagree with DeKoven's statement that "dark race and low class . . . together with the maternal itself, erupt in a troubled conjuncture at the birth of modernist narrative" (*Rich* 67), I would point out that Melanctha, Jane, Jeff, and Jem are all remarkable for their light skin, while Jeff is an upwardly-mobile professional. The narrator perpetuates a pigmentocracy by insisting that Melanctha's white blood entitles her to better treatment than the dark-skinned Rose (48), while Jane "had much white blood and that made her see clear" (59). At the same time, Melanctha's proclivity for sexual abandon links her to a primitivism defined by "an exuberant enthusiasm for the simple, the at-once innocent and sexually uninhibited" (DuCille 201). Looking at Jeff's model childhood and his middle-class pretensions, on the other hand, contemporary black readers might well have recognized him as a figure who should be condemned as "less than authentically black" (DuCille 198).[24] Indeed Jeff embodies what Stein's Harvard professor, Munsterberg, somewhat patronizingly observes of the dilemma of the nascent black middle class: "the real tragedy is not in the lives of the most miserable, but in the lives of those who wish to rise, who feel the mistakes of their fellow-negroes and the injustice of their white opponents, who desire to assimilate everything high and good in the culture about them, and yet who know that they do not, strictly speaking, belong to such a culture" (171). Jeff does not seem to feel his oppression particularly keenly, but he certainly expresses frustration about the self-defeating behaviors he sees in his patients. Indeed, he seems rather condescending at times. Jeff's socioeconomic status constitutes an important difference between himself and the other characters in the story. Bottomley observes that lower socio-economic class "create[s], in James Baldwin's phrase, 'another country'" (10), so we could view Jeff as living in a different world from Melanctha's.

Nevertheless, although he comes from a much more stable and middle-class background than Melanctha, Jeff Campbell is of mixed blood as well, "a young mulatto" (62). Fluidity, however, has no place in Jeff's ideal schema, as he believes "you ought to love your father and your mother and to be regular in all your life, and not to be always wanting new things and excitements, and to always know where you were, and what you wanted, and to always tell everything just as you meant it" (67). This image of the family, the social personality, and the process of communication is quite Victorian, suggesting that Jeff's attitudes are rearguard as opposed to modern. Indeed, Jeff sees almost everything as capable of being sorted according to simple binary categories. When Melanctha accuses him of not "believ[ing] it's right to love anybody" (70) because love is inherently bound up with irregularities and excitements, Jeff retreats to classifications: "I certainly do only know just two kinds of ways of loving. One kind of loving seems to me, is like one has a good quiet feeling in a family when one does his work, and is always living good and being regular, and then the other way of loving is just like having it like any animal that's low in the streets together . . . and that's all the kinds of love I know" (71). The impasse Melanctha and Jeff reach over the nature of love might profitably be linked to the modernist conflict between disruptive desire and the social regulation of fixed identities. We might even choose to look at Melanctha and Jeff as representatives of two strains of modernism. Melanctha suggests the expressionist school of D.H. Lawrence, which emphasizes the mind immersed in short, energized burst of experience, blood, sex and vitalism (Cantor 80). Jeff, on the other hand, aligns himself with what will become the classical modernism of an Eliot or a Pound—analytical, rational, emotionally restrained, and marked by elitism and cultural conservativism (Cantor 80). Later Jeff will refer to the two ways of loving as "two kinds of ways of living" (93). Life is love, but only within strictly demarcated boundaries. Even further along in the story, Jeff articulates the idea that "loving is just living" (104). Reinstituting the dichotomy, however, Jeff proclaims that he had never had "any claim to know what Melanctha thought it right that she should do in any of her ways of living. All Jeff felt a right in himself to question, was her loving" (110). In other words, everything. Melanctha eventually informs Jeff that there are more than two ways of loving, as she explains, "'I do love you Jeff, sure yes, but not the kind of way of loving you are ever thinking it now Jeff with me. I ain't got certainly no hot passion any more now in me" (120–121).[25] Melanctha's recognition of diminished fervor stands in stark contrast to the black primitivist icon of modernist eroticism, and her subject position is a complex one. Some elements of Melanctha's characterization draw on gross stereotypes of black female sexuality (Ammons 103). It is important to note, however, that Stein simultaneously subverts such caricatures, notably by portraying Melanctha as much more mature and complex than Jeff in her world view and her self-knowledge.

Melanctha knows that there are different ways of loving: love with hot passion, love without hot passion, the love of women for women, and the love of women for men. She also subverts gender norms by occupying the space of both disciple (with Jane) and teacher (with Jeff), and by seeking Jeff out as a potential love interest as opposed to passively waiting for him to notice her. For his part, Jeff Campbell is not particularly manly. Women are attracted to him because "he was so strong, and good, and understanding, and innocent, and firm, and gentle" (75), but he does not seem capable of sustaining a long-term relationship with a woman. Further, he seems as much concerned that Melanctha "had a good mind" (76) as he is with any kind of physical attraction, and he looks to Melanctha as someone who "could surely really teach him" (76). He later exults in his status as Melanctha's pupil, boasting, "You can't say ever, Melanctha, no can you, I ain't a real good boy to be always studying to be learning to be real bright like my teacher" (94). Jeff's attraction to Melanctha is, in fact, predicated on his information about her, so that when he finds out from Jane about Melanctha's wandering with "the different men, white ones and blacks" (84), Melanctha suddenly "seem[s] very ugly to him" (84). Melanctha characterizes Jeff's ensuing silence as "'one of the queer ways you have to be good'" (84),[26] and concludes: "'you ain't man enough to deserve to have anybody care so much to be always with you'" (85). Melanctha, on the other hand, occupies the power position. She is, figuratively speaking, "on top" (Poirier 30) in her association with Jeff. She initiates the relationship and she calls the shots. By stating that Jeff is not sufficiently manly to merit constant attention, Melanctha implicitly compares him unfavorably to herself, "a man like me," to use Stein's own words (qtd. in Pierpont 80). Later, Melanctha remarks, "'modest, that certainly is a queer thing for you Jeff to be calling yourself even when you are laughing'" (107). The text gives no overt indication that

Jeff is not heterosexual, and he certainly professes to tell it "straight" (99). Hence, among other things, "queer" seems to signify contradictory impulses. When we consider Stein as projecting parts of herself onto Jeff as well as onto Melanctha, the picture becomes even more complicated. Stein did not engage in the male pseudonymy which marked Cather's and Larsen's first published works, but she shares their use of male surrogates. Stein's use of Jeff appears much like Cather's creation of Jim Burden (and Niel Herbert), since in both cases a lesbian writer speaks through the voice of a man in love with a woman with whom he cannot sustain a love relationship. This is not to say that "Melanctha" is a coded text in which Stein employs Jeff as a mouthpiece for her own frustrated attempts to secure a long-term relationship with a beloved woman. Rather, different ways of loving are linked to fluid gender boundaries and to characters who occupy complex subject positions.

The nature of love relationships is further interrogated in the text by Stein's insistence that love is not just subject to fate—it is subject to law. Throughout "Melanctha" romantic affiliations which take place outside the bounds of "regular" marriage (e.g., Melanctha and Jane, Melanctha and Jeff, Melanctha and Jem) are continually held up to those which are legally sanctioned (e.g., James and "Mis" Herbert, Rose and Sam). At times it seems as though legal marriage is more important than almost anything else. On the first page of the text, we are told that "Rose had lately married Sam Johnson," while "Melanctha Herbert had not yet been really married" (47). Thus Rose receives legitimation and power in spite of the fact that the narrator deems her much less deserving than Melanctha. The narrator expresses indignation at the irony whereby "this unmoral, promiscuous, shiftless Rose [was] married . . . to a good man of the negroes, while Melanctha with her white blood and attraction and her desire for a right position had not yet been really married" (48). Rose squares her history of promiscuous behavior with her belief in acting properly with a verbal sleight of hand: "You know very well Melanctha that I've always been engaged to them" (49). Eventually Rose decides "it would be nice and very good in her position to get regularly really married" (49) and does so. Melanctha, on the other hand, comes to wish to marry a bad man of the mixed-race, but he leaves her. This abortive engagement constitutes a disruption of the Victorian marriage plot or the female *bildungsroman*'s heterosexual happily ever after. It also has important ramifications for nationality. Melanctha's story does not become "an official narrative of American identity" because she cannot become part of a "traditional American family" (Wald 253, 246).

It is interesting to note that even though Jeff and Melanctha constitute a heterosexual couple, they never speak of marriage and their relationship shares qualities with that of a homosexual one. For one thing, Melanctha and Jeff are intensely closeted. Taking again Sedgwick's assertion that secrecy creates a closet (205), we might observe that Melanctha and Jeff keep their growing attraction for each other concealed, not knowing whom they are hiding from or even what exactly they are seeking to cover up. The omniscient narrator describes Melanctha and Jeff as if they were children hiding from an amused parent, noting that "they always acted together, these two, as if their being so much together was a secret, but really there was no one who would have made it any harder for them" (83).

The ostensibly heterosexual relationship between Melanctha and Jeff unfolds in much the same way as the same-sex relationship between Melanctha and Jane did. Melanctha enjoys wandering with different types of men, but the narrator reports that "it was not from the men that Melanctha learned her wisdom. It was always Jane Harden herself who was making Melanctha begin to understand" (59). In the beginning of the relationship, the older woman possesses both knowledge and power, but with time Melanctha becomes ascendant. Again in her relationship with Jeff Campbell, Melanctha begins by yearning for Jeff while he remains aloof. As the narrator explains: "he held off and did not know what it was that Melanctha wanted. Melanctha came to want him very badly" (62). During this time, Melanctha comes to "feel his power with her always getting stronger" (72). When Jeff and Melanctha first start wandering together, "Melanctha never talked much" (78). By the time the relationship is on its last legs, however, "Jeff was always very silent with Melanctha. . . . Jeff never had much to say to her. Now when they were together, it was Melanctha always did most of the talking" (111). This quote provides a good example of Stein's repetition with a difference. Jeff's silence is not a regular silence. He is "very silent" which suggests a particular kind of silence. It is a qualitative and meaningful silence, not merely the absence of sound. Melanctha is "always . . . very pleasant in her talk" (112) to Jeff, but such kindness brings him scant comfort, as was the case with Melanctha's diligent attentions to Jane's welfare. Once Jeff has accepted that Melanctha does not really love him, he "was never any more a torment to Melanctha, he was only silent to her" (118). Again, the idiom is significant: Jeff is not *silent with* Melanctha, but *silent to* her.

Jeff has nothing to say to Melanctha in part because he has no claim on her. Marriage is, among other things, a property relation, and Melanctha and Jeff try to develop a sense of possession in spite of the lack of legitimation for their love, an attempt that ultimately proves unsuccessful. Early in the relationship, Melanctha is glad to claim "her Jeff Campbell" (90), while Jeff starts feeling protective towards "his Melanctha" (95). Already we know, however, that this nascent possession will ultimately disintegrate. Indeed, before too long Melanctha's attempt to assure "my own boy Jeff Campbell" (104–105) of her undying love falls flat because Jeff knows that "something . . . was not right now in her" (105). Jeff captures the irony of using possessive terms of endearment when he states, "'Good-bye Melanctha, though you certainly is my own little girl for always'" (109). Afterwards, Melanctha begins to wander again, once again with girls at first (107). Although Jeff and Melanctha each claim the other as his or her own, the relationship lacks a certain element of accountability. Hence when Melanctha resumes her wandering, Jeff does not question her about it: "Jeff Campbell always felt strongly within him, he had no right to interfere with Melanctha in any practical kind of a matter. There they had always, never asked each other any kind of question. There they had felt always in each other, not any right to take care of one another" (109–110). The continual tension between freedom and possession ultimately results in the relationship falling apart. Although Melanctha and Jeff care for one another, they will not take care of each other.

In some ways, it seems that the relationship had been doomed from the start, that Melanctha and Jeff embody contradictory impulses which cannot peacefully co-exist for any sustained period. While Melanctha wanders in a continuous present, Jeff allows the past to hold sway over his impressions and emotions. Melanctha's history changes the way Jeff views his present relationship with her. In its interrogation of history and the relationship between the past and the present, "Melanctha" displays a modern and modernist sensibility, at least in one important way. According to Cantor, "modernism was a revolt against Victorian culture" (12), and therefore against Victorian modes of thinking. One such pillar of Victorianism was historicism, a generalized faith in the relevance of history to the present (Cantor 12). Consistent with the notion that knowing something's or someone's past can provide insight into a present condition, Victorian historicism posited a unitary self which remains consistent across time (Cantor 12). In Victorian fashion, Jeff tries to make sense of Melanctha's past promiscuity and to square this with her current protestations of love for him, but his reasoning ability is unequal to the task. He cannot immerse himself in feelings and disregard rational explanations, and so when his logic fails him he is lost.

Jeff's inability to comprehend the complexity of Melanctha prefigures the limitations another Herbert has in accepting a richly unpredictable woman, namely Niel Herbert and Marian Forrester in Cather's *A Lost Lady*.[27] Jeff continually tries to explain Melanctha in terms of binaries, as he says with a frown: "'Sometimes you seem like one kind of girl to me, and sometimes you are like a girl that is all different to me, and the two kinds of girls is certainly very different to each other, and I can't see any way they seem to have much to do, to be together in you'" (80). The repetition of the word "girl" has important ramifications for how Jeff conceptualizes (or fails to understand) Melanctha. A "girl" stands in contrast to a woman, just as a "girlfriend" is not a wife. Hence Jeff suggests that their relationship has an immature quality to it. At the same time, "girl" suggests the paternalism found in Jeff's status as powerful doctor. If we look at "girl" as an ironic appellation, we might note that the term is often used for maidens or workers, while Melanctha is sexually knowledgeable and chronically unemployed. Finally, "girls" resonates with "hired girls," a term that could refer to ethnic heroines, domestic servants or prostitutes.[28] "Girls" can mean many things, and Jeff cannot figure out what kind of girl Melanctha is. As a solution, Jeff proposes that Melanctha "'tell me honest . . . which is the way that is you really, when you are alone, and real, and all honest'" (81). Again later, Jeff asks Melanctha, "Can't you help me any way to find out real and true . . . the way I should be acting" (93). In this way, Jeff fails to question the assumption that Melanctha is her truest self when she is alone. What Stein might be suggesting is the importance of social constructions of identity, that perhaps we have no essential or true self that exists in isolation. Ultimately Jeff concedes that "Melanctha was too many for him" (103). He is unable to move beyond this realization, and the relationship continues its downward spiral. An epiphany comes for Jeff when he tells Melanctha, "no man certainly ever really can hold your love for long times together. You certainly Melanctha, you ain't got down deep loyal feeling, true inside you" (107; see also 113).

For Jeff, complete honesty comes naturally, as he acknowledges: "I am always honest. . . . It's easy enough for me always to be honest. . . . All I got to do is always just to say right out what I am thinking" (74). Melanctha appreciates Jeff's honesty (74) but is incapable of duplicating it. And although Jeff accuses Melanctha of not being honest with him, she does not seem actively dishonest. Further, Melanctha's lifelong inability "to tell a story wholly" (57) might spring from a recognition of the limitations of communication as opposed to forgetfulness or dishonesty. Instead of viewing the situation in terms of truth and falsehood, we might surmise that the binarism of truth and falsehood does not adequately encompass Melanctha's world view. In discussing *The Autobiography of Alice B. Toklas,* Catherine Stimpson notes that ultimately we cannot "draw . . . reliable distinctions between true and false" ("Lesbian Lie" 163), and I would suggest that the foundations for a fictional autobiography are right here in "Melanctha." Applying Bettye Williams's conclusions about the problematic autobiographical fiction of Nella Larsen, it seems possible to say of Stein and Melanctha as well, "perhaps . . . fiction was another way of telling the truth" (54). As the "anguished" *Q.E.D.* showed (Pierpont 83), Stein would not be able to write with passion, fulfill her needs for self-expression, and communicate her thoughts (e.g., through publication) by trying to faith-fully recreate the facts. Rather, her methods would need to be indirect, at times counterintuitive, and her truth would be multiple as opposed to unitary. Ruddick implies as much when she asserts that she "believe[s] that a text can be polysemous and still have themes, or 'patterns of meaning'" (*Reading* 7). The passing Melanctha who uses parts of many stories instead of telling one wholly and accurately is an embodiment of Stein's realization.

When Jeff compromises his integrity, he, like Melanctha, begins to pass. Deciding that Melanctha's feelings are more important than his commitment to honesty, Jeff realizes that "he never could be honest now . . . for always every moment now he felt it to be a strong thing in him, how very much it was Melanctha Herbert always suffered" (95). Jeff cannot show Melanctha "his true feeling" (96), and he begins to act in ways that are inconsistent with how he feels inside. As a result, "he never could be very strong inside him" (96). As Jeff loses his trust in Melanctha, his stance on honesty changes, as the narrator reports: "now Jeff never wanted to be honest to her" (111). The rela-tionship finally ends after Melanctha tells Jeff that she does not feel passion for him (121), and he resolves "never [to] go anywhere any more to meet her" (122). Jeff is devastated by Melanctha's disclosure but he seems almost re-lieved to escape from the uncomfortable position that he has felt forced to as-sume. They part amicably, with Jeff promising to be "like a brother to her always . . . [and] a good friend" (122).

Melanctha then moves from her attachment to Jeff to a fondness for Rose Johnson. Although Rose is lazy and selfish where Jeff is hard-working and generous, she resembles Jeff in being "always strong to keep straight" (118). Melanctha's desire to please Rose is queer, as the narrator remarks: "why did the subtle, intelligent, attractive, half white girl Melanctha Herbert, with her sweetness and her power and her wisdom demean herself to do for and to flatter and to be scolded, by this lazy, stupid, ordinary, selfish black girl. This was a queer thing in Melanctha Herbert" (118).[29] One possible answer to this question is that Rose allows Melanctha to escape a part of her history and return to her childhood past. In Rose's eyes, Melanctha's relationships with Jane and Jeff never happened: "all Rose knew about Melanctha was her old life with her mother and her father" (119).

Melanctha exults in her new-found freedom to wander with Rose and to meet "new men" (123). Although Rose tries to dissuade her from flirting with white men, they satisfy a certain need for her. Melanctha returns to her younger days by enjoying the company of men who "never meant very much to [her]. It was only that she liked it to be with them, and they knew all about fine horses, and it was just good to Melanctha, now a little, to feel real reckless with them" (124). She experiences "pleasant days" (124), but she is still plagued by feeling "blue . . . and want[ing] somebody should come and kill her" (125). Feeling herself falling, Melanctha "clung to Rose in the hope that Rose could save her" (125). Rose tolerates Melanctha's attachment for a time ("Rose always was, in her way, very good to let Melanctha be loving to her" [125]), but soon decides to displace her friendship with Melanctha in favor of marriage. As a result, Melanctha finds herself homeless once again, since "Rose Johnson never asked Melanctha to live with her in the house, now Rose was married" (127), and "it could never come to Melanctha to ask Rose to let her" (128). Thus Melanctha's relationship with Rose echoes her childhood and her relationship with her mother. Melanctha turns to Jeff when her mother dies; when Rose abandons her, Melanctha embarks on another ill-fated relationship with a man.

Realizing that Rose will "no longer help her," Melanctha looks elsewhere to "see if she could find what it was she had always wanted" and happens upon "a young buck, a mulatto" (128). After one chance meeting and before knowing his name, this man becomes "her mulatto" (129), a phrase which suggests that this relationship will be plagued by the same possession issues as Melanctha's romance with Jeff. Jem Richards appears quite different from Jeff, though he does resemble some of the other significant men in Melanctha's life. He is manly and "a straight man" (129) who gambles and pays off his debts. Like Melanctha's childhood friend, John the coachman, Jem knows "all about fine horses," and like Melanctha's father, Jem demonstrates "successful power" (129). If Melanctha has looked to Rose as a mother figure, perhaps she sees an idealized father in Jem, who seems like the stuff of fairy tales. He is gem-like, flashy, "dashing" (129), "swell" (130), and often worth a lot of money. He gives Melanctha a ring and promises her marriage. At the same time, he also confuses her, as she finds herself in Jeff's position of not understanding what her lover wanted (133). As Jem's betting luck (and his confidence in his own strength) diminishes, Melanctha is thrown back upon Rose for companionship, though "Rose could now never any more be a help to her" (136). Melanctha returns to help Rose have her baby, and as when she was tending her mother in her final illness, "Melanctha did everything that any woman could" (132; see also 134). She puts all her energy into "waiting on Rose till she was so tired she could hardly stand it" (134), but her work is without recompense. Melanctha helps Rose deliver the baby, which dies shortly thereafter, and her relationship with Jem continues in its downward spiral.

Just as Jeff lost patience with Melanctha's inability to conform to his ideals of fidelity, integrity, and truthfulness, Rose eventually breaks off the friendship when she concludes that "Melanctha no way is really honest" (137). Melanctha feels unready to go off into the world alone again, but Rose refuses to claim Melanctha as her friend. Melanctha still "badly needed to have Rose always there to save her" (138), but Rose proclaims that "I hear more things now so awful bad about you, everybody always telling to me what kind of a way you always have been doing so much, and me always so good to you, and you never no ways, knowing how to be honest to me" (138). Having been banished, Melanctha feels devastated and realizes that she "wanted Rose more than she had ever wanted all the others" (139). Jem leaves her as well, and the narrator tells of her death shortly thereafter.

In "Melanctha," Stein interrogates and dismantles a series of binaries, including knowledge and understanding (71), thinking and feeling (76, 90, 101, 102), inside and outside (95, 102, 110, 114), true and false (96, 97, 111, 112), dark and light (99, 100), memory and forgetfulness (107, 113). I disagree, however, with the critics who wish to see Stein as replacing binaries with tertiaries. Such a reading still reinforces the idea of discrete categories. Benstock, for example, argues that "Melanctha" constitutes "a version of *Q.E.D.*, rewritten into a heterosexual rather than a homosexual triangle" (152; see also 178). First of all, how can anyone talk about a heterosexual triangle when heterosexuality is inherently dualistic? Taking a classic example, we might observe that the triangular relationship between Arthur, Guinevere and Lancelot was both heterosexual and homosexual (or at least homosocial): Arthur is married to Guinevere, Guinevere has an affair with Lancelot, and Lancelot loves Arthur. In "Melanctha," I would start by asking who exactly constitutes the three legs of the triangle. Melanctha and Jeff are a given, but who else—Jane Harden? Rose Johnson? Jem Richards? Even granting that someone could make a case for which character should be considered the third,[30] the triangular quality of the relationship would be difficult to demonstrate. The point is that Stein has removed us from plane geometry altogether.[31]

Just as "Melanctha" need not be read solely as a revision of *Q.E.D.*, the title character's untimely death from "the consumption" (141) need not be read solely as fatalism, naturalism or pessimism.[32] Rather, it is possible to see Melanctha as being "consumed" when she is no longer needed. Stein employs a discursive position while it is useful to her and then moves on. Indeed, we might argue that Stein—like an early literary mentor, George Eliot—needed to kill off a part of herself as a survival mechanism, a way for the whole self to keep on living.[33] In Rosemarie Bodenheimer's reading of Eliot's highly autobiographical *The Mill on the Floss*, for example, Eliot's drowning of Maggie

Tulliver represents the drowning of Eliot's own younger self. While Carol Gilligan sees renunciation as a theme throughout the novel and particularly in Maggie's death (148–49), Ruby Redinger views the ending of the novel as "regenerative" (419). Yet other critics fault Eliot for not allowing her heroines the kind of triumphs over patriarchal adversity which she herself experienced (Heilbrun 73), and the same could be said of Stein's killing off Melanctha. As Benstock suggests:

> had Stein's personal life been tormented and self-destructive, had her art consisted of a few desperate poems written in honor of Sappho, had she not proclaimed her talents to all who would listen, she would have become a lesbian cult figure and been patronized by a heterosexual public that considered her pathetic. Instead, she was resented by her brother and others for surviving so well. Survival for Stein included surviving as a Jew, and some have questioned the means by which that survival was effected. (190)

Unlike Melanctha, Stein survives and eventually flourishes. With "Melanctha," her first published text, Stein both sets the nineteenth century to rest and resolves the troubling issues of sexual orientation which consumed *Q.E.D.*[34] She also sets the stage for the texts that would make up her 1930s, post-avant-garde period. Eliot leaves us with a mature woman—not a martyr and not a victim—but a woman who knows her own mind, makes her own choices, and carries them through. Thus *The Mill on the Floss,* which stands at the threshold of Eliot's career as a woman writer, embodies a dawning, not a death knoll. Melanctha dies of consumption, and Stein bids farewell to her Jamesian masculinity and her sexual insecurity. As Stein is engaged in finding a publisher for *Three Lives,* Alice comes to Paris and Stein's mature life begins.

LIES, DAMN LIES, AND AUTOBIOGRAPHIES

The ties between "Melanctha" and *The Autobiography of Alice B. Toklas* are significant. Abraham points out that the latter is Stein's "first narrative since *Three Lives,* twenty-six years before" (108), while Barbara Will argues that the lesbian triangle initially broached in *Q.E.D.* (and taken up by "Melanctha") is most effectively resolved in *The Autobiography of Alice B. Toklas* (220). Further, Dearborn suggests a connection by pronouncing the "Gertrude Stein" character one of Stein's "most successful heroines" along with Melanctha (178). Questions of identity, inside and outside, and the nature of relationships recur in *The Autobiography of Alice B. Toklas,* as well. And yet despite these similarities and continuities, both Stein and the scholars who study her have tried to perpetuate a rupture or phase theory approach to her work. Thus "Melanctha" is deemed important because of its status as a full-fledged modernist narrative, the birth of a century, and a literary text inspired by modern art. Following "Melanctha," however, Stein enters her "middle" or "avant-garde experimentalism" phase (DeKoven, *Rich* 68). When Stein returns to narrative, it is to write money-making, "secondary" texts of questionable literary merit (Haas 111).[35] I wish to emphasize the continuities as opposed to the rupture.

Like "Melanctha," *The Autobiography of Alice B. Toklas* is a narrative but not a novel, a fictional text based on the real-life experiences of people Stein knew but not confined to the facts of their lives. While *The Autobiography* is not the straightforward autobiography its title claims (i.e., non-fiction written by the subject about her life), Stein does eventually provide us with some guidelines for how to read and evaluate her text. In "coming out" as the true author, Stein offers a precursor for her narrative strategy:

> About six weeks ago Gertrude Stein said, it does not look to me as if you were ever going to write that autobiography. You know what I am going to do. I am going to write it for you. I am going to write it as simply as Defoe did the autobiography of Robinson Crusoe. And she has and this is it. (252)

Precisely because this comparison is uttered lightly and without explanation, it demands interrogation; indeed it provides some important clues as to Stein's technique and purpose. Defoe's book, *The Life and Strange Surprising Adventures of Robinson Crusoe, of York, Mariner,* does not make its claim to autobiography in its title, but rather in its preface, which insists that "the story is told with modesty, with seriousness, and with a religious application of events to the uses to which wise men always apply them. . . . The editor believes the thing to be a just history of fact; neither is there any appearance of fiction in it" (25). Among other things, Stein's avowed intention to write like Defoe contains an acknowledgment that "Alice B. Toklas" is as fictional a creation as "Robinson Crusoe" (even though both are based on real people, namely Alice Toklas and Alexander Selkirk). While critics have commented on the constructed quality of the fictional figure called "Gertrude Stein" (Dearborn 178, Marren 152), it seems equally important to point out that "Alice B. Toklas" is a created character who happens to share the name of a real person. Indeed, we might imagine a prefatory warning along the lines of "the persons in this book are purely fictional, though in all cases names of living people have been employed." By creating fictional avatars of both herself and her beloved, Stein implicitly questions the possibilities of mimetic representation and the non-fiction narrative. As Marren points out, "in a passing autobiography the fraudulence of the convention of faithful representation is particularly obvious, and so our sense of what is 'natural' must transform itself" (169). Stein even questions the ultimate knowability of the self.[36] On a literal level, the term "autobiography" refers to "a biography written by the subject about himself or herself . . . [and focusing] on the author's developing self" (M.H. Abrams 15). Clearly, *The Autobiography of Alice B. Toklas* does not fulfill these expectations, and this disappointed and outraged some of Stein's readers. The backlash prompted by Stein's text indicates that some of her disgruntled contemporaries felt angered or deceived by her broad application of the term. Arthur Lachman, for example, argues that Stein's text, "her autobiography, which she thinly veiled as *The Autobiography of Alice B. Toklas*" (4), shows her "inordinate vanity" and "almost morbid craving for recognition" (8). Other readers accepted *The Autobiography* for what it was—autobiographical fiction. In a 1941 letter, Arnold Ronnebeck recalls, "when I think back on pp. 120 and the following of Alice B.'s Autobiography, pages on which my name appears many times, I smile, because I know you know it was not true, and I will not sue you" (355).[37]

Defoe's novel engendered controversy and Stein's text lost her several friends, but an example of a similar literary exploit which did not cause such a furor is *The Autobiography of S.S. McClure,* which is now considered a part of Willa Cather's oeuvre. Cather's and Stein's situations are not completely analogous. McClure told Cather his story and she went home and wrote about it, as opposed to Stein's simply writing the story as she thinks Alice perceived it. Furthermore, Cather did not appear in McClure's story and does not seem to have any ulterior motives in writing it, whereas readers have seen the main purpose of *The Autobiography of Alice B. Toklas* as Stein's self-aggrandizement. Nevertheless, we might acknowledge that Cather claimed that the experience of speaking as a man paved the way for Jim Burden's narration of *My Antonia,* while the voice of Alice allowed Stein to return from avant-garde incomprehensibility to narrative readability and to resolve some troubling dynamics in her earlier work.

Wagner-Martin points out that "just as Defoe's work had created an angry sensation, catalyzing fierce debates over *truth* and *fiction, author* and *protagonist,* so *The Autobiography of Alice B. Toklas* unloosed critical battles that continue still" (*Favored* 202). In other ways as well, Stein's text offers uncanny parallels with Defoe's. While *Robinson Crusoe* invokes the trope of middle-class economic salvation (i.e., "how I went out in the world and God made me financially successful"), *The Autobiography of Alice B. Toklas* is the first book of Stein's that brought her any money at all. Further, *Robinson Crusoe*'s status as a providential narrative prefigures the motif of fate or destiny which also runs through *The Autobiography of Alice B. Toklas*. Examples of this motif can be seen most clearly in the case of the bells which Alice hears each time she meets a real genius, Picasso's portrait of Stein, and the cannon which represented to Picasso and Stein all that they were trying to do. Even before starting to tell about "my arrival in Paris" (6), Alice announces her firm conviction of Stein's genius:

> I may say that only three times in my life have I met a genius and each time a bell within me rang and I was not mistaken, and I may say in each case it was before there was any general recognition of the quality of genius in them. The three geniuses of whom I wish to speak are Gertrude Stein, Pablo Picasso and Alfred Whitehead. I have met many important people, I have met several great people but I have only known three first class geniuses and in each case on sight within me something rang. In no one of the three cases have I been mistaken. In this way my new full life began. (5)

I quote this passage at length because it invokes both the trope of fate and that of a providential rebirth. In the case of Stein's portrait, Alice makes small talk with Picasso by complimenting his work, and he responds: "Yes . . . everybody says that she does not look like it but that does not make any difference, she will" (12). Picasso here claims to have presaged what Stein will come to look like, and Stein agrees. The artist and the subject—insiders, geniuses, prophets—are the only ones who are immediately satisfied with the results of so many sittings. Finally, the cannon episode, which recurs throughout Stein's later oeuvre in varied forms (Abraham 81), appears in *The Autobiography of Alice B. Toklas* in the following manner. When Picasso, Eve, Stein and Alice first see a camouflaged cannon, Picasso comments, "C'est nous qui avons fait ca . . . it is we that have created that." The narrator agrees with Picasso's assessment, noting, "and he was right, he had. From Cezanne through him they had come to that. His foresight was justified" (90). The trope of fate or destiny functions here both on the level of Picasso's (and Stein's) foresight in his formal experimentation and on the level of the narrator's willingness to see a causal line of creation.

Fate, destiny and causality operate within a male spiritual/psychological universe in Defoe, but *The Autobiography of Alice B. Toklas* departs from this paradigm by offering a female-oriented alternative.[38] Although people tend to think in free associations, Robinson tells a linear, chronological story to show the order of providence—God is in control. This strictly chronological narrative stands in stark contrast to the digressive, associative recollections which characterize the structure of *The Autobiography of Alice B. Toklas* (Marren 159). Furthermore, while Crusoe keeps time carefully and meticulously (and narrates his story accordingly), Toklas and her autobiography offer an uneven sense of time in that there is no fixed ratio between time elapsed and number of pages the text devotes to its narration. Stein persistently calls attention to years, perhaps to show that the numbers do not work out. The biggest disparity comes in Alice's pre-Paris life, which receives a scant three pages of mention; Stein's does not fare much better with sixteen. The four years of 1903–07 receive thirty-nine pages, a page-per-year ration of 9.75; the following seven years have a page/year ratio of only 8.0. The war years introduce proportionately more material, with a ratio of 12.25, and the following thirteen years are described in a much less dense 4.5 pages per year. Nor does Stein's and Picasso's belief that more happened when they were younger suffice to explain the differential. Alice recalls "hearing Picasso and Gertrude Stein talking about various things that had happened at that time, one of them said but all that could not have happened in that one year, oh said the other, my dear you forget we were young then and we did a great deal in a year" (6). The eleven years between 1903 and 1914 have a collective ratio of 8.6, but the time span from 1907–1918 has a ratio of 9.5 (though both are admittedly much higher than the 4.5 of the last thirteen years). Defoe employs a linear exposition that ultimately yields a providential design, but circles, tangents, and crossovers prevail to create a meaningful pattern in Stein's female-oriented spiritual autobiography.

   Robinson Crusoe was among the earliest English novels. *The Autobiography of Alice B. Toklas,* on the other hand, is distinctly not a novel. Still, we might say that if Defoe's text confirmed the birth of the novel, Stein's heralded the advent of modern autobiography. DeKoven identifies "Melanctha" as modernist but declares that Stein subsequently moved into avant-garde experimentalism (*Rich* 68). I would add that Stein returns to modernism (as DeKoven describes it) in her 1930s narratives and autobiographies. DeKoven differentiates modernism and experimentalism in the following manner: "modernist writing *constitutes itself as* self-contradictory, though not incoherent: incoherence is the province of avant-garde experimentalism and some postmodernism" (24). While not all critics would agree that Stein's more experimental works are incoherent, I think that Stein's autobiographies are both self-contradictory and intelligible. In *The Autobiography of Alice B. Toklas,* for example, selves are constructed, mediated, multiple, and performative. Time is fluid, circular, repetitive, and disruptive. In addition, while *The Making of Americans* has been read as ethnic autobiography (Sollors 255), I believe the rubric could be fruitfully applied to *The Autobiography,* as well. Burch argues that "ethnic novelists, perhaps even more than other writers, saw their world through the prism of personal experience" (58); Stein ups the ante by seeing her world through her experiences and presenting her world through how she perceives her lover to have seen her experiences. While Stein's act of adopting Toklas's voice brought criticism upon her for appropriation and deception, we might also see this act as a strategy for mediation. Lowe points out that "one function of canonization is the resolution of material contradiction through a narrative of formation in which differences—of gender, race, nationality, or sexuality—are subsumed through the individual's identification with a universalized form" (52–53). Thus we might argue that Stein employs the form of autobiography in order to free up space for a narrative of difference constructed by an expatriate Jewish lesbian writing during a nativist, masculinist, anti-Semitic period. Similarly, Dearborn points out that "midwiving and mediation" (31) are often prerequisites for ethnic authorship (31), further noting that sometimes the author is herself the "mediator, working between two cultures" (38). An American in Europe, a Jew surrounded by Gentiles (not to say fascists), a lesbian seeming to participate in the cult of masculinity, and the self-proclaimed "grandmother of the modern movement" (qtd. in Wagner-Martin, *Favored* 154), Stein occupies the position of mediator and/or midwife. In this context, we can evaluate Stein's final paragraph as an ironically placed (or an inverted) statement of intention. What we need to do, of course, is to go back and read the text again, this time knowing that Stein is the author. And then again, knowing that Stein is writing in the tradition of the elusive Defoe.

The Autobiography of Alice B. Toklas might also be read as a story in Benjamin's sense, specifically in opposition to the classification of "novel." Although Benjamin's point is precisely that the Great War has removed the storyteller from the midst of society while the novel has supplanted the story (84, 87), Stein's text represents an important exception to (or at least a modification of) that claim. Benjamin observes that "men returned from the battlefield [of WWI] grown silent—not richer, but poorer in communicable experience" (84), but women (namely Stein and Toklas) seem to have returned with ample stories.[39] *The Autobiography of Alice B. Toklas,* not a novel and not an autobiography in the traditional sense of the word, draws on the strengths of storytelling which Benjamin deemed dead approximately twenty years earlier. The chatty, familiar tone of Stein's text shares an object of storytelling as Benjamin defines it, in that it "does not aim to convey the pure essence of a thing, like information or a report . . . but sinks the thing into the life of the storyteller, in order to bring it out of him again" (91–92). In the

case of *The Autobiography of Alice B. Toklas*, we have two storytellers, the author (Stein) and the narrative "I" (Toklas). In its elision of time through alin-
earity, repetitions, and tangents, the text also distinguishes itself as more story
than novel (Benjamin 99).

Like all good stories, *The Autobiography of Alice B. Toklas* raises at least
as many questions as it answers. One question that it brings to the fore is what
it means to write the autobiography of one's beloved. Stein's appropriation of
Alice's voice is playful or even deceitful, but it is also risky. Fuss argues that deploying essentialism is not inherently dangerous, but rather "what is risky is
giving up the security—and the fantasy—of occupying a single subject position and instead occupying two places at once" (19). This simultaneous occupation of several discursive positions is exactly what Stein successfully
manages in *The Autobiography of Alice B. Toklas*. Drawing on the ideas of
queer theorists like Dollimore and Berlant, we might argue that Stein occupies the position of a beloved Other as a way to express her feelings of love towards and her desire for possession in a more socially acceptable manner.[40] In
this way, Stein's narrative "seeks to move beyond the self/other, 'I'/ 'not-I' binarism" (Fuss 33) by confusing author, narrator, and protagonist beyond
recognition. Indeed, James Breslin contends that Stein "creates *herself* through
the *external* perspective of Alice" (152, emphasis added). Along similar lines,
a chapter heading that does not include Stein but applies to what she attempts
in *The Autobiography of Alice B. Toklas* is Morgan's "Writing the Self From the
Outside-In," which "refers to authors who—because of race, ethnicity, or sexual persuasion—have had to work through a kind of dual oppression. Doubly
marginalized, twice silenced, these writers . . . have had to negotiate a particularly complex relationship to their cultural positioning in order to establish
a valid identity and to discover a speech that would serve them" (13). The
voice of Alice brings Stein from (literary and sexual) margin to mainstream
(i.e., popular writing and traditional marriage).

Issues of spatial positioning and queer identity are further seen in the
thematic recurrence of the inside/outside motif in *The Autobiography of Alice
B. Toklas*. Alice ends her prefatory remarks by promising to "tell you how two
americans happened to be *in* the heart of an art movement of which the *outside* world at that time knew nothing" (28; emphasis added). And yet their insider status is continually called into question because they are Americans
outside America, women in an intellectual/artistic world dominated by men,
lesbians amidst the Paris cult of masculinity, and Jews in an anti-Semitic
Europe.[41] Alice comments that Stein "always was, she always is, tormented by
the problem of the external and the internal" (119). Perhaps Stein's liminal
status and persistent concerns with borders link her to the subjects of

Gambrell's study of women modernist insider/outsiders, "whose value consisted in their simultaneous distance from and intimacy with the subjects of their own inquiry" (4–5). In this case, it would seem that Stein's act of adopting Alice's voice serves to dramatize her own status as insider-with-a-difference. This voice provides Stein with the psychological space she needs to bring her experiences out of herself in the form of intelligible language. In order to write about herself, she needs to leave herself, so to speak, just as many of her peers discovered the need to leave a geographical home in order to articulate their sense of it (Urgo 56, 65).

Stein, of course, was one of those Americans who wrote about her homeland from abroad. Thus it is not surprising that, like her personal identity, Stein's national identity as it emerges in the course of *The Autobiography of Alice B. Toklas* is marked by shifting affiliations. Alice recalls that "later I often teased her, calling her a general, a civil war general of either or both sides" (16). This attribution suggests that Stein's American identity was fluid in terms of regional loyalty. Whereas Nebraska retains an almost exclusive claim to Willa Cather, no single place in America is particularly connected with Gertrude Stein. Ironically, Stein's capacity to identify with all America is not a very American trait, at least as Blair conceptualizes Americanism: "As a matter of course most Americans find it easy to identify themselves with one side or the other of many available sets of distinctions: one party or the other, one region or another, one team or its opponents, one group or its rivals" (7). Thus Stein's potential for being a leader on either side of the Civil War suggests a broadness of national identification that is paradoxically un-American. Stein's status as (im)migrant/expatriate, on the other hand, marks her as particularly American according to Urgo, who argues that "the single experience . . . that defines American culture at its core is migration" (5). In both her childhood and her adult life, Stein developed and maintained a "migratory . . . consciousness" (Urgo 13).

Whether or not Stein should be considered as American as she seemed to think herself, *The Autobiography of Alice B. Toklas* was a roaring success. Part of its resonance might be attributed to the fact that American cultural studies began in the twenties and came into prominence in the thirties (Gleason, *Speaking* 190), so that Stein's chatty memoir about Americans abroad met with an eager audience. Further, Stein managed to avoid falling victim to a nativist double standard articulated by Fairchild: "we expect all foreigners to be assimilated in the United States and blame them if they are not; we do not expect any American to be assimilated in a foreign land, and blame him if he is" (172). As a child, Stein assimilated fully to her American surroundings, apparently fulfilling her father's injunction that she and her siblings "should

forget their french and german so that their american english would be pure"
(74). She remained steadfast in her identification as fully American, going so
far as to suggest that living in France made her more so. Thus to Fairchild's
claim that "America is the best country in the world—for Americans" (174),
Stein might add that America is the best country to identify oneself with, but
"'a parent's place is never the place to work in'" (Benstock 12). America can
be home, but not office.

An American identity was valuable to Stein in other ways, as well. In *The
Autobiography of Alice B. Toklas,* for example, gender identity and nationality
converge to create further space for non-threatening difference. Alice relates
that Vollard, the picture dealer from whom Gertrude and Leo first bought
Cezannes, "explained to every one that he had been visited by two crazy americans and they laughed and he had been much annoyed but gradually he found
out that when they laughed most they usually bought something so of course
he waited for them to laugh" (32). As an American, Stein can be dismissed as
"crazy" instead of having to make sense; as an American with money, Stein is
someone to pay attention to. Similarly, after telling how "Mildred Aldrich had
a distressing way of dropping her key down the middle of the stairs where an
elevator might have been . . ." (35–36), Alice adds that "only americans did
that" (36). Americans are allowed to be clumsy and to refuse to adapt. They are
also a "third sex" type of category, as Picasso observes: "ils sont pas des hommes,
ils sont pas des femmes, ils sont des americains. They are not men, they are not
women, they are americans" (49). Given the gender freedom of third-sex status, Stein can then proceed to normalize her own gender identity and sexual
orientation. Indeed, throughout *The Autobiography of Alice B. Toklas,* Stein
makes matter-of-fact what might otherwise be considered scandalous, unnatural, or marginal. In rehearsing Stein's experiences in medical school and her
ultimate decision to leave without taking her degree, Alice observes that "she
always says she dislikes the abnormal, it is so obvious. She says the normal is so
much more simply complicated and interesting" (83). Once in Paris, Stein sets
up a traditional household in which she, the genius, is waited upon and attended to by Alice, her wife. Alice's discussion of the wives of geniuses she has
sat with comes early in the text, as if to situate her as a wife (and thereby situate Stein as a husband/master and a genius).

Along similar lines, Marren conceptualizes the "Gertrude Stein" of *The
Autobiography of Alice B. Toklas* as an identity "created . . . by a passing subject" (152). She further argues that this "passing 'I'" functions as a solution to
the question of "how might Gertrude Stein herself be represented in such a
way that her embodiment—as a woman, as a lesbian—will not preclude public recognition of her status an artist and an intellectual?" (164). To this I

would add that Stein is also a Jew, while a highly visible strand of modernist geniuses are Gentiles. Furthermore, as Cantor has pointed out, T.S. Eliot, Ezra Pound, and Wyndham Lewis were all "violently anti-Semitic" (128). Cantor attributes the "anti-Semitic strain in Modernism" to the fact that Jews "were seen as the arch-representatives [and] . . . as the arch-beneficiaries of that liberal historicist culture so disliked by Modernism" (129). At the same time, Jews were condemned by anti-modernists "as the arch-fiends of Modernism, who were eroding traditional European Christian and national culture" (129). In order to establish herself as a member (or, as she would have it, a leader) of the modern literary world and also to secure a popular audience, Stein became a passing subject in terms of her Jewish roots.

On the one hand, it seems questionable to impute that Stein was a Jew passing for WASP. She had been given at least a rudimentary Jewish education (Wagner-Martin, *Favored* 16), and she certainly identified herself as Jewish, declaring in a college essay that "a person was 'a Jew first and an American only afterwards . . . ' [and] emphasiz[ing] that 'race feeling' was 'an enlargement of the family tie'" (Wagner-Martin, *Favored* 34). Further, during the heyday of her 1920s salon, Stein made little attempt to downplay her Jewishness. Wagner-Martin suggests that "posing as the wise expatriate Jewish American, approaching fifty, Stein created herself as the great, undiscovered American writer" (*Favored* 162–63). By 1928, she had proclaimed herself "'the most famous Jew in the world'" (Wagner-Martin, *Favored* 185). Similarly, Alice was quite Semitic in appearance, and Stein made no attempt to hide either their Jewish heritage or the nature of their living arrangements from the many visitors who attended her salon.

Nevertheless, Stein persists in disseminating internalized anti-Semitism in *The Autobiography of Alice B. Toklas*. Early in the text, "Alice" relays the following incident:

> Gertrude Stein who has an explosive temper, came in another evening and there were her brother, Alfy and a stranger. She did not like the stranger's looks. Who is that, said she to Alfy. I didn't bring him, said Alfy. He looks like a Jew, said Gertrude Stein, he is worse than that, says Alfy. (11)

Here Stein engages in the most gross forms of stereotyping, constructing as Other, someone who may or may not even belong to a stigmatized group, of which Stein is herself a member. Wagner-Martin relays an even more outrageous incident, which occurred when Bryher visited Stein's salon in the 1920s: "Stein described [her] as 'an ethical Jewess . . . rather a rare type'— although Bryher was not Jewish" (*Favored* 155). Although one Jew's act of saying another person looks like a Jew need not inevitably be construed as a put-down (many people remarked on Alice's Semitic features, for example), Stein's comment about Bryher draws attention to one of the many paradoxes of Stein's identity politics. As Blanche Wiesen Cook has observed, "'she was Jewish and anti-Semitic'" (qtd. in Benstock 19). Not all of Stein's friends and visitors accepted her Jewishness as a positive attribute, so perhaps she put down other Jews (or Gentiles, as the case might be) in order to deflect attention from her own ethnicity. Indeed, Bravig Imbs recalls how a mutual friend would say of Stein during this period: "'Gertrude is the most un-Jewish person I ever knew. She is so dangerous and tolerant and has such a magnificent brain. Those aren't Jewish traits'" (126–7). The fact that Imbs felt compelled to establish that Stein did not display typical (or stereotypical) Jewish attributes or behaviors indicates that Stein's social milieu did not always accept her ethnic ties. To establish and maintain her position as Queen Bee in the world of modernist male geniuses, Stein might have felt it necessary to de-emphasize this aspect of her personal history. In her life, Stein owns herself and her ethnic heritage, but in the text meant to give her a public (written) voice, she retreats to anti-Semitism. Extrapolating from Berzon, who argues that African-Americans who severed themselves from their African roots engaged in passing (6), we might conclude Stein's act of rejecting her ethnic heritage is a form of passing, as well. Certainly, Stein's actions also seem to suggest that her self-creation at times required her to deny her descent to establish the "consent relations" (Sollors, *Beyond* 223) which can situate her within a male, white, Christian heterosexual tradition. *The Autobiography of Alice B. Toklas* shows discomfort with Stein's Jewish identity, and one which is not resolved by the act of writing the text. Arguably she does not begin resolve this tension until she writes *Everybody's Autobiography.*

In the first line of her own introduction to *Everybody's Autobiography,* Stein offers the following straightforward explanation for her title: "Alice B. Toklas did hers and now anybody will do theirs" (1). The title seems playful and egotistical in equal measure. Its underpinnings are also profoundly threatening to an American identity. Americans are individualists, and an autobiography is the life story of a (single) self. Everybody's autobiography is different from everybody else's. The notion that one book could suffice for everyone (or that Stein equals everybody) is both preposterous and psychically threatening, and yet Stein plows right ahead. We might also note that Alice did not do hers, Gertrude did "Alice's" and now anybody is not doing theirs—Gertrude is doing everybody's. Furthermore, given the logic of Stein's first line, the book should have been called Anybody's Autobiography, but Stein opts for the more inclusive term. Stein soon broadens the field of autobiography by announcing (in a line that gets its own paragraph), "anything is an autobiography but this was a conversation" (3). Clearly Stein has not developed any more respect for the conventions of the genre since her *The Autobiography of Alice B. Toklas* days. Further, Stein, the self-proclaimed genius, attests that "autobiography is easy like it or not autobiography is easy for any one and so this is to be everybody's autobiography" (4). If it is easy for anyone, why does Stein fritter away her talents on something so trivial? And if Stein means to suggest that her experiences can stand in for anybody's and everybody's, then she must not be as exceptional a genius as she claims. As the text progresses, it becomes clear that Stein's project is both a continuation and an elaboration of some of the major concerns in her earlier work.

Like *The Autobiography of Alice B. Toklas, Everybody's Autobiography* is not a novel: "an autobiography is not a novel no indeed it is not a novel" (200). And as Benjamin earlier pronounced the death of the storyteller, Stein here deems the novel a dead art. At the same time, Stein seems to revive the art of storytelling by structurally accentuating the importance of the oral tradition in her "very talky" text (Poirier 27). Stein believes "the novel as a form of writing is dead" and advises "all the young ones now to write essays, after all since characters are of no importance why not just write meditations, meditations are always interesting, neither character nor identity are necessary to him who meditates" (104). Characters and depth psychology are hallmarks of early modernist writing—Stein's own "Melanctha" is in fact an excellent example of a character study—but Stein has clearly given up on character as a mode by now. Indeed Stein anticipates the postmodern rejection of the depth model (Dollimore 64). In a similarly postmodern move, Stein paraphrases a French acquaintance who remarks that "every generation that is every two years is completely a different thing now everything is so confused . . ." (205). She later takes credit for this realization herself, as she announces, "any two years can make a generation" (314). Such fragmentation of what had traditionally been a relatively large unit (i.e., the generation) suggests Stein's belief that no one is connected to anyone else in a meaningful way. It also pulls the foundation out from under discourses like ethnic literature, which draw heavily on the metaphor of generations, particularly in terms of first- and second-generation immigrant conflict (Sollors, *Beyond* 208; Dearborn 73). Still, Stein does not dispense completely with such forms. An autobiography is not a novel, and an autobiography by an expatriate Jewish lesbian is not necessarily an ethnic novel. *Everybody's Autobiography* does, however, employ and play with some of the conventions of both genre and sub-genre.

One example of a playful twist on ethnic women's autobiography is Stein's emphasis on food. While the "hungry heroine" is a common figure in

ethnic tales of the rise from ghetto to American Dream (Dearborn 80), Stein
tells the reader about all the significant meals she and Alice ate during their
six months in America: "I will of course always tell everything we ate" (179).
On a more serious note, Stein offers an alternative to immigrant portrayals of
America as the Land of Opportunity: "I used to be fond of saying that
America, which was supposed to be a land of success, was a land of failure.
Most of the great men in America had a long life of early failure and a long
life of later failure" (88).[42] Stein's own experience had been the opposite—her
early years of relative obscurity were seemingly wiped out by her immense and
almost instant popularity following *The Autobiography of Alice B. Toklas* and
her subsequent lecture tour. Stein comes into her own as a celebrity, but it is
clear that much of her American success stems from the fact that she is a vis-
itor and not a resident.

This success has been as disarming as it has been pleasurable, and it has
had some unpredicted effects on Stein's perception: "it seems very long ago
and it is long ago because at that time I had never made any money and since
then I have made some and I feel differently now about everything, so it is a
long time ago four years ago that I wrote The Autobiography of Alice B.
Toklas" (44). A shifting sense of time amidst a desire to connect with one's
roots are, in fact, hallmarks of ethnic explorations. Indeed, Dearborn identifies the central problem of ethnicity as the "relation of the individual to his
ancestor, or . . . to time" (182). Stein has been dealing with time throughout
her 1930s narratives, and she explains in "A Transatlantic Interview, 1946"
that she wrote in the present in order to make time cease to exist: "I did it un-
consciously in The Autobiography of Alice B. Toklas, but I did it consciously
in Everybody's Autobiography . . ." (20). Just as Stein offered an uneven ratio
between time elapsed and pages devoted to narration in *The Autobiography of
Alice B. Toklas,* she purposely disrupts the mimetic quality of *Everybody's
Autobiography* by reminding us that the events she narrates took place in the
past. For example, in the midst of her "America" chapter, Stein talks about
meeting Jacques Viot, "the day before yesterday" (216). The past and the present impinge on one another. She then spends a few paragraphs speaking about
lecturing in Chicago, only to flip back to the "present" of writing the text by
stating, "I find out just today and in Paris that Americans and Europeans are
different. Two things happened to me today" (217). After musing on the differences between Americans and Europeans (which, I might add, Stein had
found out previously and remarked upon on multiple occasions), Stein returns to her earlier narrative with a casual, "so we stayed our two weeks in
Chicago . . ." (218)—as if the episode of helping some Americans in Paris
stood in causal relation to Stein's and Toklas's time in Chicago. Later in the

same chapter, when Stein is telling about "leav[ing] for California in an airplane," she comments that "just now" (i.e., the present of writing the book) "a great many are getting killed in the airplanes," observes that she and Toklas were not killed, and continues with her narrative (288). Breslin notes that *The Autobiography of Alice B. Toklas* "provides not—as Stein seems to have thought—a mere submission to the conventions of autobiography but an intense and creative struggle within them" (149), since autobiography is "necessarily retrospective" and Stein strives to create a "continuous present" (150); the same can be said of *Everybody's Autobiography.*

In a continuous present, the subject is always changing. This makes the task of producing a single autobiographical subject a difficult one. Indeed, Stein does not even try, as Will points out: "in its refusal to produce a coherent autobiographical subject that will mirror authorial presence, *Everybody's Autobiography* poses a major challenge to textual constructions of identity as fixed or essential, and to a phallocentric organization of knowledge dependent upon the exclusion of some 'feminine' Other" (243). Further, instead of focusing on the relation of the autobiographical subject to outside events, Stein contends that "the real ideas are not the relation of human beings as groups but a human being to himself inside him and that is an idea that is more interesting than humanity in groups, after all the minute that there are a lot of them they do not do it for themselves but somebody does it for them and that is a darn sight less interesting" (213). Hence the philosophical quality of *Everybody's Autobiography.* Stein seems to write as much for her own edification as for any desire to transmit information to posterity. This "autobiography" does not offer a unitary subject or a clear sense of time and events.

For a text which consistently denies the relevance of clear-cut categories, *Everybody's Autobiography* contains several surprisingly forthright statements of binary absolutes, beginning with the declaration, "if you win you do not lose and if you lose you do not win, at least if you win or if you lose it seems so" (9). Like winning and losing, thinking and speaking are conceptualized as disparate elements in a polarized field, as Stein reflects: "when I write I write and when I talk I talk and the two are not one, no not for any one and when they come near being one, then the inside is not inside and the outside is not outside and I like the inside to be inside and the outside to be outside, it makes it more necessary to be one" (271–72). Thinking and speaking, inside and outside, are further related to the realms of private and public, a major concern for a writer who cherishes her privacy and who has recently been thrust into the public spotlight: "Well anyway when you say what you do say you say it in public but when you write what you do write you write it in private if not you do not write it, that is what writing is, and in private you are you and in public you are in public . . ." (301). Stein also draws a connection between the inside/outside dichotomy and the notion of identity by insisting that "the thing is like this, it is all the question of identity. It is all a question of the outside being outside and the inside being inside" (48).

Inside/outside boundaries are linked to national and ethnic identity in this text, as well as in *The Autobiography of Alice B. Toklas*. Once again, Stein is neither purely inside nor completely outside of any given category. For example, she is neither a model American (native born, raised, and residing) nor an acknowledged expatriate. Instead we might think of the "Gertrude Stein" of *Everybody's Autobiography* as a cross-cultural or trans-Atlantic mediator. Stein clearly identifies as an American, both before and after her lecture tour. In excusing herself for not wanting to make the trip, Stein insists that identification is more important than actual location, asserting that "after all I am American all right. Being there does not make me more there" (115). Having visited America, Stein affirms, "I am clear I am a good American, I am slow-minded and quickly clear in expression, I am certain that I see everything that is seen and in between I stand around but I do not wait, no American can wait. . . . Americans can neither serve nor wait . . ." (310). She cannot make America her permanent home, however, because Americans are too needy. In explaining why she remains in France, she observes that "the reason is very simple their life belongs to them so your life can belong to you" (105). She further observes that "in France everybody reads everything aloud. In America they talk over the radio but they do not read aloud. . . . I like to read with my eyes and not with my ears. I like to read inside and not outside" (168). Stein's position— identifying with one country and living in another—allows her to view both cultures from a distance, and perhaps to offer a greater understanding of both.

Although Stein did not embark for America with the plan of becoming a mediator or translator for two countries, her trip might be viewed as permitting her to re-establish her connection to America, its Founding Fathers and its traditions. Having dismissed generations as so frequent as to be meaningless, Stein nevertheless contends that fathers are omnipresent: "Well feudal days were the days of fathers and now once more these days are the days of fathers" (144). Fathers, and implicitly Founding Fathers, lead Stein to thinking about biological and ethnic fathers, as well. Hence, Stein further suggests that "the Jews and they come into this because they are very much given to having a father and to being one and they are very much given not to want a father and not to have one, and they are an epitome of all this that is happening the concentration of fathering to the perhaps there not being one" (146–47). Stein is still not ready to acknowledge that Jewish fathers are part of her history, however. Her language distances her from the group she describes, as if she were not, in fact, one of its members. Stein's gradual acknowledgment of her own status as a Jew occurs within the context of another ethnic group, African-Americans.

Having attended a party for "Negro intellectuals" hosted by Carl Van Vechten, Stein offers the following thoughts:

> I know they do not want you to say negro but I do want to say Negro. I dislike it when instead of saying Jew they say Hebrew or Israelite or Semite, I do not like it and why should a Negro want to be called colored. Why should he want to lose being a Negro to become a common thing with a Chinaman or a Japanese or a Hindu or an islander or anything any of them can be called colored, a Negro is a Negro and he ought to like to be called one if he is one, he may not want to be one that is all right but as long as he cannot change that why should he mind the real name of them. . . . Well its name is Negro if it is a Negro and Jew if it is a Jew and both of them are nice strong solid names so let us keep them. (206)

This passage is rich with insights into Stein's attitude towards race, ethnicity and the power of naming. First of all, Stein expresses what must be seen as a personal affront to hearing Jews spoken of as Hebrews, etc. Thus she speaks as a member of one group (Jews) and believes that this authorizes her to comment on another group (African-Americans). Secondly, Stein anticipates cultural theory by about sixty years in observing that African-Americans are not the only "people of color." She then argues that specificity and uniqueness should be privileged above broader identification—Americans of African descent should be pleased to use a term which refers to them and not to other groups. Stein proceeds to offer an essentialist view of racial and ethnic identification as an attribute which "cannot [be] change[d]" and should therefore be accepted.[43] Finally, Stein deems both "Negro" and "Jew" "nice strong solid names," suggesting a certain equality; her rhetorical coupling of the two groups further strengthens the ties between her black characters in "Melanctha" and her own Jewish roots.

At the same time that she perceptively enumerates some parallels between black and Jewish experience, Stein shows a pronounced lack of insight into the power relations entailed in naming, particularly as they apply to who gets to name the Other. She sees "a Negro . . . [or] a Chinaman or a Japanese or a Hindu or an islander" (206) as something one is, but in fact such identities can be willfully chosen or forcibly assigned. William Petersen notes that identities are ideally chosen by individuals, but he also admits that "each person is also influenced by social factors over which he or she has had no control. . . . We do not choose (entirely) how others will regard us or what, even despite our best intentions, they may ascribe to us" (41). Stein herself (wrongly) attributes Jewish status to certain hapless Gentiles, though we do not hear of any instances in which someone "calls [her] a Jew" as Kathleen St. Peter does Louie Marsellus (*PH* 85). Clearly Stein, author and shaper of words, occupies a more privileged position than the African-Americans she urges to accept their identity as she has accepted hers.

In spite of the parallels she sees between black and Jewish experience, Stein is not a proto-Civil Rights activist. Instead of considering her own history and well-being as somehow conjoined to that of people of color and therefore using her voice to speak out for silenced people on the margins, she basically uses these observations as a way to understand and an excuse to talk about herself. After attending an all-black theatrical performance, Stein comments that "negro actors act anything so naturally . . . publicity does not hurt them because they can be what anything makes them and it does not make anything else of them because they are the thing they are then. So it is not acting it is being for them, and they have no time sense to be a trouble to them" (288). Here Stein attributes chameleon-like characteristics to black people, suggesting that they have little backbone and little ability to differentiate real life from make-believe. Her comment about time draws on negative stereotypes of black workers as lazy, immature, and carefree. Stein, on the other hand, is deeply concerned with issues of publicity and the public self, particularly now that she has returned to the United States. America is defined by a fundamental striving for legibility, as Stein explains: "in America they want to make everything something anybody can see by looking. That is very interesting, that is the reason there are no fences in between no walls to hide anything no curtains to cover anything and the cinema that can make anything be anything anybody can see by looking" (202). Ironically, race is something that many (white) people have historically thought they could see by looking, when in fact people of color have successfully passed for white throughout American history. This observation suggests that such legibility made Stein feel vulnerable. Indeed, one's public identity can only be a source of vulnerability in a visual culture. Wagner-Martin argues that Toklas was "afraid of slander" and homophobia, while Stein "was afraid of anti-Semitism" (*Favored* 209). Perhaps Stein felt that racism, because it is more openly discussed, was less insidious than anti-Semitism. At any rate, the popularity and acceptance the women achieved on their American tour seems to have bolstered Stein's comfort with her ethnic roots, even if it did not make her substantially more understanding of other forms of minority status.

By the time she finished writing *Everybody's Autobiography* in 1937, Stein seemed "intent on being Jewish," a shift which Wagner-Martin finds consistent with Stein's personality: "[Stein's] claiming her Jewishness with such pride in the midst of the secrecy and persecution that shrouded most of Europe seemed more brave than foolhardy. Above all, it seemed characteristic" (*Favored* 230). Although Wagner-Martin attributes a certain intentionality to Stein's growing identification, Stein sometimes seems naive or reckless in her lack of concern for the anti-Semitism building around her. In her wandering, associative style, Stein off-handedly chats about friends, daily occupations, and fascism:

> So I wandered with Basket and Pepe and I enjoyed myself and I took to gardening and it was a great pleasure I cut all the box hedges and we have a great many and I cleared the paths more or less well, the box hedges I did very well and then the weeds came up in the garden and we had corn the Kiddie who sends it to us says now we must not give it to any fascists but why not if the fascists like it, and we liked the fascists, so I said please send us unpolitical corn, and Bennett Cerf and Jo Davidson came to see us and we called for them in Geneva and got lost getting out of Switzerland the way we always do. (318–19)

Stein wants unpolitical corn, but, as she certainly knew, boundaries are not always easy to enforce. Hence as *Everybody's Autobiography* winds down, we find Stein in a characteristically paradoxical position, accepting her own Jewishness and liking the fascists she encountered.

Stein's attitude about Jews and her own ethnic roots indicates growth and change on her part, while the paradoxes and self-contradictions inherent in her words and her situation suggest continuity. By the end of her second autobiography, Stein decides that perhaps the first was not an autobiography and the second is not a sequel: "And now I almost think I have the first autobiography was not that, it was a description and a creation of something that having happened was in a way happening not again but as it had been which is history which is newspaper which is illustration but is not a simple narrative of what is happening not as if it had happened not as if it is happening but as if it is existing simply that thing. And now in this book I have done it if I have done it" (312). She acknowledges the blurry line between that which is "described" (i.e., that which is objective, outside, real) and that which is created (i.e., that which is fictional, constructed, originating inside the self). She decides that she did not create the continuous present in *The Autobiography of Alice B. Toklas,* but thinks that she did that more effectively in *Everybody's Autobiography.* Also at the end of this text, Stein aligns herself with painters whose "pictures are trying to escape from the prison of framing," noting that "all those so far have tried it have gone dead in not giving birth to it" (322).

Stein wants her work to escape the confines of genre, of categories like money-
making and real, of periods like early and late or avant-garde or narrative. She
is a "grandmother" now, but she is still trying to give birth. Stein knows quite
well that *The Autobiography of Alice B. Toklas* was hugely successful, but she
offers a rare glimpse of her capacity for humility when she states, "I guess it
was a great success" (327). She reflects that "it is a peaceful thing to be one
succeeding" (327), but peace does not necessarily make for great art. Indeed
her next autobiography will be about war—*Wars I Have Seen.*

DOES SIZE MATTER? OR, BIG LITTLE DOGS

Everybody's Autobiography is a sequel to *The Autobiography of Alice B. Toklas,*
and Stein writes it as if it picks up exactly where the latter left off. In fact, *The
Geographical History of America* falls between the two. Although Gleason
states that the concept of identity did not come into articulation until after
WWII (*Speaking* 137), Stein was fully engaged in puzzling out its nuances in
this 1936 text. One might even go so far as to include Stein in the category of
Jewish intellectuals who played a major role in theorizing ethnicity and identity (Gleason, "American" 108). Gass links Stein's "attempt to identify
America with modernity" (5) to her desire to create a continuous present,
pointing out that "geography would be the study appropriate to it: mapping
body space" (8–9). This "mapping [of] body space" constitutes for Stein yet
another form of experimentation with multiple discursive positions. *The
Geographical History of America* is philosophical and reflective, and Haas includes it in the category of "Entity: Really Writing" (115), in contrast to *The
Autobiography of Alice B. Toklas* and *Everybody's Autobiography,* examples of
mere "Identity: Audience Writing" (111). Still it is not an island unto itself,
disconnected from Stein's other narrative texts or from the explorations of her
contemporaries.

The Gertrude Stein who wrote *The Geographical History of America* and
the "I" who speaks it are not unlike the Willa Cather who wrote *The Professor's
House* and the Professor whose viewpoint is privileged. Cather had recently
won a Pulitzer Prize and achieved popular and financial success when she set
about creating the disillusioned and anti-consumerist Godfrey St. Peter. Stein
had become an instant celebrity and finally started making money with *The
Autobiography of Alice B. Toklas,* and her work was finally assured of a publisher (and therefore an audience) when she pondered "the problem of personal identity" (Gass 16) and the effect fame would have on her writing.
Similarly, the only house Cather's Professor ever considers home is a cramped,
rented one, and Stein spends a lifetime "liv[ing] . . . in hotels, ships, trains,
rented rooms . . ." (Gass 14). On a thematic level, St. Peter ponders issues

such as "science as a phase of human development" (*PH* 68) and the nature of human intellect, while Stein's text delves into "the Relation of Human Nature to the Human Mind." St. Peter reflects that "the fact is, the human mind, the individual mind, has always been made more interesting by dwelling on the old riddles, even if it makes nothing of them" (68) and concludes his ruminations with his now-famous pronouncement: "art and religion (they are the same thing, in the end, of course) have given man the only happiness he has ever had" (69). Stein certainly "dwell[s] on the old riddles" in *The Geographical History of America,* contemplating (and reiterated in a repetition-with-a-difference form throughout) "what makes religion and propaganda and politics" (46).[44] These issues might not be of primary interest to Stein, but she cannot ignore them; indeed "religion and propaganda and politics" have become the subject of art.

Like *The Professor's House, The Geographical History of America* is a formal experiment for the author. Stein's work, while "in no sense a volume of philosophy" is nevertheless "philosophically . . . the most important of her texts," perhaps best conceptualized as "the stylized presentation of the process of meditation itself, with many critical asides" (Gass 23, 23–24, 23). Addressing the seemingly redundant passages in the text, Gass explains, "we repeat when we think . . . [and] the style of *The Geographical History of America* is often a reflection of this mental condition" (33). The structure of *The Geographical History of America* is also characteristically American if we consider it in light of Blair's thesis of American modularity. Arguing that "Americanness" is not "what people believe (or say they believe)," but "tendencies in the way life within it is organized" (8), Blair proceeds to define modularity as "when the Americans take something the Europeans had always considered as a whole . . . and break it up" (11). Some examples of modularity which Blair offers include Whitman's poetry and the work of blues/jazz musicians. Whitman, he explains, "left behind the ruling European conceptions of sequential and holistic literary structure in favor of modular openness" (62). Similarly, blues and jazz demonstrate modularity because "both are essentially add-on structures without inherent pointing toward any foreseeable climax" (76). Arguably, Stein's text belongs in this category, as well. Instead of offering a coherent, unitary history of the country (starting, perhaps, with Plymouth or Jamestown and continuing through to the Great War or the stock market crash), Stein offers a fragmented "geographical history," which is literally all over the map.[45]

If we place her work within the context of the modularity that partially defines Americanism and the formlessness that partially defines modern writing, it seems perfectly sensible for Stein to conclude that "there is no reason why chapters should succeed each other since nothing succeeds another, no now any more. In the old novels yes but not new any more" (82). She further states, "why is it not necessary to have chapters and if in spite of it not being necessary one does have them why do they not have to follow one another" (83). In *The Geographical History of America*, Stein offers chapters, plays, scenes, volumes, pages, parts and autobiographies—all numbered (but few arranged consecutively) and many used more than once. The text is narrative in that individual sentences make sense, but there is no single story or overarching plot to speak of.[46] At one point, Stein offers a morality-play-like interlude in which the characters are "identity, human nature, human mind, universe, history, audience and growing" (146). She also provides a few more traditional narrative episodes, such as "the story of Bennett" (72), but one would be hard pressed to offer a synopsis of *The Geographical History of America*.

Nevertheless, in writing about America, Stein simultaneously claims the country as her own and leaves her mark on it. While *The Professor's House* delves deeply into issues of possession, Stein offers the following meditation on the language of ownership: "How is America. Very well I thank you. This is the reply. If you say I thank you that means that in a way it belongs to you. Very well I thank you" (67–68). Despite her *de facto* expatriation, Stein exerts a claim on America merely by answering for it, or in this case, by writing about it. She defines herself as an American, and no one can say otherwise. Stein offers her own bid for why "a Geographical history is important" (47), but in typical form she does not write *a* geographical history—she writes *the* geographical history. Stein never spells out what exactly her project entails, but she does say that we will recognize it when we see it. As she explains, "when suddenly you know that the geographical history of America has something to do with everything it may be like loving any man or any woman or even a little or a big dog" (84). Once again showing a Whitmanian influence, Stein situates her work by invoking a portrait of the Everyman who loves Anyman (or -dog).

In addition to writing in the tradition of Whitman, Stein repeatedly situates herself in relation to other geniuses. Indeed, *The Geographical History of America* begins with Stein aligning herself, the speaking "I," with two extraordinary American males, both of whom are linked in the popular imagination with revolution and freedom: "in the month of February were born Washington and Lincoln and I" (45). Such cataloging implies a more-than-healthy ego in Stein, along with an identification with ideological Americanism, freedom, and equality. Indeed, Fuchs points out that particularly in its early years, "what distinguished the American national spirit, character, and identity was not sectarian religion or ancestry but a culture of politics" (21), clarifying that "for Jefferson, American identity was a matter of American ideology . . ." (56). Having compared herself to two quintessential American symbols, Stein immediately proceeds to insist that "these are ordinary ideas" (45). Broadening her identification from American heroes to international literary greats across the centuries, Stein offers the following linkage: "think of the Bible and Homer think of Shakespeare and think of me" (109). When she tries to contextualize her writing within her own time, Stein can only rhetorically (and repeatedly) wonder "why is it that in this epoch the only real literary thinking has been done by a woman" (210; see also 216–17, 220). In contemplating her status as an American, a writer, and a genius, Stein also finds a prototype for her own position vis-a-vis nationality, namely that she is of her country but not in it. Thus she observes, "Theodore and Franklin Roosevelt like Napoleon and Louis Napoleon even though they belonged to the country to which they belonged were foreign to it" (127). Stein, "non-expatriate" (Spencer 204) but non-resident, is similarly foreign to the country to which she belongs.[47]

Establishing a cross-cultural and longitudinal context for her project is one strategy that Stein employs in order to conceptualize her sense of personal identity. Another method towards this end is Stein's introduction of two mantras which recur throughout the text: "what is the use of being a little boy if you are going to grow up to be a man" (50), and "I am I because my little dog knows me" (99). While the former interrogates the relationship between the child and the adult self (i.e., personal identity over time), the latter invokes the relationship between personal identity and audience. In addition to interrogating identity, human nature, and the human mind, both of these ritualistically repeated lines further expand the explorations of discursive positions which Stein attempts in "Melanctha" (writing about black, lower-class characters) and *The Autobiography of Alice B. Toklas* (writing as Alice). Here it would seem that Stein's interest is in expanding the generic, perhaps presaging her decision to write another book about herself and call it *Everybody's Autobiography*. In the case of "little boy [who is] . . . going to grow up to be a man," Stein continues, "and yet everybody does so unless it is a little girl going to grow up to be a woman" (50). This line occurs only once, though, so it seems that the boy growing up to be a man suffices to summarize everyone's developmental pattern. Stein further articulates her broad use of the generic when she says, "any man that is women and children" (58). In this case, it is difficult to discern whether "any man" includes "women and children," or whether "women and children" substitutes for "any man." Gass clarifies the first mantra and connects it to the second in the following way:

> When Gertrude Stein wrote that there was little use in being born a lit-
> tle boy if you were going to grow up to be a man, she did not intend to
> deny causality or the influence of the past. She did mean to say that when
> we look at our own life, we are looking at the history of another; we are
> like a little dog licking our own hand, because our sense of ourselves at
> any time does not depend upon such data, only our 'idea' of ourselves
> does, and this 'idea,' whether it's our own or that of another, is our iden-
> tity. Identities depend upon appearances and papers. Appearances can be
> imitated, papers forged. (37)

Thus in Gass's estimation, Stein's real concern is with the impossibility of per-
petuating a fixed identity when people are constantly changing and when the
accouterments of identity are so easily altered.

    While I see the merit in Gass's reading of the "little boy," I think he stops
short of a thorough analysis of the "little dog." Stein describes the reciprocal
relationship between the little dog (the audience) and the speaking "I" in terms
suggestive of the mirroring which occurs between a mother and a child—the
little dog's recognition confers identity upon the speaking "I." At the same
time, Stein acknowledges the tenuousness of relying on a outside source for affirmation: "I am I because my little dog knows me, but perhaps he does not
and if he did I would not be I. Oh no oh no" (100). Upon further examination, cause and effect are not always clear, as Stein points out: "*If* I am I *then*
my little dog knows me" (102; emphasis added). Whereas Stein initially suggested that the dog's recognition confers identity, she here implies that the
speaking "I" must have an identity as a prerequisite for the dog's acknowledgment. She then proposes that perhaps the little dog's knowing "does not prove
anything about you it only proves something about the dog" (103), eventually
concluding that "I am I because my little dog knows me, even if the little dog
is a big one, and yet the little dog knowing me does not really make me be I no
not really because after all being I I am I has really nothing to do with the little dog knowing me, he is my audience, but an audience never does prove to
you that you are you" (104–05). Since the little dog is a figure for an audience
and "any dog has identity" (134), we might assume that this discussion has
been entirely hypothetical. At this point, Stein gives her first indication that
this mantra is not wholly of her own creation: "the old woman said I am I because my little dog knows me, but the dog knew that he was he because he
knew that he was he as well as knowing that he knew she" (134). Stein herself
had several dogs, as any reader of her "autobiographies" is well aware. Thus it
seems that the little dog of *The Geographical History of America* functions on
several rhetorical levels simultaneously—generic ("a dog" [46] and "any little
dog" [48]); specific (the old woman and her little dog); and personal (Stein's

standard poodle, Basket). I will point out, however, that Stein's primary attachment was not to a little dog, but rather a big one. Stein had Chihuahuas, as well, Byron and Pepe, but the only dog she mentions in this text is Basket.[48] In proposing that any dog, even a big one, can serve the purpose of "my little dog," Stein is pushing the generic one step further.

In addition to offering broad new forms of the generic, Stein further expands the definition of autobiography by writing a slew of them (172–84). Most people write a single autobiography (or perhaps several consecutive volumes on a particularly noteworthy life), but Stein provides many autobiographies, and indeed, multiple versions entitled "autobiography one" (179). Even when Stein unhinges autobiography from its traditional definitions, however, there are limits to what the genre can do. Because it is inherently dependent on an audience, autobiography cannot communicate entity:

> Become Because.
> Beware of be.
> Be is not what no one can be what no one can see and certainly not
> what no one can say.
> Anybody can say be.
> Be is for biography.
> And for autobiography.
> No not for autobiography because be comes after.
> So once more to renounce because and become. (184)

In her interrogation of the tension between the desire to create a narrative of the self and the impossibility of producing a unitary self to narrate, Stein prefigures Butler's argument which questions the "popular discourse on gender identity that uncritically employs the inflectional attribution of 'being' to genders and to 'sexualities'" (*Gender* 21). While Butler insists that "within the inherited discourse of the metaphysics of substance, gender proves to be performative—that is, constituting the identity it is purported to be" (*Gender* 24–25), Stein seems to be saying that the self is similarly performative or constructed. Furthermore, the self is constructed only in the context of an audience. Autobiography is about the self, but not for the self. Paradoxically, perhaps, one writes an autobiography for an audience. When Stein does offer a few lines of autobiography it is not under that rubric but rather "the story of my life" (187). Stein begins with, "at that time I had no dogs" (188). By this she means no pets, but also no audience. Stein had a second best, "a family," but it is dispensable, as she points out, "they can be a nuisance in identity but there is no doubt no shadow of doubt that that identity the family identity we can do without" (188). Little dogs and national ties, on the other hand, are imperative.

If size does not matter for the "little dog" in question, it does matter for the United States itself: "in the United States there is more space where nobody is than where anybody is" (45). Gass agrees with the aptness of Stein's decision to write a geographical history. He clarifies that in a rootless, migratory country such as the United States, "sometimes one feels there's nothing but geography . . . and certainly a geographical history is the only kind it can significantly have" (13). Stein further explains that history is an appropriate genre, since "big countries cannot really make poetry because they do not cannot all when they say the same thing feel as they do" (202). Along similar lines, Stein's former professor, Munsterberg, observes that "a nation which in every decade has assimilated millions of aliens, and whose historic past everywhere leads back to strange peoples, cannot with its racial variegation inspire a profound feeling of indissoluble unity" (5). America is not the setting from which to produce great literature, but as a subject it provides discursive positions for Stein to work from. Indeed, Stein's literary strategies in some ways epitomize Berlant's definition of American nationality and the American Dream: "to be American . . . would be to inhabit a secure space liberated from identities and structures that seem to constrain what a person can do in history" (*Queen* 4). Stein rejects traditional history and traditional conceptions of identity in one fell syllogistic swoop: "identity is history and history is not true because history is dependent upon an audience" (139). As an alternative, Stein creates herself and re-conceptualizes history not as the past but as a realm of possibility dependent on the presence of an audience.

In spite of its vast size and its frontier tradition, America is no longer empty, as Stein acknowledges: "leave well enough alone means nothing now because nothing is alone" (168). Indeed, we might observe that Stein's world view has (predictably) changed dramatically in the thirty years since "Melanctha: Each One as She May." Another important shift which occurs between the publication of "Melanctha" and that of *The Geographical History of America* has to do with the fact that Stein is no longer struggling for money and fame. While "Melanctha" establishes links between living and loving, Stein here adds, "now anybody who loves money and anybody who loves loves money anybody who loves loves to have money" (48). Having a paying audience causes Stein to question the paradoxical relationship between the intrinsic and the extrinsic worth of art: "as long as nothing or very little that you write is published it is all sacred but after it is a great deal of it published is it everything that you write is it as sacred" (53). Having an audience seems preferable to obscurity (just as wealth seems preferable to poverty), but it also has the potential to lessen a work's spiritual value precisely in proportion to the financial value it bestows.

Audience is also related to the inside/outside dichotomy which Stein addresses in "Melanctha" and in her various autobiographies. Indeed, Harriet Chessman claims that all of Stein's work struggles with "the communication between an 'I' and a 'you,' between an author (or a work) and a reader" (137). Thinking about human nature and the human mind in terms of inside and outside, Stein insists, "if the human mind is in then it is not out" (113). Public speech is also differentiated from private writing, as Stein explains: "what is the difference between write it and tell it. There is a difference you can tell it as you write it but you can tell it and not write it" (117). Along similar lines, "when inside is inside it sees outside but it is inside" (180). Inside and outside are separate but not equal, and they are not always clearly defined. At times Stein conceptualizes the two as a binary either/or (e.g., the human mind is either in or out), but at times there seems to be space for a more fluid both/and (e.g., inside can see, if not be, outside). In this way, Stein seems to share the experience of the subjects about whom Gambrell writes that "if modernist women 'insider-outsiders' were compelled to circulate constantly among discrete intellectual formations addressing a series of different audiences with different agendas, then frequent self-revision can be read, in part, as a defense, a necessary evasion" (33–34). Stein's audiences included the American public, her fellow artists and geniuses, and herself (not to mention her big little dog). Thus we might conclude that Stein's repetitive meditations serve the purpose of allowing Stein to speak as her selves as opposed to being limited to (defining and) speaking as herself.

Indeed, Stein toys repeatedly with the notion that a unitary self could be developed and sustained over time. For example, she reflects that "when I was one that is no longer one of one but just one that is to say when I was a little one, but not so little that I meant myself when I said not one" (172). Here Stein plays with the slippage between speaking of "one" as an age, as a generic person, and as a specific individual. Moving from her childhood to her Radcliffe days, Stein recalls, "when I was at college I studied philosophy that was it they did not know what they saw because they said they saw what they knew, and if they saw it they no longer knew it because then they were two. . . . The minute you are two it is not philosophy that is through it is you" (178). If philosophy cannot resolve the tension between seeing and knowing in order to present a coherent identity, neither can religion: "You see that is what religion means when it says two in one and three in one and so religion can try to be one in one. . . . So after all then even in religion one is not one" (179). One is not one in Stein's oeuvre either, as her many versions of "autobiography one" (179) imply. Thus Stein conceives of the self as multiple, as fluid and as a potential object for wordplay.

Stein plays with words, but she also recognizes their power. Indeed, language has important links to both nationality and identity. In terms of nationality, Massa and Stead point out that "for the American, more than for the Englishman, language and the construction of national identity have been inter-involved" (4), while Anderson insists that language both creates and enables the solidarity of a nation (154). Gass offers a summary of Stein's particularly American linguistic attributes, including "her natural American bent toward self-proclamation and her restless quest for truth" (20). He further suggests that Stein ultimately defined herself "as an eccentric, dilettante, and gossip, madwoman, patron, genius, tutor, fraud, and queer—the Mother Goose of Montparnasse" (20). In addition, nationality and sexual orientation are intertwined in Stein's writing and ideologically, as Berlant comments, "linked complexly to the enigma of consensual sex is that of consensual nationality, which similarly involves theories of self-identity, of intention, and of the urge to shed the personal body for the tease of safe mutual or collective unboundedness" (*Queen* 171). Stein qualifies her immersion in "collective unboundedness" by raising issues of legibility: "It is wonderful how a handwriting which is illegible can be read, oh yes it can" (183).[49] Here she literally refers to the fact that only Alice, her beloved, can decipher her longhand manuscripts, but she also highlights the fact that not everyone can accurately read and comprehend all aspects of a multifaceted person like herself. For example, Stein's homosexuality is not necessarily "something legibly written on the body" (Edelman 9), or, for that matter, something clearly written on all Stein's texts. At the same time, Stein insists that "anything that is anything can be read again" (233). In other words, multiple readings from multiple perspectives produce multiple texts.

Bringing the discussion full circle, we can observe that language plays a crucial role in the construction and maintenance of personal identity, as well. Indeed, Stein might well have agreed with Dollimore's reading of Shakespeare's Caliban as creation and creator of language at the same time: "Caliban curses as an effect of language itself. . . . He possesses no essential nature, perverted or true, but an identity partly formed in and by language. . . . It is within and by that language that he is made or made able—created/coerced—to curse" (109). In *The Geographical History of America*, Stein essentially writes herself into continuing existence, as an American, as a genius/hero/artist, as a lesbian, and as a person. Through repetition and continual re-working of philosophical and epistemological issues, Stein "become[s] her own literary progenitor" (Blankley 208). The meditations which comprise *The Geographical History of America* do not come together as a definitive and unambiguous treatise, however, and the text ends with a prime example of the "willful inconclusiveness, inscribed within the textual sequences" of Gambrell's women modernists (184): "I am not sure that is not the end" (*GH* 235).

Outspoken and ambitious though she was, Gertrude Stein did not believe that she possessed the key to ultimate, unchanging truths. Her "strong impulse towards *self*-revision" (Gambrell 32), which links her to other women modernist intellectuals, led her to accept growth and change, inconsistency and contradiction, not just as part of life but as a condition of life. Indeed, we might observe that Stein's various avatars demonstrate both continuity and transformation—Melanctha and Jeff of "Melanctha," the "Gertrude Stein" of *The Autobiography of Alice B. Toklas,* the narrator of *Everybody's Autobiography,* and the speaker of "I am I" in *The Geographical History of America.* Furthermore, Stein employs a host of marginal, liminal, and transitional figures, including the mixed-race individual, the cosmopolitan, and the Wandering Jew. Hence, Stein uses innovative forms and fluidity of identity.

Stein claims to have written "for myself and strangers" (qtd. in Poirier 25), but she was part of a literary and artistic movement, as well. She wrote within and against traditions simultaneously (Dearborn 55), and considered herself to be centrally involved in the forging of new ones. Although she would have been the first to call her work ground-breaking, she was not one for social causes. As "Alice" relates of Stein's decision to leave medical school without her degree, "her very close friend Marion Walker pleaded with her, she said, but Gertrude Gertrude remember the cause of women, and Gertrude Stein said, you don't know what it is to be bored" (*ABT* 82). Stein did not seek out female protégées, devoting her attention to her male peers while charging Alice with entertaining (and protecting her from) the tedious wives of geniuses, but she served as an important literary role model for Nella Larsen. While Stein never considered herself part of a community of women, she was working in ways that were analogous and complementary to her literary contemporaries like Cather and Larsen. Stein unhinges the concept of identity, allowing for looser and more fluid representations of nationality, ethnicity, geographical movement, and gender. Through innovative forms and narrative styles she actively participates in the (female, lesbian, expatriated American) quest for self-expression, the ability to resolve "the problem of the external and the internal" (*ABT* 119) once and for all.

Chapter Four
"The Mixedness of Things": Nella Larsen

Willa Cather, Gertrude Stein, and Nella Larsen all showed a sustained interest in how "geography, migration, and identity" (Yohe 1) converge to shape human experience. Although the three writers are generally studied within the rubric of distinct and non-overlapping sub-fields, all three moved in intersecting personal and professional circles. To begin with, author and photographer Carl Van Vechten, who introduced many of his friends to one another, sustained a long-term friendship with each woman. Mabel Dodge sent Van Vechten to Stein with a letter of introduction 1913, and the ensuing relationship lasted until Stein's death, with Van Vechten acting as literary agent as well as personal champion.[1] Van Vechten also praised Cather's work and the two had a friendly relationship from 1912 at least through the mid-1930s, when Cather finally allowed Van Vechten to photograph her. Van Vechten photographed Larsen, as well, along with being a close friend and literary mentor from 1923 to Larsen's virtual disappearance from the literary and social scene following her husband's death in 1941. He discussed Stein's work with Larsen and tried to interest his publisher, Knopf, in both Stein's and Larsen's work. Along with publishing both *Quicksand* and *Passing* in 1928 and 1929, respectively, Knopf became Cather's friend and publisher in 1920 and served in both capacities until the end of Cather's life.

In addition to having close relationships with some of the same people, Cather, Stein and Larsen displayed some similar personal patterns. All spent formative time in Europe but retained a sense of themselves as Americans. Further, each writer believed in the possibilities for and took an active role in her own self-creation. Manifestations of this shared predilection include fudged birth years, new names or nicknames, and alternative narratives of personal history.[2] Not surprisingly, these biographical similarities extend to literary affiliations, concerns, and techniques, as well. From a thematic perspective, Larsen's treatment of identity is evocative of Stein's "Melanctha";

stylistically, Larsen writes in Cather's demeuble tradition, offering a deceptively simple prose style and dense, concise imagery. Indeed, Walter White compares Larsen to Cather in his 1928 letter supporting Larsen's Guggenheim application (Davis 295). Also like Cather, Larsen employs a male protagonist in a short story (Davis 180) and engages in male pseudonymy.[3] In Larsen's case, the disguise is two-fold, as Wall observes of Larsen's story, "The Wrong Man," "if the male pseudonym obscures the author's identity, so too does the absence of racial markers in the text" (86). Hence Larsen scholars, like their equivalents in Cather studies and Stein studies, tend to read Larsen's work as coded and multivalent.

Representation—what is communicated, how, and by whom—is a key concern of all three writers. In particular, all three see the complexity and potential problems inherent in men's attempts to portray women. Cather dramatizes this situation in her irony-laden *A Lost Lady* (1923), a novel which shows an idealistic young man's failure to comprehend a richly contradictory older woman. As Cather was finishing her book about Niel's inability to capture and pin down the essential Marian, she was having her own portrait painted by Leon Bakst, commissioned by the Omaha Public Library. In spite of his best efforts, Bakst was unable to give the citizens of Nebraska a likeness of their native daughter: "he went on painting desperately at the portrait, sitting after sitting, while all the while it grew worse—stiff, dark, heavy, lifeless—everything that Willa Cather was not . . ." (E. Lewis 132). In life, as in literature, men's attempts to comprehend and represent women produce a disappointingly "grim portrait" (O'Brien, *EV* 240). Picasso did not fare much better with his portrait of Stein. She was happy with his rendition, but few other people have been, and it is certainly telling that Picasso had to blot out Stein's head and repaint it from memory in order to complete the canvas. In the *The Autobiography of Alice B. Toklas,* Picasso comments to Alice that Stein would eventually grow into her portrait. While this assertion implies the genius of foresight, it is worth noting that Picasso, who "struggled with the subject mightily" (Pierpont 83), was incapable of painting the woman as she was—he could only offer his version of the woman as she would be. Larsen's Helga Crane is also the subject of a painting which distorts her appearance. Looking at Axel Olsen's depiction of her, Helga is repelled by the "disgusting sensual creature with her features" (*Q* 89). Her aunt and uncle are unpleasantly startled as well. When Larsen tackles representation of women by men, the additional factor of how whites represent blacks complicates the issue.[4] Hence Carby notes that "the section of the novel [*Quicksand*] set in Copenhagen confronted directly the question of the representation of blacks by whites" (171). Furthermore, Larsen explores how white-identified black women represent (and create) other black women. Thus, in *Passing*, which McCoy reads as "the emblematic tale of Irene Redfield's colonization of Clare Kendry" (71), "the narrative is driven not so much by Clare's hidden racial life as by Irene's predilection for reading Clare an indeterminate free space upon which to construct escapist narratives—narratives that help her to alleviate the multiple pressures Irene herself experiences in being black, female, and bourgeois in 1920s America" (72). In this way, Larsen looks at many dimensions of the problem of representation, simultaneously sharing the preoccupations of her predecessors and moving beyond their work.

Larsen's positionality also links her to Gambrell's intellectual insider/outsiders. Larsen traveled among the black social elite, but she also moved in white intellectual and artistic circles. Her friends were both white and black, and she consistently resisted pigeonholing. Thus Larsen illustrates what Gambrell calls "*multiple* affiliation: serial or simultaneous connections to more than one formation—and in many cases, to competing formations" (24). Indeed, Larsen's life embodies the dilemma Gambrell poses: "what . . . does it mean to be affiliated with a school, movement, or discipline in which one would, under more usual circumstances, occupy the position of 'Other' . . ." (12). Gambrell's paradigm complicates Lewis's assessment that Larsen had a "determination to write about cultured Afro-America from the inside" (D. Lewis 140). Here Lewis fails to recognize that Larsen was not wholly on the inside, as Davis notes: "after she became a celebrity, she attended fashionable parties, openings, teas, and cabarets, yet she remained primarily an observer, highly visible, but rarely the center of attention" (7). Martha Cutter picks up this ambivalence in Larsen's texts as well. She observes that, in *Quicksand,* for example, Helga feels torn between what marrying James Vayle would offer in terms of social status and what being Mrs. James Vayle would entail in terms of social conformity. Helga "longs to be an 'insider,' [but] she also feels smothered by the prospect of adapting herself to a particular social role" (Cutter 77). In Larsen's case, even identifying as black or white required complex negotiations. Sollors observes that black narrators "have illustrated how external definitions by racial categories persistently interfere with individual definitions from the inside" (*Beyond* 192), while Washington asks further, "what happens to a writer who is legally black but internally identifies with both blacks and whites, who is supposed to be content as a member of the black elite but feels suffocated by its narrowness, who is emotionally rooted in the black experience and yet wants to live in the whole world not confined to a few square blocks and the mentality that make up Sugar Hill?" (162). We might attempt to offer an answer to these questions by looking at how Larsen tried to situate herself professionally and artistically.

Well-read and eclectic in her interests,[5] Larsen took up some of the same questions (and utilized some of the same techniques) as Cather. Larsen's texts, published in the late 1920s, are stylistically of a piece with the mid-1920s demeuble novels Cather wrote after her world broke in two.[6] Larsen also takes up Cather's experiments with narrators, especially unreliable ones, and with portraying an ironic distance between a narrator and the author. While neither Cather nor Larsen is read as a high modernist writer, both share thematic concerns with mainstream modernism. For example, Cantor identifies a "rejection of absolute polarities" (38) and an attendant emphasis on interaction as characteristics of modernism. In Cather, "the sun [lies] like a great golden globe in the low west [, w]hile . . . the moon [rises] in the east, as big as a cart-wheel" (*MA* 206); Cather introduces binaries in order to undo them. Surely this is also what Larsen's preoccupation with the "mixedness of things" (Davis 243) suggests. Furthermore, modernist writing utilizes microcosms and particle physics, showing "a penchant for the fragmented, the fractured, and the discordant" (Cantor 36–7). Cather uses microcosms in her Bohemian Family of Man (the Shimerdas of *My Antonia*) and in her Professor's symbolically-charged house, while she protests the encroachments of science by speaking through St. Peter. Married to a physicist, Larsen shows more patience for science; her microcosms employ science as a tool, thus taking up Cather's question and moving beyond her answer. For example, Helga's Harlem, where "black figures, white figures, little forms, big forms, small groups, large groups, sauntered, or hurried by" (*Q* 58), presents a cross-section of America, as does the Negro Welfare League dance in *Passing*. Such analogies as "her atom of friendship" (*Q* 5) clearly draw on Larsen's knowledge of modern science. Finally, both Cather and Larsen created episodic texts which utilize flashbacks, letters, and out-of-body experiences, and which structurally underscore the fragmented and fluctuating identities of the characters they portray.

Larsen also shares goals and approaches with Stein, whom she actually names as a literary mentor. It is unclear, however, whether she ever actually met Stein or if their acquaintance was strictly epistolary. Wagner-Martin reports that Larsen visited Stein's Paris salon sometime in the mid 1920s, bringing a letter of introduction from Carl Van Vechten (*Favored* 177). Davis, Larsen's biographer, makes no mention of this visit, however, and Larsen's letter to Stein suggests that the two had not met as of February 1928. Along with a copy of her newly-published *Quicksand*, Larsen enclosed the following note:

Dear Miss Stein—

I have often talked with our friend Carl Van Vechten about you. Particularly about you and Melanctha, which I have read many times.

And always I get from it some new thing—a truly great story. I never cease to wonder how you came to write it and just why you and not some one of us should so accurately have caught the spirit of this race of mine.

Carl asked me to send you my poor first book, and I am doing so. Please don't think me too presumptuous. I hope some day to have the great good fortune of seeing and talking with you. (Gallup 215–16)

From this letter, we might conclude that Stein and Larsen had not actually met.

This is only one of several discrepancies amongst critics as to the facts of Larsen's life. Another example is Larsen's trip to Copenhagen as a young adult: Cheryl Wall states that Larsen never really visited Denmark as she had claimed (92), while Washington accepts the story of Larsen's studies abroad (161). Davis endorses neither version. Although she reports that "no documents have surfaced that would indicate that Larsen studied in Copenhagen, and no records support her claim of having lived in Denmark as a teenager," Davis stops short of discrediting Larsen's claim, noting that "Larsen may well have departed for Denmark during 1909 and returned before the fall of 1912" (67–68). The important issue in the vexed history of Larsen scholarship is the fact that Larsen continually "invented" herself (Ammons 185). Like Stein, Larsen creates multiple versions of herself and perpetuates them. While Stein "created herself as the great, undiscovered American writer" (Wagner-Martin, *Favored* 162), Larsen, like her character, Helga, "is a self-made woman, self-made in the sense that she has invented herself" (Davis 276). Furthermore, Larsen fabricated much of what she allowed others to know about her personal history (Larson xi–xii). Although her novels draw on autobiography, much of the time Larsen spent revising her texts was devoted to "the process of reinventing fact" (Davis 296). Her novels are thus doubly fictionalized, since the "facts" of Larsen's life are largely fiction and then Larsen subjects these to literary fictionalization.

Whether or not Stein and Larsen met in person, Larsen's awareness of modern science and modernist experimentation suggests that Larsen shared Stein's interest in modernity. Also like Stein, Larsen seems ahead of her time in some ways, anticipating certain postmodern tenets. By *Everybody's Autobiography,* Stein begins to explore the disappearance of the depth model and the fragmentation and multiplication of generations. For her part, Larsen represents identity in a way that is consistent with Fuss's conception of postmodernism: "the postmodern identity is frequently theorized as an atomic identity, fractured and disseminated into a field of dispersed energy. The appeal to metaphors drawn from modern physics is not unsuggestive: one visualizes the subject as a highly charged electronic field with multiple identity particles bouncing off each other, combining and recombining, caught in an interminable process of movement and refiguration" (103). Furthermore, conceptualizing identity in a way that reflected her own experience necessitated some negotiations on Larsen's part, as Gilroy has observed of people with ties to both Africa and Europe (1). Nella Larsen, Helga Crane, Clare Kendry and Irene Redfield all attempted to do so with varying success. Hence Larsen is included in Gilroy's list of "notable black American travelers" whose journeys "had important consequences for their understanding of racial identities" (17–18).[7] Clearly Larsen wrestled with issues that are still quite relevant to people of mixed or multiple heritages.

Before applying such terms as modernist or proto-postmodernist to Larsen's work, it seems appropriate to consider her work within the contemporary rubric of ethnic autobiography. Ethnic and/or immigrant writers sometimes seem to be a few steps behind the mainstream in literary trends. As Ferraro points out, ethnic realism, seemingly a holdover from American realism in the nineteenth century, was still going strong during the high modernist period (1, 58). Larsen's membership in a black elite striving for middle-class success situates her in much the same place as Cather and Stein, in spite of the fact that she was nearly twenty years their junior. Accordingly, Victorian mores seem to have been at least as influential for Larsen as they were for Cather and Stein. Indeed, as Davis states, "although [Larsen] treats the emergence of a woman's sexuality in both of the novels, she does so partially with the attitudes toward sex and sexuality that are more in keeping with Victorian mores and manners and that are at odds, rather than compatible, with the new, Freudian ideas an of the world of the 1920s that also influenced her thinking about sexuality and psychology" (328). Along similar lines, Cutter observes that Helga uses her sexuality but also represses it and "recoils" from it (84), much like Cather's Jim Burden. Furthermore, while Mary McManus contends that Larsen's work demonstrates a shift away from nineteenth century "strictures of slavery and the preoccupation with racial uplift" (80), I would point out that Larsen does not break from nineteenth-century modes completely.

While Larsen (like Cather and Stein) rejected certain elements of her mother's world, she was not granted complete acceptance into the rarified world of the traditional (white male) artist, either (Ammons 10). Unlike Cather and Stein, Larsen's relationship to art and history were complicated by race. Larsen was never a full part of her mother's world not only because of the changes that came about with the transition from the Victorian period to the modern period, but also because her white mother displayed such ambivalence towards this black child born out of wedlock. Hence Larsen sought "approval from male power-brokers as an exceptional female . . . [and] saw herself as being in competition with other women for finite rewards" (Davis 14). Larsen wanted to earn professional respect on her own terms and not within the sub-categories created by race and gender (i.e., black writer, woman writer). David Palumbo-Liu explains that such an attitude is typical of "the ethnic artist [who] aspires to join the dominant's universal culture, to slough off 'ethnic' and solely identify as 'artist'" (194). Touching on the phenomenon by which Larsen sought to recreate herself and offer a new version of the truth in her fiction, Palumbo-Liu observes that "it is no accident that the possibilities for construct-ing a minority self as no longer subordinate to, but part of, the dominant are sustained most vigorously in the realm of art, and particularly the world of *fic-tion*. . . . On the other hand, the dominant can withhold such possibilities and place upon the minority subject a set of de-limited sites of representation within the supposedly open field of the universal" (193). It was precisely these limitations that Larsen sought to free herself from through her fiction.

QUICKSAND: THE HEART OF AN IMMENSE DARKNESS

Larsen defined herself as a writer—"Nella Larsen, novelist" (Davis 2)—and sought to situate herself as part of a literary tradition. It is interesting, there-fore, that Gertrude Stein, one of the few writers Larsen actually identifies as a literary mentor, was not yet widely read. Nevertheless, Larsen's "poor first book" (qtd. in Gallup 216) indeed shows the influence of Stein's first pub-lished text, though that influence may not manifest itself overtly. As Davis suggests, Larsen's "embedding of Stein's 'Melanctha' into the narrative gestures toward a gendered search for voice and actualization" (275). Thus it is on the underlying level of subtext that Larsen most clearly takes lessons from Stein. The protagonists of both "Melanctha" and *Quicksand* share salient (and more obvious) features, however. To begin with, both Melanctha Herbert and Helga Crane are American mulattas with a light-skinned (in Helga's case, white) mother and a dark-skinned, unscrupulous absentee father. Both women lose their mothers at a relatively young age, and neither seems to find the loss particularly wrenching. Parents provide little emotional support and offer meager financial resources. Consequently, "all her life long, [Melanctha] loved and wanted good, kind and considerate people" (*TL* 72), and "all her life Helga Crane had loved and longed for nice things" (*Q* 6). These seemingly modest goals prove difficult to attain, as Melanctha undercuts her own efforts towards security and advancement by "always losing what she had in wanting all the things she saw" (*TL* 50), while Helga battles a "ruthless force, a qual-ity within herself, which was frustrating her, had always frustrated her, kept

her from getting the things she had wanted. Still wanted" (11). Both protagonists also have trouble creating a correspondence between inner and outer realities. Thus, Melanctha's inability "to tell a story wholly" (*TL* 57) finds an
analog in Helga's difficulty in being honest with those around her. Helga re-
sorts to telling "angry half-truths" (26) to Dr. Anderson, and she heeds Mrs.
Hayes-Rore's advice to conceal her white origins by saying only that her
mother is dead and leaving curious minds to "fill in the gaps to suit [them-
selves]" (41). Perhaps in part due to their communication difficulties,
Melanctha and Helga are often seen as detached from other people and from
any specific landscape. Melanctha is characterized as an urban wanderer,
while Helga responds to the necessity of seeking employment in Chicago by
wandering (27, 32). She is offered the opportunity to make money by knowing white and black men (as Melanctha does with "the different men, white
ones and blacks" [*TL* 84]), "but the price of the money was too dear" (*Q* 34).
Because of their detachment from people, Melanctha and Helga are puzzling
to their acquaintances. Melanctha is "mysterious" (*TL* 50, 61), like her
mother was before her (*TL* 50, 52), while Helga cultivates a certain "mysteriousness" in Copenhagen, a trait which had manifested itself in America as an
"air of remoteness . . . so disastrous to her friendships" (74).

In addition to depicting a character much like Stein's Melanctha, Larsen
offers representations that share Stein's racism and deployment of stereotypes.
Helga observes of the Naxos administration that "these people yapped loudly
of race, of race consciousness, of race pride, and yet suppressed its most delightful manifestations, love of color, joy of rhythmic motion, naive, spontaneous laughter" (18). Here Larsen's incisive criticism of the hypocrisies and
ironies of the black middle class combine with her willingness to perpetuate
the image of the carefree black person with "the free abandoned laughter that
gives the warm broad glow to negro sunshine" (*TL* 63). Helga also demonstrates internalized self-hatred when she expresses disdain for the common
blacks around her, deploring "the care-free quality of their laughter [which]
roused in her the desire to scream at them: 'Fools, fools! Stupid fools!'" (53).
Attending a vaudeville show in Copenhagen, Helga is "filled with a fierce hatred for the cavorting Negroes on the stage" (83), suggesting that despite ve-
hement protestations to the contrary, Helga is as concerned with racial uplift
as the next person. Although Larsen disparaged uplift,[8] she was held account-
able by her peers. Even Larsen's endorsement of Stein's racist appropriations
suggests that Larsen had a mixed identification.

Larsen never sought Cather out as an acquaintance as she did Stein, and
she does not mention Cather as an influence. Nevertheless, Larsen's work is
compared to Cather's by Larsen's friend Walter White (Davis 295), who also

suggests that Larsen and Cather might have had a similar audience (Davis 217).[9] Furthermore, on a structural level, Larsen's novels share Cather's use of the journey motif. In *My Antonia,* for example, the action moves from train car to New York (Preface), from Virginia to rural Nebraska (Book 1), from the country to the town of Black Hawk (Book 2), from the town of Black Hawk to the city of Lincoln (Book 3), and finally back to the Burdens's old homestead and the Cuzaks's new one (Books 4 and 5). *Quicksand* consists of a similar set of journeys, as Helga moves from the southern Naxos to Chicago, from Chicago to New York, from New York to Copenhagen and back again, and finally, from New York to Alabama.[10] In addition to linking Larsen to Cather, journeys situate Larsen within the milieu of other black women writers, since "metaphors of travel recur in writing by Harlem Renaissance women" (Wall xiv).

In Helga Crane's case, travel means crossing. Crossing has multiple connotations, including geographical movement (e.g. crossing the ocean, the Great Divide, or the Mason-Dixon Line), hybridization, breaching of boundaries, and religious piety.[11] The motif of crossing is important in Cather's *The Professor's House,* as well as in *My Antonia.* Helga is like Godfrey St. Peter, who travels frequently, both geographically and in his mind, and the notion of crossing/crosses is foregrounded throughout *Quicksand.* For example, *Quicksand's* epigraph comes from Langston Hughes's poem, "Cross."[12] Furthermore, Helga herself is a cross, a hybrid born of a mixed marriage. Throughout her life, she continually crosses geographical lines, occupying the position of both migrant and immigrant. Although Helga's travels within the United States would normally be considered migration as opposed to immigration, Helga (like Larsen) seems to consider the South a foreign country. Along these lines, both Thomas Hammond and Lewis refer to southern black migrants as "immigrants" (138; D. Lewis 221). By any definition, Helga is a potential immigrant when she goes to Copenhagen for an extended visit and perhaps to marry a Danish citizen. In another vein, the cross invokes Christianity. From a religious standpoint, Helga comes to accept the cross of Christ and will presumably die a martyr. Additionally, taking "cross" in the sense of "to cross out," we might apply further Clemmen's observation that *Quicksand* ends with "a negation of life by life" (458) to our analysis of crossing in Larsen's text. Crossing out can also work as atonement—Helga's pious suffering in Alabama somehow makes up for her days as a "scarlet 'oman" and a "pore los' Jezebel" (112). Finally, crossing is linked to passing, and while Helga never passes for white in the traditional sense of the expression, she does pass for other things.[13]

Part of what allows Helga to pass is her cosmopolitanism, which has produced in her an awareness of other ways of being. In her status as a cosmopolitan, Helga once again shares important features with Cather's Professor and with St. Peter's Jewish son-in-law, Louie Marsellus. Throughout *Quicksand,* Helga moves uneasily between a positively-inflected cosmopolitan mobility and its negative counterpart, a disturbing sense of rootlessness. She is the modernist wanderer, the expatriate American and the Wandering Jew— free to move, consigned to homelessness.[14] In this sense she occupies a quintessential American position: "passage itself, in other words, defines for Americans either psychically or actually what it means to be an American" (Urgo 55). While Yohe contends that "Larsen's characters are on journeys which never end; they never attain clear senses of identity or find places where they can belong" (12), I am not sure that Helga's ultimate goal (or what Larsen means to champion) is rootedness. Rather, it seems equally likely that Helga's/Larsen's ideal world would be one which could accommodate flexibility and transitivity instead of insisting that everyone fit into a unitary, essentialist category. Like Cather's St. Peter, who reflectively tries to figure out how to make peace with his several avatars and how to go on living in an imperfect world, Helga struggles with the Sisyphean task of finding her place and the subject position which most fully captures her essential self.

In creating Helga Crane, Larsen builds on "Melanctha," drawing from Stein's characterizations, her use of a racially ambiguous heroine, and her deployment of racial stereotypes. Further, *Quicksand* evokes Cather's *My Antonia* and *The Professor's House* in the attention it pays to journeys, cosmopolitanism, and boundary crossing. At the same time, Helga's story is very much her own. An attractive and attracting heroine, Helga, a schoolteacher at a southern school for black children, commands the reader's attention from the onset of the novel. Larsen begins with a carefully framed scene in which Helga, "a slight girl of twenty-two years, with narrow, sloping shoulders and delicate, but well-turned, arms and legs" (2), sits "alone in her room, which at that hour, eight in the evening, was in soft gloom" (1). She seems "well fitted to that framing of light and shade" (2), but she is not well fitted to her present occupation: "the South. Naxos. Negro education. Suddenly she hated them all" (3). Helga's unhappiness comes about over time, as she "had taught in Naxos for almost two years, at first with the keen joy and zest of those immature people who have dreamed dreams of doing good to their fellow men. But gradually this zest was blotted out, giving place to a deep hatred for the trivial hypocrisies and careless cruelties which were, unintentionally perhaps, a part of the Naxos policy of uplift" (5).[15] This three-chapter segment sets crucial foundations for the future pattern of Helga's life.

Naxos is assimilationist in its philosophy and practice.[16] Starting with "savages from the backwoods" (12), the institution systematically makes its students over into upstanding citizens who will be a credit to the race. Helga perceives Naxos as "a big knife with cruelly sharp edges ruthlessly cutting all to a pattern, the white man's pattern" (4). The diction here echoes Melville's "The Tartarus of Maids," which describes an outsider narrator's trip to a "whitewashed factory" (2456) where "machinery—that vaunted slave of humanity—. . . stood menially served by human beings, who served mutely and cringingly as the slave serves the Sultan" (2458). The "sheet white" maids who work at the paper factory seem to be "their own executioners; themselves whetting the very swords that slay them" (2460). Despite a colleague's insistence that Naxos is better than most places, offering "pretty good salaries, decent rooms, [and] plenty of men" (14), Helga cannot remain where she feels surrounded by the sterility born of mindless imitation. Color has been outlawed in this school for colored children, but Helga can see through the prohibitions to realize that "bright colours *were* fitting and that dark-complexioned people *should* wear yellow, green, and red. Black, brown, and gray were ruinous to them, actually destroyed the luminous tones lurking in their dusky skins" (18). Like the supervisors in Melville's story, who only accept asexual women as potential employees, the puritanical matrons at Naxos ban sensuality and sexuality. Indeed, just as Melville links women's sexuality with death, Larsen portrays an institution bent on upholding the worst in Victorian mores.

Naxos remains Victorian in its attitudes towards sex, and its intellectual paradigm is profoundly anti-modernist: "it tolerated no innovations, no individualism. Ideas it rejected. . . . Enthusiasm, spontaneity, if not actually suppressed, were at least openly regretted as unladylike or ungentlemanly qualities" (4). Striving to make its students and teachers into model African-Americans, Naxos squelches individuality. Although individualism is a highly-touted tenet of American culture, Munsterberg observes that individuality rarely flourishes in American society: "a stranger is at once struck by the tendency to uniformity which arises from the belief in general equality. The spirit of comradeship is unfavourable to individual differentiation, no matter whether it is a question of a man's hat and necktie to his religion and his theory of the universe" (553). As a teacher in Naxos, Helga expresses sympathy for her students, "those happy singing children, whose charm and distinctiveness the school was so surely ready to destroy" (5), but she feels unable to change the system.

The Naxos approach is also basically that of the broader Americanization movement, which was most faithfully carried out roughly between the turn of the century and 1920 (Gleason, "American" 84). Americanization called for "immigrants . . . to become new people" (Gleason, "American" 82). In the classic case of Mary Antin, for example, the transition from "immigrant" to "American" involves being born again (Salvaterra 29). Furthermore, the process of Americanization requires time and intentionality (Fairchild 222), but Helga refuses to be converted to the Naxos way—"she hadn't really wanted to be made over" (7). At the same time, Helga feels black-balled, as if she could not have obtained acceptance even if she wanted it, because of her lack of family connections: "if you couldn't prove your ancestry and connections, you were tolerated, but you didn't 'belong'" (8). In this way the Americanization movement and the sensibility of an emergent black elite converge around a preoccupation with origins and lineage. Helga knows she is not good immigration, so to speak—"she was, she knew, in a queer indefinite way, a disturbing factor" (7). Her unwillingness and inability to be assimilated is signified in the text by the adjective "queer."

At the time Larsen was moving in literary circles and writing her fiction, "queer" was evolving as a term to "mark . . . the differences between the still emerging categories of 'homosexuality' and 'heterosexuality' . . . though its new meaning was a fluid one" (Lindemann, *Queering* 2).[17] Older meanings also in play during this period include, "strange, odd, peculiar, eccentric, in appearance or character . . . [and/or] of questionable character, suspicious, dubious . . . [and/or] any difficulty, fix, or trouble, bad circumstances . . ." (qtd. in Lindemann, *Queering* 143, n. 2). "Queer" recurs as an adjective throughout *Quicksand,* appearing no fewer than ten times in this 135-page novel. While Deborah McDowell offers a convincing reading of queer overtones in *Passing,* no one has questioned Helga's heterosexuality, nor do I intend to do so. I will suggest, however, that Larsen purposefully invokes the transitivity, inversion and blending implicit in any discussion of homosexuality in her creation of Helga Crane. Helga is fully aware of the double standard that is in operation at Naxos, whereby "you could be queer, or even attractive, or bad, or brilliant, or even love beauty and such nonsense if you were a Rankin, or a Leslie, or a Scoville; in other words, if you had a family. But if you were just plain Helga Crane, of whom nobody had ever heard, it was presumptuous of you to be anything but inconspicuous and conformable" (8).

To Helga's observation, we might add Berlant's contention that, "in contrast to the zone of privacy where stars, white people, and citizens who don't make waves with their bodies can imagine they reside, the immigrant to the United States has no privacy, no power to incorporate automatically the linguistic and cultural practices of normal national culture that make life easier for those who can pass as members of the core society" (*Queen* 192). Because Helga is not of a first family, she does not have the right to be different. She is not an established southerner (like her Atlanta-born and bred fiancé, James Vayle), so her status is much like the hypothetical immigrant Berlant describes. Helga tries to observe the Naxos dress code and thereby gain some measure of approval and acceptance, but her peers disapprove of her wardrobe, considering "the colors . . . queer" (18). For her part, Helga agrees that some colors are queer. Meeting Naxos principal Robert Anderson for the first time, Helga reflects, "'Queer . . . how some brown people have gray eyes. Gives them a strange, unexpected appearance. A little frightening" (20). Here the conjunction of queerness with Anderson foreshadows that he will be a site of sexual questions and identity issues. Indeed, Helga will eventually come to contemplate having an illicit affair with Anderson. In the meantime, given her inassimilable queerness and her refusal to be "naturalized" (7) to the Naxos way, Helga has no choice but to leave Naxos.

When Helga finally comes to the conclusion that Naxos is not for her, the decision is described as a sort of anti-conversion, a premonition of her born-again experience at the end of the novel. Having determined to cease in her persona as a Naxos teacher, Helga undergoes a rebirth, and the second chapter begins with Helga waking "unrefreshed and with that feeling of half-terrified apprehension peculiar to Christmas and birthday mornings" (10). Something new and different is about to happen, and Helga does not know whether it will be for better or for worse. Although the day feels like Christmas, Helga does not have a worshipful attitude. Rather, she seems to be a born-again anti-Christian like "God-free" St. Peter (Skaggs 76). Indeed, it is the memory of a visiting white preacher who recently spoke at Naxos that pre-cipitates (and steels) Helga's decision to leave the school. Helga gives in to her frustration with Naxos "with an odd gesture of sudden soft collapse, like a per-son who had been for months fighting the devil and then unexpectedly had turned round and agreed to do his bidding" (5). This scene suggests the stan-dard good girl/ bad girl (Madonna/ whore) dichotomy, a binary model which will constrict Helga throughout the text. If Helga is not working for heaven, then she must be working for the devil. In addition to introducing this di-chotomy, the Naxos section of the text sets out several other important the-matic foundations for the novel as a whole: the tension between individuality and the establishment, Helga's simultaneous desire to fit in and to stand out, the allure and revulsion inspired by elite groups, and the vitiating presence of hypocrisy in people Helga wishes to admire. Further, this section establishes "queer" as a key term, a signifier of blurred boundaries, liminality, and dis-turbing emotions. Finally, it is important to note that Helga resolves her dif-ficulties at Naxos by leaving, by running away. This is a particularly American strategy, according to Urgo, who asserts that "What all Americans share is . . . a sense that flight or relocation is in itself of tremendous utility. If nothing else, move" (58).

Helga's first major journey takes her back to her birthplace and raises questions about home and family. Returning to Chicago, Helga experiences "a queer feeling of enthusiasm" (30), a nascent sense of belonging. Here "queer" signifies an uneasy and shifting relationship with people who should offer acceptance but do not. Helga's only living family member, her Uncle Peter, has married a woman who "plainly wished to dissociate herself from the outrage of [Helga's] very existence" (29). Mrs. Nilssen quickly reminds Helga that she has no home and no family in Chicago, unequivocally stating, "you mustn't come here any more. . . . And please remember that my husband is not your uncle" (28–29). Yohe concludes from this episode that racial identity is stronger than blood kin ties (85), while McManus points out that "home space" is both "ambiguous" and "equivocal" (151). When her family connections fail her, Helga tries alternative sources for companionship and assistance. Helga's first attempt to find "a church home" (Wall 113) leads her to the Negro Episcopal Church, where the good Christians ignore her, prompting Helga to "distrust . . . religion more than ever" (34). Initially, at least, neither Helga's family nor her "brothers and sisters" of the cross will provide her with love or money.

As much as Helga wants friendship and a feeling of belonging, money is her first priority. Money was "the most serious difficulty" (6) in Helga's plan to leave Naxos, and obtaining money quickly becomes her primary concern in Chicago. Money and movement become linked at this point. In order to make money, Helga travels with Mrs. Hayes-Rore to New York. Money is thus both catalyst and reward, since Helga is given a good job in New York and chooses to relocate there. In the comfort of Anne's beautifully-appointed home, Helga tries to deny the importance and power of money. She nonchalantly comments that "'money isn't everything. It isn't even the half of everything,'" proposing that "'it's only outside of Harlem among those others that money really counts for everything'" (46). Here an ironic distance clearly emerges between character and author. First of all, we know that money was indeed very important to Helga and will be again, as she finds herself first with much more (in Copenhagen) and later with much less (in Alabama) than she presently possesses. Secondly, Helga's ambivalent attitude towards money reflects the tensions that Larsen (like Cather and Stein) experienced between money, art, and audience.[18] Davis points out that Larsen's version of the American dream "included making money" as a novelist (217). Although Larsen wanted to write carefully crafted and critically acclaimed works of literature, "her dream did not carry with it a place for herself in a bohemian world of artists; rather, it was an updated version of the dream of a middle-class woman to achieve status, position, and money within the upper social echelons and, in her case, in both the black and the white worlds" (Davis 217). Helga knows she wants money and enjoys living well, and yet financial security is not enough to give Helga a sense of having found her place in the world.

The proverbial rich man has a hard time earning his way to heaven, and the comfortably-appointed Helga Crane finds New York another kind of hell. She takes pleasure in attending devilish gatherings, such as the cabaret. In the cabaret scene, Helga "descend[s] through a furtive narrow passage into a vast subterranean room[,] . . . one of those places characterized by the righteous as a hell" (58). Here she gives herself up to "the reek of flesh, smoke, and alcohol," realizing "that not only had she been in the jungle, but . . . she had enjoyed it" (59). Larsen here uses imagery suggestive of Dante's *Inferno*, an interesting counterpoint to her earlier evocation of "The Tartarus of Maids." Indeed it would seem that Helga's move from Naxos to New York has been a shift of hells, from the hell of maids to the hell of jungle creatures. Within the hell of New York, Helga firmly establishes herself on the devil end of the devil/angel binary. Hence in spite of making two significant geographical journeys (Naxos to Chicago and Chicago to New York), Helga finds herself playing similar roles and returning to familiar subject positions.

Regardless of her improved financial circumstances and her vibrant social life, Helga finds her current positionality ultimately dissatisfying. Neither money nor the excitements of Harlem can keep Helga from becoming bored. What seems like perfect happiness quickly gives way to Helga's characteristic and enigmatic "restlessness" (47). Like St. Peter, who at first seeks physical causes for his falling out of love with life, Helga "consult[s] a physician, who, after a long, solemn examination, said that there was nothing wrong, nothing at all. . . . All interest had gone out of living. Nothing seemed any good" (47). Helga's woes stem from psychological rather than physical causes, of course, but she cannot consider that her troubles are internal rather than external and she acts accordingly. When nothing seems any good, Helga moves on. Once again, money, an emblem of physicality, becomes the catalyst for Helga's relocation. When she receives her inheritance from Uncle Peter, Helga decides to travel to Copenhagen to see her mother's sister and her husband. Although "money as money was still not very important to Helga" (54), she comes to believe that money can bring her freedom from racial oppression (55) and decides to buy a steamer ticket.

In Copenhagen, Helga recognizes that "always she had wanted, not money, but the things which money could give, leisure, attention, beautiful surroundings. Things. Things. Things" (67). Larsen had read Theodore Dreiser (Davis 311), so Amy Kaplan's observation about Sister Carrie might easily be applied to Helga: "wanting to be different takes the form of longing to have more, as identity is defined by the power to spend money" (149). To the end of making herself different, Helga tries on a new persona. Hence her relocation to Copenhagen constitutes yet another rebirth. Waking up from an afternoon nap on the day of her arrival, Helga feels like the beggar in the opening section of Shakespeare's *The Taming of the Shrew*. As David Bevington explains of that play, "the induction sets up the theme of illusion, using an old motif know as 'The Sleeper Awakened' (as found, for example, in *The Arabian Nights*). This device frames the main action of the play, giving to it an added perspective" (108). The Copenhagen section of *Quicksand* provides a sort of inverted frame (like Tom's story in Cather's *The Professor's House*), as the chapters on either side take place in America. Being given the royal treatment without quite feeling like she deserves it, Helga experiences a "sensation of lavish contentment and well-being enjoyed only by impecunious sybarites waking in the houses of the rich" (67). Although she too begins with a sense of disbelief, she quickly joins Sly in his willingness to accept royal status:

> Am I a lord? And have I such a lady?
> Or do I dream? Or have I dreamed till now?
> I do not sleep: I see, I hear, I speak,
> I smell sweet savors, and I feel soft things.
> Upon my life, I am a lord indeed,
> And not a tinker nor Christopher Sly.
> Well, bring our lady hither to our sight,
> And once again a pot o' the smallest ale. (Induction 2.68–75)

Helga "liked it, this new life," but even more important than the physical comfort is her sense of finding her right station: "it was important, this awakening in the great high room which held the great high bed on which she lay, small but exalted. . . . This, then, was where she belonged. This was her proper setting" (67).

Paradoxically, the setting Helga considers proper is one in which she is continually made to stand out (like a turquoise in dull silver?). At first she reacts ambivalently to the prospect of having her aunt call attention to Helga's differences. The attention she receives makes her feel "like nothing so much as some new and strange species of pet dog being proudly exhibited" (70). She is a curiosity, a show-thing, a domesticated animal. It is interesting to note that Helga also becomes annoyed when the Danes treat her "'as if I had horns, or three legs'" (70). The reference to horns invokes myths about Jews, suggesting a parallel between Helga's experience and that of Jewish people. It also suggests Satan, as if Helga's Negro heritage potentially renders her a "scrimy black devil" (*P* 172). Helga claims to be hesitant about emphasizing her difference when "hitherto all her efforts had been toward similarity to those about her" (*Q* 72). This statement is only partially true and demonstrates Helga's lack of self-awareness. While she did try to fit in at Naxos, she held herself apart from the other girls at the Chicago YWCA and from the lower-class types in Harlem. In spite of her disinclination to think of herself as a toy dog, a Jew, a devil, or a cripple, Helga is happy in the knowledge that she has found her "own milieu" (74) and is proud to display her individuality.

Before too long, Helga passively "[gives] herself up wholly to the fascinating business of being seen, gaped at, desired" (74), much like the "odd gesture of sudden soft collapse" (5) that accompanied her decision to leave Naxos. Observing Helga's propensity for "posturing and . . . dressing," Davis contends that Helga "and the Dahls have, perhaps not unwittingly, used her obsession with clothes to attract men" (267). Dress is an indicator of class status but also of group membership: "dress serves not only as a criterion of difference [i.e. social status], but as a signal of identification[,] . . . a ticket of admission and a sign of belonging" (Kallen 13). Ann DuCille further points out that *Quicksand* should not be dismissed as a novel of manners solely because of the attention it pays to details such as clothing: "rather, clothes function semiotically as sexual and racial signifiers" (205). Along similar lines, McManus uses the opening scene of the novel to compare "sexual repression" with "transvestitism," as she notes, "Helga's provocative appearance signals sexual desire, but because her isolation is also apparent, dressing and posing will be the consummate act" (50). Finally, Dollimore insists that, in the early modern period, "dress underwrites not only class differences but national and racial ones also. . . . Accompanying the association between dress and class was that between dress and gender" (288–89). Helga more and less consciously chooses to use dress as a means of communicating messages about class, race, and gender.

Helga is not the only one who stands out for her dress and her difference. Axel Olsen, the portrait painter whom Helga's aunt and uncle aspire for her to marry, is like no one Helga has met before. Furthermore, he is repeatedly connected with queerness. He is an artist, as Helga immediately discerns from his "broad streaming tie. But how affected! How theatrical!" (70). How gay. Indeed, as another member of the dinner party explains, "'He's queer'" (71). Further, Olsen is "brilliant, bored, elegant, urbane, cynical, [and] worldly" (77), a real cosmopolitan. He both propositions and proposes to Helga, but it seems plausible to read Olsen as a Van Vechten-type figure, someone who has the potential to be both a married man and a homosexual. When Helga turns Olsen down, he responds "in a queer frozen voice" (88), incredulous. Soon thereafter he retreats "to some queer place in the Balkans" (90).

Olsen is largely responsible for Helga's exotic costumes, as Helga's aunt and uncle appoint him Helga's fashion consultant. In addition to molding Helga's appearance to fit preconceived notions of how an African-American woman should appear, Olsen paints a portrait which puts a specific slant on Helga. While Olsen argues that he has portrayed "'the true Helga Crane'" (88), Helga feels completely alienated from the subject of his painting. Hence Ammons's contention that "Helga Crane struggles to step out of the frames others design for her" (188) uses a telling analogy. Like Stein, who came to believe that portraits trying to escape their frames were the next wave of great art, Helga (and Larsen) sought to avoid confining scripts. Copenhagen and the expectations of her aunt and uncle prove too limiting, so Helga plans "a brief visit" to America (93).

Returning "home" to New York, perpetually homeless Helga takes up residence in a hotel, "home" to transients. Her last American residence, Anne Grey's house, is no longer available to her because of Anne's marriage to Robert Anderson. Nevertheless, Helga is glad to be back in Harlem, convincing herself that New York is more home than Copenhagen. She becomes "a little bored, a little restless" (96), but prefers the "gorgeous care-free revel" of Harlem to her "stately life in Copenhagen," which had "the heavy solemnity of a church service" (96). The analogy is a telling one—clearly Helga is still more party animal than parishioner. Furthermore, Helga uses the skills that she has honed in Copenhagen to even greater advantage in Harlem:

> Her courageous clothes attracted attention, and her deliberate lure—as Olsen had called it—held it. Her life in Copenhagen had taught her to expect and accept admiration as her due. This attitude, she found, was as effective in New York as across the sea. It was, in fact, even more so. And it was more amusing too. Perhaps because it was somehow a bit more dangerous. (98)

Helga's calculated flirtations are more dangerous because she is no longer off-limits. She is not a decorative object, but an agent of live sexuality. And she is available. Whereas the Danes found Helga's sexuality non-threatening, Anne is aware that Helga causes Anderson "to struggle against that nameless and to him shameful impulse, that sheer delight, which ran through his nerves at mere proximity to Helga" (95). She therefore resolves to make "her marriage . . . a success" (95) by any means necessary, most immediately by keeping Anderson as far away from her former friend and housemate as possible. Helga gets another chance at socially condoned, legitimate marriage when she sees James Vayle again at a Harlem party, but she is even more put off by the idea of marrying Vayle than when the two were at Naxos. Realizing that Vayle is indeed going to propose, Helga escapes as quickly as possible, telling him "laughingly that it was shameful of him to joke with her like that" (104). Immediately thereafter, Helga bumps into Robert Anderson, who kisses her passionately, making her indignant and angry. Over the next few weeks, her anger is transformed into "riotous and colorful dreams" (105) of ecstasy. Helga mentally prepares herself for the social ramifications of having an affair. Although she "wasn't . . . a rebel from society, Negro society" and "had no wish to stand alone" (107), Helga resolves to follow her passion. Having refused Axel Olsen in Copenhagen, however, Helga now experiences the rejection of her overtures to Anderson. Just as Olsen originally proposed a non-legal relationship, Helga wants to have an affair with her sometime-friend's husband. Anderson, who probably never knew of Helga's feelings, offers an apology for his drunken embrace. For Helga, this "surprising, trivial apology loom[s] as a direct refusal of the offering" (109).

Anderson's snub causes Helga to fall into an inappropriate match, the Reverend Mr. Pleasant Green. The evening after her encounter with Anderson, Helga goes wandering through the streets in a rainstorm. She seeks shelter from the wind and rain which have just caused her to fall in a gutter by entering a storefront church. In the church, the parishioners are "singing a song which she was conscious of having heard years ago—hundreds of years it seemed" (110–11), creating a link not only to Helga's childhood but to some primal experience. The primitivism of the church, while suggestive of "sexual excitement and orgasmic release" (McDowell xx), simultaneously invokes a climactic utterance in Joseph Conrad's *Heart of Darkness,* "the horror! the horror!" (1811):[19]

> Fascinated, Helga Crane watched until there crept upon her an indistinct *horror* of an unknown world. She felt herself in the presence of a nameless people, observing rites of a remote obscure origin. The faces of the men and women took on the aspect of a dim vision. "This," she whispered to herself, "is terrible. I must get out of here." But the *horror* held her. She remained motionless, watching, as if she lacked the strength to leave the place—foul, vile, and terrible, with its mixture of breaths, its contact of bodies, its concerted convulsions, all in wild appeal for a single soul. Her soul. (113; emphasis added)

Like Kurtz, Helga moves from observer to participant, until, in a moment of hesitation, Helga is "lost—or saved" and the faithful hordes close in on her (113). Furthermore, Helga, like Kurtz, will die in the savage land she has chosen for her home. While Kurtz chooses to remain deep in the Congo, where he is absorbed "into the heart of an immense darkness" (1817), Helga continues the downward path which began with a street gutter and leads her into rural Alabama.[20]

Upon her arrival in "the tiny Alabama town where [Reverend Green] was pastor to a scattered and primitive flock" (118), Helga reveals that the Naxos sensibility has not completely deserted her. Resolving "to do much good to her husband's parishioners" (119), Helga reveals her outsider status and her sense of her own superiority in conferring charity on the less fortunate and less informed.[21] Her missionary spirit does not last long, however, as Alabama becomes, like Kurtz's Congo, "an immense darkness" (Conrad 1817) which threatens to swallow her entirely. Helga surrenders herself to "the wisdom of God" and thereby receives "a queer sort of satisfaction" (126), but childbirth becomes a recurring horror without consolation (127). When Helga falls into a stupor after the birth of her fourth child, her withdrawal is conceptualized as an immersion in darkness: "nothing penetrated the kind darkness into which her bruised spirit had retreated" (128). It is also a downward motion, a descent motif: "she had gone *down* into that appalling blackness of pain" (128; emphasis added).

The final paragraphs of the novel, in which Helga contemplates escape for herself and her children, draw on the history of female slave narratives. Helga's stupor has been a coping mechanism for a body exhausted by giving birth to too many children in too short a period of time, but it might also be read as a means of transcending the bounds of gender. Once she returns to normal consciousness, Helga chooses to perpetuate her state as long as possible; it would seem that Helga finds freedom in her confinement. Like Harriet Jacobs's Linda Brent, who experiences a sense of personal empowerment by choosing to lock herself in a garret where she can see and hear things from a safe distance, Helga cherishes "that serene haven, that effortless calm where nothing was expected of her" (128). Indeed, we might consider this period between Helga's coma and her acknowledgment, "I'm back" (128), as a sort of modernist vacation. Also like Jacobs/Brent, Helga will not abandon her children, even at the cost of her own freedom.[22] She puts off her escape until some future time when she will be physically able to undertake the journey: "'I'm still,' she reasoned, 'too weak, too sick. By and by, when I'm really strong—'" (135). Generations after emancipation, Helga finds herself enslaved. And although "there was not the element of race, of white and black [because] [t]hey were all black together" (135), Helga is no less miserable. By the end, "the Helga Crane who had dominated the narrative is symbolically dead" (Davis 271). This should come as no surprise, given the text's epigraph, which foreshadows a movement towards death.

Quicksand's downward spiral emerges within a narrative that is linear in time (events are told in chronological order as they occur) and circular in geography (Helga moves from the South to a northern city, and then to Europe; afterwards she moves back to a northern city and finally returns to the South). In her multifarious crossings, her desire to understand her world and find her place in it, and her unwillingness or inability to remain firmly within any discreet social category, Helga Crane resembles Godfrey St. Peter and Melanctha Herbert. Also like Cather and Stein, Larsen works within and against the *bildungsroman* tradition. Thus, although death lurks close to the surface from beginning to end, *Quicksand* can be considered a coming-of-age novel, and one which emphasizes psychological and relational aspects of attaining maturity. As Davis has noted, the novel "interrelat[es] psychological and social forces in Helga Crane's search for definition and development" (Davis 277).[23] Consistent with this genre, Helga's mother dies when Helga is fifteen, and the text follows Helga's progress to marriage (and implicit death). Larsen does not manage to write beyond the ending in *Quicksand*,[24] but she produces a distinctively twentieth century *bildungsroman* in other ways. For example, Davis also points out that Larsen read Freud and Otto Rank, and "was taken with . . . psychological interpretations of childhood and its impact on the adult" (310). For practical purposes, Helga loses her mother at a much earlier age than fifteen since she never felt like her mother claimed her. This situation is replicated again, when, as an adult, Helga must deal with the paradox of having a family that is not intimate or familiar, but foreign. Thus, when she receives a letter from Uncle Peter, Helga looks reflectively "at the peculiar foreign script of her uncle" (53). Literally, Helga might be noting that Peter's penmanship is that of an immigrant or that his handwriting is unfamiliar to her because of the infrequency of their correspondence. On another level, however, the juxtaposition of "foreign" and "uncle" highlights the fact that Helga is not a member of an organic family. She is foreign to her birth family and they are foreign to her.

At times Helga also feels foreign to her fellow African-Americans and to the Danes in her ancestral homeland. Speaking of her peers in Harlem, Helga confidently decides that "she didn't, in spite of her racial markings, belong to these dark segregated people. She was different. She felt it. It wasn't merely a matter of color. It was something broader, deeper, that made folk kin" (55). Helga proudly considers herself a rebel, an outsider. Still, she might not be as different as she imagines. As Stephen Greenblatt has observed of the tension between containment and transgression, "[people] imagine themselves set in diametrical opposition to their society where in fact they have unwittingly accepted its crucial structural elements" (qtd. in Dollimore 285). Fitting in and finding her place really do seem to be Helga's goals, in spite of her protestations of independence. In Denmark, Helga becomes the exotic other, as her aunt explains: "'you're a foreigner, and different'" (68). Thus, the people of Denmark are not her family either. Helga recognizes that "she wasn't one of them. She didn't at all count" (70). When Helga returns to Harlem from Copenhagen, she does an about-face from her previous thoughts about her relation to American blacks, insisting that she is bound to them by "ties that were of the spirit," ties which were "much deeper" (95) than mere skin color or physical features. This bonding does not help Helga in Alabama, however, as she recognizes that "she, a poor weak city-bred thing" (125), has little in common with her husband's parishioners. Wherever she goes, Helga comes to feel foreign, marginal, outside—her mother's home, Devon, Naxos, her Uncle's home, New York, Copenhagen, Alabama. She is the "foreigner within" (Lowe 5).

This lack of connectedness has ramifications for Helga's identity. As Davis observes, "family, both the individual members related by marriage and blood who make up a domestic community and the social group through which human beings first derive a shared identity, becomes one obsession shaping her life and limiting her possibilities for constructive action" (260–61). Since Helga receives imperfect socialization from her mother and never develops a sense of herself as part of a family or a larger group, she has a lifelong struggle to figure out who she is, where she fits in, and how she can relate to other people. Gleason speaks to this phenomenon when he explains that "identification is involved in the process by which persons come to realize what groups are significant for them, what attitudes concerning them they should form, and what kind of behavior is appropriate" (*Speaking* 129). Not only is Helga's personal identity compromised, but her national identity is called into question. Writing only two years before Larsen, Fairchild contends that "nationality is acquired" by "social transmission" (42), suggesting that Helga's lack of family socialization disrupts her American identity. Helga's solution of belonging to two countries is impractical: "this knowledge, this certainty of the division of her life into two parts in two lands, into physical freedom in Europe and spiritual freedom in America, was unfortunate, inconvenient, [and] expensive" (96). Nevertheless, Helga's quest itself is American at heart. Royce insists that the search for group identity is peculiarly American: "The Americans' unsystematic desire to identify with intermediary groups—larger than the family, smaller than the nation—may be based on real or imagined descent, on old or newly adopted religions, on geographic area of origin, socialization, or residence, on external categorization, on voluntary association, or on defiance" (qtd. in Sollors, *Beyond* 175–76).

Despite her yearning for a sense of belonging, Helga repeatedly denies essentialist conceptions of race and gender.[25] Clemmen agrees that the novel as a whole "feeds into a modern movement against essentialism" (466). To begin with, it is Dr. Anderson's assertion, "'You're a lady.' . . . 'Financial, economic circumstances can't destroy tendencies inherited from good stock'" (21), that steels Helga's resolve to leave Naxos. In Copenhagen, where race does not seem to matter, Helga is criticized for claiming a black identity which her appearance seems to deny. Thus "one day an old countrywoman asked her to what manner of mankind she belonged and at Helga's replying: 'I'm a Negro,' had become indignant, retorting angrily that, just because she was old and a countrywoman she could not be so easily fooled, for she knew as well as everyone else that Negroes were black and had woolly hair" (76). Helga, like Larsen, legally takes the status of her color, but for all intents and purposes her identification is with African-Americans. Thus she tells her aunt that her marrying Olsen would be a "mixed marriage" (78), though presumably her marrying a man with two black parents would not. Dearborn has observed that intermarriage serves as both metaphor and means of Americanization (100), though she notes that "miscegenation disrupted the *idea* of family" (139).

Helga is a mulatta, the result of miscegenation and a union without legal sanction. While the implications of Helga's mulatto status have been discussed at length,[26] I am particularly interested in the ways that Larsen's use of the mulatto figure creates a bridge between mixed-race characters and members of other marginalized or minority groups. For example, Berzon's observation that some mulatto characters "seek to create a third caste in what is essentially a two-caste system" (13) suggests a kinship between the mulatto and the "third-sex" lesbian. Indeed, McLendon's contention that the archetypal tragic mulatto "is depicted as the victim of persistent longing and unattainable desires aroused by his mixed blood" (153) uses language much like that found in Radcliffe Hall's *The Well of Loneliness*.[27] For example, during the "terrible, heart-breaking months" during which Stephen Gordon becomes "gaunt with her unappeased love for Angela Crossby" (*WL* 186), Stephen bemoans the mis-matched combination of her body and her desires: "all her life she must drag this body of hers like a monstrous fetter imposed on her spirit" (*WL* 187). Recalling her first trip experience with the Paris underworld, Stephen reflects that she "never forgot . . . those haunted, tormented eyes of the invert" (*WL* 387). Further similarities include the identification of black people with the curse of Ham and Hall's depiction of homosexuals as people who bear the mark of Cain (*WL* 301; see also 352).[28] In addition, although Helga concludes that having a home in each of two countries is impractical, Stephen is advised, "'one may have two homes—many homes'" (*WL* 246). Like Helga, Stephen comes to believe that one country is insufficient to satisfy her various needs for identification, rootedness, and freedom. Dearborn offers further support for emphasizing the parallels between Helga Crane and other women who, like Stephen Gordon, do not fit neatly into prescribed categories: "the problems Larsen's heroines suffer derive from their identities as women; race functions symbolically in her novels rather than realistically, so the mulatto condition is, for instance, a metaphor for a divided self—a condition Larsen feels all women share" (59).

While I find Dearborn's argument about the importance of gender in Larsen's texts convincing, the split represented in the "divided self . . . [which] all women share" is not Larsen's only primary emphasis. The mulatto condition also provides a physical embodiment of "mixedness" (Davis 243), a prominent motif in *Quicksand.* Along these lines, mixedness is suggested by the color gray, a mix of black and white. Robert Anderson's most salient feature is his "piercing gray eyes" (22), which have a mesmeric capacity, nearly causing Helga to lose her resolve to leave Naxos; "Gray Chicago" (27) is characterized by uncertainty, ambiguity and ambivalence. Helga, "who had been born in this dirty, mad, hurrying city had no home here" (27) and no family either. In New York, Anne *Grey* appears quite secure, but, as Helga observes, she accepts white values even while she espouses black separatism. Having borne too many children to her new husband, a "rattish yellow man" (118), Helga falls into a "blackness of pain" (128), then reemerges to a gray area. In this "borderland" (128), Helga "doze[s] and dream[s] in snatches of sleeping and waking" (135). When she is comatose or only semi-coherent, Helga is protected from her husband's attentions and the pregnancies such attentions invariably produce. Returning to the world, however, confirms Helga's death: "and hardly had she left her bed and become able to walk again without pain, hardly had the children returned from the homes of the neighbors, when she began to have her fifth child" (135). Although *Quicksand* explores mixedness throughout, its ending offers only a biological certainty.

In her first novel, Larsen explores how race, gender, and nationality interact in a liminal zone named Helga Crane. Strategically employing the journey motif, Larsen looks at the relationship between physical movement, psychological space, and personal identity. *Quicksand* offers a strong heroine, one reminiscent of both Godfrey St. Peter and Melanctha Herbert, but one whose individuality cannot withstand the downward pull of such social influences as assimilation, racism, and misogyny. Helga is continually born-again, but she is never permitted to engage in the life-sustaining strategy of "dwelling in possibility," as Skaggs says of Cather's Professor (63). Larsen's second novel will return to the questions of categorization and borders, only to reaffirm the significance of permeability and fluidity and the inadequacy of binary systems.

PASSING: A CONSCIOUSNESS OF KIND

Larsen achieved moderate success with her first novel, but she was still not in a position to take risks that might alienate her publisher or offend her readership. She thought of her second novel as "Nig," but it was not to be: "someone at Knopf had suggested the change of its title because 'Nig' might be too inflammatory for a novel by an unproven writer, while 'Passing,' and the phenomenon's connection to miscegenation, would incite interest without giving offense" (Davis 306–07). In fact, passing and miscegenation give great offense indeed. Helvie observes that "there is an innate value judgment in the term [passing] which seems to imply deception. Society is suspicious of anyone whom they cannot place neatly into a predetermined category" (39). This desire to be able to categorize is matched by an insistence that categories remain consistent over time. It is not acceptable for someone whom society has deemed black, for example, to decide to occupy the subject position of a white person. Indeed, Sollors points out the irony of this situation, noting that the moral disdain for passing "seems at particular odds with a social system that otherwise cherishes social mobility and espouses the right of individuals to make themselves anew by changing name, place, and fortune, and that has produced famous *parvenus* and confidence men" (*Neither* 249–50).[29] Although the 1906 Naturalization Act allowing name changes encouraged immigrants to assume a new identity (Wald 248), African-Americans were never encouraged to make themselves anew in this way. Names could be legitimately changed through marriage, but only through legitimate marriage. Whether or not an actual union was given legal sanction, the idea of race-mixing remained threatening on several levels. Americanization takes place through the family (Wald 246, 253), and miscegenation unhinges the ideological underpinnings of family (Dearborn 139). Thus *Passing,* while not as overtly controversial as "Nig," nevertheless moves into dangerous territory.

First, however, Larsen situates her novel as part of the Harlem Renaissance. *Passing*'s epigraph, taken from Countee Cullen's "Heritage,"[30] highlights the social and emotional distance between the forced immigrant and his twentieth-century descendent. McDowell contends that this excerpt "mislead[s] the reader" (xxiv) into "plac[ing] race at the center of any critical interpretation" (xxiii) by presenting the romantic part of the poem as opposed to its far less hopeful conclusion and thereby deflecting attention from the novel's powerful (homo)sexual subtext. While I think McDowell offers a strong and convincing reading of lesbian eroticism in *Passing* (xxiii-xxxi), the epigraph also stresses another important issue in the text, namely that "heritage" consists of more than just "race." In creating a speaker who feels alienated from his ethnic origins in spite of the persistence of his skin color, Cullen offers a multidimensional view of African-American identity. The relationship between race, ethnicity, and heritage has been largely overlooked, as Fuchs has observed: "neither whites nor blacks acknowledge the ethnic character of the African-American experience. Blacks and whites usually thought of blacks in terms of race only" whereas ethnicity implies ancestral traditions (177). Along similar lines, Petersen points out that in common parlance, "race" refers to non-whites, while "ethnicity" refers to European nationalities, noting a problematic "confusion . . . between physiological and cultural criteria" (6). Taking a universalist approach, Sollors argues that "ethnicity includes dominant groups . . . and race, while sometimes facilitating external identification, is merely one aspect of ethnicity" (*Beyond* 36). Thus Larsen seems ahead of her time—not romantic or sentimental, but quite modern—in her choice of epigraphs.

It is the nature of the relationship between race and ethnicity, between present practice and ancestral traditions, and between being and performing that Larsen interrogates in *Passing*. "What is Africa to me?" is the double-edged question both Clare Kendry, who is passing for white, and Irene Redfield, who is living a model life as a "race woman" in Harlem, must face. Washington contends that "'Passing' becomes, in Larsen's terms, a metaphor for the risk-taking experience" (163), but I would further suggest that it is a scientific strategy (and one in perfect keeping with Larsen's education and interests), a means of isolating the several components of identity, including heredity, environment, social milieu and spiritual or intellectual affiliation. Clare has black blood, lives a white life, and feels spiritually connected to black people; Irene has black blood, immerses herself in black society, and aspires to white values. Both women own themselves as black at times and pass for white at others. Who is the better example of an ethnic American?

Larsen delves into "this hazardous business of 'passing,' this breaking away from all that was familiar and friendly to take one's chances in another environment, not entirely strange, perhaps, but certainly not entirely friendly" (*P* 157). But we cannot really get to the nature of racial passing without taking a more careful look at the closely related concept of ethnicity. This term is by no means uncontested in its definition; there has been much discussion over the past hundred years as to what ethnicity is, how it is transmitted, and how it relates to identity. Describing ethnicity as "'a consciousness of kind'" (57), Bottomley distinguishes it from culture or tradition (50) and from nationalism (59). She further notes that "ethnicities are imposed, as well as assumed and inherited" (60). Salvaterra adds a historical perspective when he points out that before 1970 ethnicity was considered biologically determined and heritable (39), while the 1990s view holds that "membership is not automatic. . . . [I]t is expressive of our urge to differentiate among the great masses of other humans, to select some as 'like' us and some as 'others,' not 'like us.' Foregoing membership, therefore, must be a far different matter than merely a cultural swap" (44). Gleason further explains the difference between two camps of thinking about ethnicity: "primordialists regard ethnicity as a given, a basic element in one's personal identity that is simply there and cannot be changed, while optionalists hold that ethnicity is not an indelible stamp impressed on the psyche but a dimension of individual and group existence that can be consciously emphasized or de-emphasized as the situation requires" (*Speaking* 132). Novak also states that in the United States "individuals are free to make as much, or as little of their ethnic belonging as they choose" (40). This assertion is patently untrue for African-Americans, who have not been allowed to ignore the racial dimension of their ethnicity.

In Larsen's novel, passing is dual-edged and paradoxical. People pass for different things at different points in the text, and the idea of passing is both compelling and repulsive: "'It's funny about "passing." We disapprove of it and at the same time we condone it. It excites our contempt and yet we rather admire it. We shy away from it with an odd kind of revulsion, but we protect it'" (185–86). Passing is connected with success and danger (carrying off the masquerade brings status and wealth, but detection will unhinge a life), and with convenience and embarrassment (amenities are more available to the passer, but even "the idea of being ejected from any place" [150] is extremely distasteful). The first chapter of Larsen's text makes no mention of passing, however, as the novel begins with Irene Redfield receiving a letter from her childhood acquaintance, Clare Kendry. Irene seems middle-of-the-road American, while Clare (if her letter is any indication) is something to inspire nativist fears. In this opening section, we have no indicators of the subjects' racial identifications or ethnic origins. We know merely that Irene is minding her own business, sorting through her "little pile of morning mail[, consisting of] . . . ordinary and clearly directed letters," when "a thin sly thing" intrudes (143). The offending document has a New York postmark, but it is not from a New Yorker. Written on "Italian paper" which seems "out of place and alien" (143), the letter is "mysterious and slightly furtive" (143), both for its lack of return address and for "its almost illegible scrawl" (143). Furthermore it represents a difference that cannot be ignored: "foreign paper of extraordinary size" (143). And yet in spite of these markings of otherness, Irene immediately recognizes that "some two years ago she had one very like it in outward appearance" (143).[31]

Receiving the letter launches Irene into a vivid flashback from many more than two years ago, in which she sees "a pale small girl sitting on a ragged blue sofa, sewing pieces of bright red cloth together, while her drunken father, a tall, powerfully built man, raged threateningly up and down the shabby room, bellowing curses and making spasmodic lunges at her which were not the less frightening because they were, for the most part, ineffectual" (144). The image of this child mourning for her father shortly thereafter, "weeping, swaying her thin body, tearing at her bright hair, and stamping her small feet" (144), seems to bear no relation to the sender of the "flaunting" letter written in "purple ink" (143). And yet to Irene, the dangerous letter and the "theatrical heroics" (144) are both of a piece with what she knows of Clare Kendry.

Opening the letter sends Irene into yet another reverie, and the novel begins a second time with "what Irene Redfield remembered" (146) about "'that time in Chicago'" (145). It is at this point that we receive our first clear indication that Irene is black. Having escaped the stifling heat of Chicago's streets by having tea on the roof of an upscale hotel, Irene suddenly fears that a woman at the next table "somehow kn[e]w that here before her very eyes on the roof of the Drayton sat a Negro" (150). The stranger's stares give Irene a moment's panic, but she comforts herself by recalling that white people seem incapable of correctly guessing her ethnic heritage: "they always took her for an Italian, a Spaniard, a Mexican, or a gipsy. Never, when she was alone, had they even remotely seemed to suspect that she was a Negro" (150). In this early scene, Larsen provides a conceptualization of race which draws on both essentialist and constructionist paradigms. Irene is secure in her identity as a black person—"it wasn't that she was ashamed of being a Negro" (150)—but her status is still ambiguous because other people cannot correctly place her. Presumably black people would recognize Irene as one of their own under any circumstances, and white people would know that Irene was black if they saw her in context (i.e. amongst other black people). The thought that a white person could pick her out in this situation, however, is "absurd! impossible!" (150).[32] Unfortunately this knowledge does not help Irene to see the social construction of race, namely that race, like ethnicity, is context-bound and fluid (Salvaterra 39). Instead Irene subscribes to the essentializing view of race which deems her a Negro, and she tries to categorize others according to a similarly stringent system. Studying the stranger at the next table, Irene tries to deduce from her physical appearance "some clue to her identity" (151). After the other woman identifies herself as Clare Kendry, Irene discerns a telltale sign, Clare's "Negro eyes" (161). Instead of making Irene feel a kinship with Clare, however, this facial feature makes Clare "exotic" (161) to Irene.

Clare might seem foreign or exotic, but she is in fact uncannily familiar, a neighbor Irene has not seen in twelve years. In the course of speaking with Clare, Irene learns what has happened to her since she disappeared from

Irene's neighborhood following Bob Kendry's death in a bar fight. This history is narrated at length in the novel, and it introduces important motifs that recur in the text as a whole. Clare's is a quintessential rags-to-riches story and a fairy tale. The beautiful but penniless orphan is taken into the household of her father's white aunts (the sisters of Clare's white grandfather) basically as a domestic servant. Her only ties with her former life are furtive trips to her old neighborhood, taken in moments "stolen from the endless domestic tasks in her new home" (152).[33] In time, however, the servant girl becomes mistress: Clare marries up and far surpasses her aunts in wealth and status. She works hard for her aunts, and with a little luck and a lot of pluck, Clare finds success in the form of John Bellew, a wealthy and handsome white man. As soon as she turns eighteen, Clare runs off with Bellew, leaving her aunts to assume she is "living in sin" (160) and her peers to speculate that she has become a prostitute. Among Irene's cohort, Clare's perceived straying is accounted for by her family background. Well-meaning former acquaintances reflect: "'what can you expect. Look at her father. And her mother, they say, would have run away if she hadn't died'" (153).[34] In fact, the reality is both less risqué (Clare is married) and more dangerous (Clare's husband is terribly racist) than anyone in the old neighborhood had ever imagined.

Clare is not given the admiration accorded to either a Horatio Alger hero or a Cinderella heroine because her rise is tainted by the fact that she is passing for white. The act of passing (and the deception it implies) somehow detracts from the legitimacy of Clare's rather remarkable triumph. Larsen interrogates this double standard in attitudes towards social mobility and racial passing,[35] and she marks the irony, the potential threat, and the cultural discomfort with achieving success by closeting a defining part of oneself with the word "queer." Clare's aunts, for example, are strange old birds, "queer" (159), and queerness reappears throughout *Passing*. As Butler avers, "that Larsen links queerness with a potentially problematic eruption of sexuality seems clear" (*Bodies* 176). Clare describes her aunts with the adjective "queer" because of their hypocrisy regarding illicit sex: "for all their Bibles and praying and ranting about honesty, they didn't want anyone to know that their darling brother had seduced—ruined, they called it—a Negro girl. They could excuse the ruin, but they couldn't forgive the tar-brush" (159). Because of this situation, we might conclude that Clare has been passing for most of her life. As a child, she never fit in with her peers because of her father's mysterious situation: "Clare had never been exactly one of the group, just as she'd never been merely the janitor's daughter, but the daughter of Mr. Bob Kendry, who, it was true, was a janitor, but who also, it seemed, had been in college with some of their fathers. Just how or why he happened to be a janitor, and a very inefficient one at that, they none of them quite knew" (154). As a teenager in her aunts' home, Clare feels the need to hide her from neighbors as well. In this light, Clare's decision to cross the color line seems a logical continuation of earlier patterns rather than the radical break Irene considers it.

One indication that Clare has not broken entirely from her former life is her desire to find old acquaintances. Having returned to Chicago on one of her husband's business trips, Clare hopes to reconnect with her past and to bring the past and the present together. To this end, Clare invites Irene to join her and her husband for dinner. Irene pleads other engagements, and Clare corrals her into promising to come for tea the following Tuesday. Much against her better judgment, Irene actually goes. Upon arriving, Irene discovers another childhood acquaintance, Gertrude Martin. Gertrude was never a friend, and the fact that she too had married a white man (though not under false pretenses) causes Irene to acknowledge her with "an unsympathetic, almost harsh voice," as she thinks to herself, "great goodness! Two of them" (165). The social dynamics at the tea create fluctuating alliances, a tense undercurrent beneath an external calm, for the tea is perfectly arranged. Clare pours "the rich amber fluid from the tall glass pitcher into stately slim glasses, which she handed to her guests, and then offered them lemon or cream and tiny sandwiches or cakes" (168). All these forms and manners cannot gloss over the discomfort produced when these three women, who really have very little in common except for a childhood passed in the same neighborhood, are put in a social situation. The major wedges between them are class and racial identity. Clare is by far the wealthiest and most cultured of the group. Her husband has amassed a large fortune, and the two of them travel all over the world; she even speaks in "a voice remotely suggesting England" (151). Next in the socio-economic scale is Irene, a member of Harlem's black elite. Her husband is a successful physician and she has traveled to Europe, but she is rooted in the limited sphere of a specific section of New York City. Gertrude Martin has married a white man, but she does not seem to have gained much status in this way. She "looked as if her husband might be a butcher" (167), as indeed he is. Gertrude's husband has become primary owner of what was once his father's store and the store itself has relocated to another street, but Gertrude is clearly not on the same socio-economic level as Clare or Irene.

If Clare and Irene share a basically comparable class status, Clare and Gertrude have in common the fact that both married white men (though Fred Martin is aware of his wife's race and John Bellew is not). They also share a fear of giving birth to a dark-skinned baby. Just as Clare "nearly died of terror the whole nine months before Margery was born," Gertrude was "scared to death too" (168) before giving birth to her twin boys. Both agree that "nobody wants a dark child" (168). Here Irene steps in to emphasize her distance from this clique, calmly announcing, "'one of my boys is dark'" (168). Gertrude tries with embarrassed discomfort to ascertain whether this was a surprise, but Irene cuts her no slack: "her husband, she informed them quietly, couldn't exactly 'pass'" (168).

The tea-time conversation is intended to be light and polite, so Clare accordingly tries to shift the topic to the safer ground of old acquaintances. An interesting exchange takes place as the three women reminisce about a man named Claude Jones:

> Gertrude shrieked with laughter. "Claude Jones!" and launched into the story of how he was no longer a Negro or a Christian but had become a Jew.
>
> "A Jew!" Clare exclaimed.
>
> "Yes, a Jew. A black Jew, he calls himself. He won't eat ham and goes to the synagogue on Saturday. He's got a beard now as well as a moustache. You'd die laughing if you saw him. . . ."
>
> Clare's laugh tinkled out. "It certainly sounds funny enough. Still, it's his own business. If he gets along better by turning—"
>
> At that, Irene, who was still laughing her unhappy don't-care feeling of rightness, broke in, saying bitingly: "It evidently doesn't occur to either you or Gertrude that he might possibly be sincere in changing his religion. Surely everyone doesn't do everything for gain." (169)

This conversation is particularly telling. First of all, Larsen once again brings up Jewishness as a counterpoint to African-American experience.[36] Secondly, Gertrude clearly thinks that Negro identity and being a Jew are mutually exclusive. She does not speak of Claude's converting to Judaism, but rather makes the essentialist proposition that Claude has "become a Jew." This is seen mainly in Claude's behavior, namely his abstention from eating pork and his observing the Jewish Sabbath by attending services. Claude cannot change his skin (or the shape of his nose) but he grows a beard, additionally providing a physical symbol of his new state. Gertrude takes these changes as indicative of the fact that Claude has become a new person. Clare, on the other hand, sees Claude's conversion as a matter of "turning" Jew, suggesting transformation and a certain fickleness. Perhaps Claude had a Jewish side lying dormant in his psyche, waiting for the proper conditions to trigger its release. Or perhaps he has metamorphosed into a Jew this time, and next time he will "turn" something else. Only Irene sees Judaism as a religion alone—a matter of personal beliefs—and rebukes the others for not considering the possibility that Claude is motivated by something other than personal gain or constitutional weirdness. None of the women offers a perspective that is completely accurate. Judaism encompasses both ethnic and religious aspects (Gleason, *Speaking* 242), but being black and being Jewish are not at all mutually exclusive. Etienne Balibar speaks to this gap in conceptualization that the three women evidence when she notes that "*the distinction between 'minorities' and 'majorities' becomes blurred* in a number of ways. First of all it is blurred because a growing number of individuals and groups are not easily inscribed in one single ethnic (or cultural, linguistic, even religious) identity" (53). Irene, Clare, and Gertrude cannot agree upon a single way to conceptualize Claude's identity, and the conversation falters under Irene's self-righteous declarations.

When "race or other thorny subjects" (170), such as religion, produce too much tension, Clare once again tries (unsuccessfully) to steer the conversation in safer directions. At this point, any pretense of politeness is shattered as Clare's husband comes home and greets her with an off-hand "Hello, Nig" (170). John Bellew is a fairly non-descript man, "a tallish person, broadly made. . . . His hair was dark brown and waving. . . . His steel-grey opaque eyes . . . mov[ed] ceaselessly between thick bluish lids" (170). He is not unattractive, but he is not completely manly either, as "he had a soft mouth, somewhat womanish, set in an unhealthy-looking dough-coloured face" (170). When Clare introduces her husband to her guests, her eyes reveal "a queer gleam" which Irene cannot interpret (171). The queerness spreads as Bellew launches his attack on "the black scrimy devils," prompting Gertrude to emit "a queer little suppressed sound, a snort or a giggle" (172). Bellew is not wholly masculine and the three women are not white—queerness marks the blurred borderlines. Irene suppresses her rage because of "some dam of caution and allegiance to Clare" (173) and meets Bellew in his attempt "to be agreeable" (173). Irene even admits that Bellew is relatively likable, "a fairly good-looking man of amiable disposition. . . . Plain and with no nonsense about him" (173). Shortly thereafter, Irene and Gertrude manage to extricate themselves. Leaving the Bellews's hotel, Irene and Gertrude become the third possible combination of alliances as the two discuss their anger at Clare for putting them in such a situation and speculate about the details of Clare's dangerous life. Ultimately, however, Irene wishes to stand alone. She begs off traveling back to her father's house with Gertrude and reflects on the afternoon herself. The next day she heads back to New York. Destroying the letter that Clare sent her by means of explanation, Irene "turn[s] her thoughts to her own affairs. To home, to the boys, to Brian" (178).

On the surface, Brian Redfield seems completely unlike John Bellew, and yet he too is connected with queerness, namely an "old, queer, unhappy restlessness" (78) which overtakes him from time to time.[37] Moreover, he too has features that hint at effeminacy. Irene spends much time and mental energy trying to suppress Brian's wanderlust, and she also engages in semantic acrobatics to convince herself of Brian's rugged masculinity. He is "extremely good-looking," but, as Irene is quick to insist, not "pretty or effeminate" (183). Nevertheless, even Irene will acknowledge that Brian's attitude towards his female patients is both atypical and unnerving: "'Brian doesn't care for ladies, especially sick ones. I sometimes wish he did. It's South America that attracts him'" (173). Proud as she is of Brian's "pleasant[ly] masculine" (184) traits, Irene tries to shelter her boys, prompting Brian to accuse her of "trying to make a molly-coddle" of them (189). When Junior learns about sex from schoolmates, Irene tells Brian that he has "picked up some queer ideas about things" (189). Queerness (and the boundary blurring it implies) has no place in Irene's respectable and regimented household.

In general Irene seems happy with her husband, though he is not always up to her standards of proper bourgeois manners. Irene experiences a daily irritation as Brian eats his morning toast "with that audible crunching sound that Irene disliked so intensely" (185),[38] but she does not comment. Like Grandmother Burden and Lillian St. Peter, Irene ignores what she does not want to know or act upon (Marren 118). While Brian wants his sons to become aware of reality at the earliest possible opportunity, "Irene wants to deny racism as a shaping presence and instead envision a neutral, benign landscape" (Marren 133). Thus Brian considers lynching a suitable topic for dinnertime conversation, while Irene wants her sons's "childhood to be happy and as free from the knowledge of such things as it possibly can be" (231).

Brian and Irene take different approaches to more abstract matters, as well. In response to Irene's musings about why Clare stays married to a bigot, Brian merely comments, "'If I knew that, I'd know what race is'" (185). Irene seeks rational explanations, but Brian realizes that some things are beyond logic.[39] Shortly thereafter, it is Brian who proposes totalizing explanations, while Irene sees more complex interactions at work. To Irene's pondering of the paradox of passing, Brian responds, "'Instinct of the race to survive and expand.'" "'Everything can't be explained by some general biological phrase,'" Irene protests, but Brian gets the last word: "'Absolutely everything can. Look at the so-called whites, who've left bastards all over the known earth. Same thing in them. Instinct of the race to survive and expand'" (186). From a strictly biological perspective, Brian is right about the survival and expansion of a human gene pool. Taking race and culture into consideration, however, it becomes clear that no recognizable "race" survives or expands from the hybridization produced by miscegenation (through passing or through bastardization). The logical conclusion to be drawn from Brian's argument is actually the impossibility of purity—ethnic, racial, or cultural. As Bottomley has pointed out, "obviously, with so many people constantly on the move throughout world history, there can be no such thing as a 'pure' culture, let alone a pure 'race'" (42–43). Irene does not answer Brian, but she clearly does not accept his explanations.

Whether or not she can say for sure what race is, Irene feels compelled to protect Clare because of an "instinctive" (227) race loyalty. Irene recognizes that "she had to Clare Kendry a duty" based upon "those very ties of race, which, for all her repudiation of them, Clare had been unable to completely sever," simultaneously acknowledging that "Clare Kendry cared nothing for the race. She only belonged to it" (182). Irene sees "racial identity" (209) as fixed, not performed or chosen. In this way she would seem to agree with Larsen's contemporary, Commons, who asserts, "race differences are established in the very blood and physical constitution" (7). Clare is black, and therefore Irene must protect and help her. It does seem odd, however, to lump white-identified Irene together with passing-for-white Clare within the category of "black." Still, if we take a biological perspective again, we might note that this taxonomy is appropriate, at least to the degree that black people in America are the product of an intermixing of any number of African national and ethnic groups, as Urgo elaborates: "not even the late twentieth-century term *African-American* can assign the ethnic roots of black Americans to a specific location. African American, understood as an ethnicity, must trace its origins to the middle passage itself" (96). Clare and Irene share this common origin, such as it is. Hence, they are somehow aligned.

Just how and why black people are related to one another in the text is not clear, however. Irene and Clare misinterpret each other's actions and attitudes in part because each holds a different opinion about the nature of group- and self-identification. Irene feels connected to Clare because of a shared race, and yet Clare does not seem to honor (or even acknowledge) the alliance. In Irene's opinion, Clare has "no allegiance beyond her own immediate desire" (144). Irene sees this tendency as a fault in Clare, but perhaps what Larsen means to interrogate is the nature of the bonds that exist solely on the basis of race. While Irene seems to think that race is the basis of group identification, she might be proposing a false source of unity or solidarity. To speak of "the race" (225) as Irene does might be to make the same mistake as sociologists who speak of an "ethnic group," falsely implying a cohesion and a group awareness not necessarily present (Petersen 2).

Irene certainly considers race as delineating a group, but, as Young has pointed out, "race or nationality can also be fruitfully conceptualized as a seriality" (206).[40] In a seriality, people interact with their environment as independent agents; the fact that some people come into contact with similar environmental elements does not make for group identification (Young 199). When the world positions Clare as white (or Irene as white, for that matter), she does not belong to the seriality of black women. When Clare chooses to come to Harlem to immerse herself in a black world, however, she "move[s] and act[s] in relation to practico-inert objects that position" her as a black woman (Young 205).[41] Young takes note of this phenomenon when she points out that "which, if any, of a person's serial memberships become salient or meaningful at any time is a variable matter" (207). A group, on the other hand, suggests "a collection of persons who recognize themselves and one another as in a unified relation with one another" (198). Furthermore, a group "forms around actively shared objectives" (199). When Clare tries to get involved with the Harlem social life, she seeks to become part of a group. Her race alone, however, neither presupposes a group nor provides automatic membership.

In addition to challenging Irene's definitions of race and race feeling, Clare disrupts Irene's sense of social propriety. The mobility she achieves through passing for white enables and encourages her to pass across age and class boundaries as well. She does not always act like an adult, "happily amus[ing] herself with Ted and Junior" (208) when she visits the Redfield household. If the boys are not upstairs in their playroom, Clare shows a perfect willingness to "descend to the kitchen and . . . spend her visit in talk and merriment with Zulena and Sadie" (208). Clare descends the social ladder by socializing with lowly servants, a behavior that Irene finds inappropriate and even threatening. Irene would not stoop to such indiscretions, and Clare is— by virtue of her husband's wealth and position and her assumed race—of an even more elite socio-economic group.

Irene's attitudes towards respectability and security are consistent with what we know of her as a younger woman. She still "care[s] about such things" (157) as acting in perfect taste and avoiding being conspicuous, as Clare is quick to surmise. Gertrude also immediately assesses that Irene is "'just the same. . . . Not changed a bit'" (165). In New York, Irene insists that Clare should not seek her out because such behavior is "'terribly foolish, and not just the right thing,'" prompting Clare to respond, "'you haven't changed a bit. The right thing!'" (195). This impasse Clare and Irene reach over the relative importance of excitement and propriety duplicates the rocky relationship between Stein's Melanctha Herbert and Jefferson Campbell.[42]

Indeed, Larsen shows her debt to and admiration for Stein in her second novel as well as her first by deploying thematic elements and developing characters reminiscent of those in "Melanctha." Here, however, Larsen makes a fuller attempt to move beyond Stein's answers. Most noticeably, Larsen avoids negative racial stereotypes, offering instead a thorough deconstruction of the notion of race itself. Some similarities between Stein's doppelganger and Larsen's include the fact that Melanctha and Clare both had abusive fathers, while Irene and Jeff had happy childhoods. Indeed Irene would probably agree with Jeff that "you ought to love your father and your mother and to be regular in all your life, and not to be always wanting new things and excitements, and to always know where you were, and what you wanted, and to always tell everything just as you meant it" (*TL* 67). Melanctha does want excitements, of course, as does Clare, while for Irene "safety [and] security . . . were all-important" (195). Irene correctly suspects that Clare "was yet capable of heights and depths of feeling that she, Irene Redfield, had never known. Indeed, never cared to know" (195). The dynamics in the relationship between Clare and Irene are also similar to those that Stein creates between Melanctha and Jeff. When they are first reunited in Chicago, Irene talks (like Jeff) and Clare listens (like Melanctha). Thinking about it in retrospect, Irene realizes that "she hadn't asked Clare anything about her own life," allowing her to sit "motionless" (155), drinking it all in. Commenting on Larsen's literary debt to Stein, Davis suggests that "Clare . . . owes her passive nature in part to . . . Melanctha," further proposing that interactions between Melanctha and Jeff provide one prototype "for the bipolar relationship between Clare and Irene Redfield" (311). Because of the tension that marks their association, Jeff and Melanctha part ways and reunite several times in the course of the story, particularly in correlation to Jeff's moods and attitudes towards Melanctha's wandering. Similarly, Irene both "encounter[s]" Clare in Chicago and "re-encounter[s]" her in New York, and her feelings for Clare repeatedly vacillate between intense dislike (and the wish to break off all contact with Clare) and intense warmth. Indeed, the warmth of this relationship is another example of how Larsen moves beyond Stein. Whereas Stein uses Jeff in part as a way to talk about one woman's attraction to another woman (as Cather uses Jim Burden), Larsen explores the ramifications of the female-to-female gaze head-on.[43] Davis further observes that "the themes and central characters of *Passing* suggest that Larsen interpreted the 'complex and desiring' Melanctha Herbert, Stein's protagonist who 'wanders' in search of 'wisdom,' as an embodiment of the acute invisibility and vulnerability of those who belong to many worlds and whose inability to discover a 'right position' results from the failure of others to perceive and, therefore, to 'read' them competently" (34). Like Melanctha, Clare is neither a pure victim nor a wholly responsible person. Both women die at the end of the text, but they are neither passive martyrs nor active agents of their own destinies. Furthermore, in both *Passing* and "Melanctha" passing is structurally underscored by narrative strategies. Cutter suggests that "Clare's problematic passing presents the ultimate mechanism for creating 'a perpetual present'" (76). Although Cutter takes this term from Roland Barthes, we might observe that it is much like the continuous present that Stein spent much of her career trying to formulate and to make a reality in her texts. Hence in her second novel, Larsen both acknowledges her legacy from Stein and, in some ways, exceeds that legacy.

Clare's reserve provides another link to the "mysterious" Melanctha (*TL* 50, 61), as "she still remained someone apart, a little mysterious and strange" (209). It also aligns her with Larsen who was, "as an old friend tactfully put it, 'a good pretender'" (Davis 10). Clare passes for white, and her general mannerisms are conceptualized as "acting, not consciously, perhaps—that is, not too consciously—but, none the less, acting" (182). Socializing in Harlem circles, Clare has no "object[ion] to appearing a bit pathetic and ill-used, so that people could feel sorry for her" (209). By the last section of the novel, Brian too is passing—for attentive husband, for involved father, for happy and successful Harlem physician, and possibly for straight.[44] Like Godfrey St. Peter, "Brian . . . had withdrawn. The house contained his outward self and his belongings" (224). It also becomes clear that Irene is passing for model racewoman and mother. She claims altruism and high-mindedness but eventually admits that security is her real god (235).

Thinking strictly of racial passing, Clare wonders "why more coloured girls . . . never 'passed' over" (158). "Passed over" connotes a permanent transition, such as passing over the bridge to heaven (or hell) when one dies.[45] The passer's condition would thus be a permanent and irreversible one. As Clare's own life demonstrates, however, passing is not always permanent, as in "just passing through." It can mean adopting a whole new way of life and breaking radically from the past, or it can mean trying on different subject positions and changing them when the time seems right. Irene's crossing the color line and then crossing over again provides yet another example of temporary passing, that is, passing for convenience.[46] Reflecting on the concept of passing in general, Ginsberg offers, "passing is about identities . . . [and] passing is also about the boundaries established between identity categories and about the individual and cultural anxieties induced by boundary crossing" (2). As if to structurally underscore the motif of boundary crossing, Larsen's text continually crosses back over itself, particularly through the use of flashback.

Irene's meeting Clare in Chicago, the central narrative strand of "Encounter," is told as a flashback. A key scene in "Reencounter," which deals with Clare's time in New York, also utilizes a backward-looking mode: the Negro Welfare League dance is relayed as an incomplete retrospective account. The chapter begins: "the things which Irene Redfield remembered afterward about the Negro Welfare League Dance seemed, to her, unimportant and unrelated" (203). Each of the following three paragraphs opens with, "She remembered . . ." (203–04). Occupying the outsider/observer position together, Irene and white author Hugh Wentworth apply an analytical eye to the microcosm of humanity before them. [47] As Wentworth relates, "'Everybody seems to be here and a few more. But what I'm trying to find out is the name, status, and race of the blonde beauty out of the fairy-tale'" (204–05). Faced with the multitudes, Wentworth seeks to classify, to pigeonhole according to traditional categories. Clare's dance partner, the unusually dark-skinned Ralph Hazelton, serves as a counterpoint to Clare's blondness, producing a "study in contrasts" (205). The exotic apparently resides on either end of the color spectrum; whereas Irene had previously deemed Clare's whiteness exotic, she here surmises that Ralph's attractiveness to women lies in his dark exoticism. Dancing with men like Ralph produces "'a kind of emotional excitement[,] . . . the sort of thing you feel in the presence of something strange, and even, perhaps, a bit repugnant to you; something so different that it's really at the opposite end of the pole from all your accustomed notions of beauty'" (205). Irene's explanation recalls Ginsberg's comment about the anxiety produced when individuals threaten to traverse boundaries between well-established categories of identity (2). Dancing with Ralph is exciting precisely because of the proximity (and potential blending) of dark and light. The danger of the situation only adds to its appeal. Following up on Hugh's comment about Ralph's dancing partner, Irene challenges Hugh to guess Clare's race, insisting, "'you usually know everything. Even how to tell the sheep from the goats. What do you think? Is she?'" (206). Hugh admits himself defeated, as he responds, "'damned if I know! I'll be as sure as anything that I've learned the trick. And then in the next minute I'll find I couldn't pick some of 'em if my life depended on it'" (206).

This conversation is revealing both for its content and for the concepts embedded in the speakers' words. Both Irene and Hugh utilize an essentializing and totalizing definition of race. Race, African-American status in this case, is something one either is or is not. We might further observe that "name, status, and race" is an odd conjunction of attributes. Names are given at birth, but can easily be changed, both legally and informally, through marriage or through choice.[48] In addition, names can be both descriptive and prescriptive, though what one is called is only indirectly related to what one is. In some cases the connection is ironically and tragically closer than one might suspect—Bellew's calling Clare "Nig" is a case in point. Status is equally complex and has any number of connotations and denotations: free or slave, married or single, friendly flirt or professional courtesan, and socio-economic class. In a society that champions upward mobility and the self-made man, status should be changeable. And yet for African-Americans who try to pass, this glorification of mobility disappears (Sollors, *Neither* 249–50). Finally, race is fixed and knowable according to the paradigm accepted by Irene and Hugh, but not by everyone. Irene can read people, but the transmission is one-way. Blacks can always recognize each other, but whites can only sometimes recognize blacks. The reason, as Irene smugly informs Hugh, is that whites do not pass for black and this makes all the difference (206).[49] Irene and Hugh both seek to place people within discrete categories based on social and biological features. Ultimately, however, "race and history and metaphysics do not enforce an identity" (Appiah 108).

Identity is particularly fluid among certain types of people, and Clare fits into two such types. She is a cosmopolitan and a "metropolitan man."[50] Clare is a world traveler and a cultured person, a creative and flexible thinker. She is also a city-dweller who can keep calm in dangerous or trying situations, "react[ing] with [her] head instead of [her] heart" (Simmel 48), who appreciates money, and who views her own life with a certain detachment and objectivity. She remains somewhat aloof and mysterious, even when among friends. Furthermore, it is the city itself which facilitates the fluidity of Clare's identity. Indeed passing largely is a metropolitan phenomenon both because of the anonymity offered by cities and because of the opportunities cities present to occupy several non-overlapping worlds simultaneously. As Park notes, cities "encourage the fascinating but dangerous experiment of living at the same time in several different contiguous, but otherwise widely separated, worlds" (126). Taking a historical perspective, Sollors similarly observes that "[racial passing] thrived in modern social systems in which, as a primary condition, social and geographic mobility prevailed, especially in environments such as cities or crowds that provided anonymity to individuals, permitting them to resort to imaginative role-playing in their self-representation" (*Neither* 247–8).

Cities facilitate Clare's successful passing; furthermore, Clare's ability to carry off the masquerade places her in a quintessential American subject position. Berlant explains that using "ambition or plastic surgery or assimilation . . . or . . . interracial marriage to a more racially and class-privileged person" can increase a person's chances of becoming "a member of the core national culture" (*Queen* 217). Clare has certainly undergone a transformation in her rebirth as Mrs. John Bellew, and the perks of such a socio-economic position lead Clare to claim "'that it's even worth the price'" (160). Furthermore, Clare's transience and lack of roots position her as distinctively American since the "experience of change, mobility, and loss of contact with the past" (Gleason, *Speaking* 169) largely creates and defines American identity.

Like any good American, Clare resents anything that holds her back from the pursuit of happiness. In an ironic foreshadowing, Clare descries the fact that she cannot participate in Harlem events while her husband is in town: "'Damn Jack! He keeps me out of everything. Everything I want. I could kill him! I expect I shall, some day'" (200). Irene dryly cautions Clare to "be reasonable," pointing out that "there's still capital punishment . . . [and] everything must be paid for" (200). While Clare's sense of being an American centers around freedom, Irene's strong identification as an American comes more from rootedness. Although she contemplates "some European school for Junior next year" (190), she determinedly vows that "she would not go to Brazil. . . . She was an American. She grew from this soil, and she would not be uprooted" (235). Irene's protestations of American pride are rather suspect, as Berlant points out by questioning: "what kind of body does American national identity give her, and how does the idea of this body solve or salve the pain that the colonized body experiences?" ("National" 112). Marren explains Irene's American pride by noting "that romanticization preserves in Irene a sense of organic identity with the nation" (141). In any case, it is clear that Clare and Irene have different senses of what it means to be an American. Whereas Clare embodies the American ideals of social and physical mobility, individualism, and self-creation (along with living out a rags-to-riches story), Irene displays loyalty to American ideology (see Munsterberg 5; Gleason, "American" 62) and espouses a willingness to uphold the laws, customs, and aims of her (white) country.

The two women also offer competing versions of what it means to be a mother. They do agree, however, "'that being a mother is the cruelest thing in the world'" (197). Larsen read Kate Chopin (McManus 191), and Clare shares Edna's priorities: "'Children aren't everything. . . . There are other things in the world, though I admit some people don't seem to suspect it'" (210).[51] Irene, on the other hand, admits, "'I know very well that I take being a mother rather seriously. I *am* wrapped up in my boys and the running of my house. I can't help it'" (210). Irene's self-image is wholly bound up in her role as mother, wife and homemaker, and yet she too has priorities beyond her family. Towards the end of the novel, Irene realizes "that, to her, security was the most important and desired thing in life. Not for any of the others, or for all of them, would she exchange it" (235). By the same token, Clare does not wholly disregard the well-being of her family. Consideration for her daughter's welfare slows Clare's urge to leave her husband and move to Harlem, though it does not squelch it entirely. As Clare explains, "'Margery? . . . If it wasn't for her, I'd do it anyway. She's all that holds me back. But if Jack finds out, if our marriage is broken, that lets me out. Doesn't it?" (234). Like Helga Crane in Alabama, Clare wants to escape from the confines of being a mother and a wife. Also like Helga (and like Harriet Jacobs's Linda Brent), Clare speculates about how to achieve her freedom while causing the least amount of damage to the people who depend on her.

The more Clare thinks about leaving her own family, the more she seems to take up residence with Irene's. Irene becomes increasingly uncomfortable with Clare's continued presence in her household and her social milieu. Not unlike her creator, Irene feels threatened by other women's achievements or capabilities. As Brian becomes more friendly towards Clare, Irene feels the need to belittle her. Aligning herself with Hugh Wentworth, Irene contends that Clare does not have the intellect to keep up in cultured company: "'She isn't stupid. She's intelligent enough in a purely feminine way. Eighteenth-century France would have been a marvelous setting for her, or the old South if she hadn't made the mistake of being born a Negro. . . . Clare has got brains of a sort, the kind that are useful too. Acquisitive, you know. But she'd bore a man like Hugh to suicide'" (216). In her quest for control and security, Irene moves from hoping that Bellew will learn that Clare "was spending all the time that he was out of the city in Black Harlem" to awaiting the moment when Bellew would discover "that his wife was a Negro" (225). Irene does not want Bellew to divorce Clare. She needs Clare thoroughly out of the way, and so she shamefully contemplates "if Clare should die" (228). The last thing Irene wants is for Clare to be free—"if Clare was freed, anything might happen" (236). Significantly, she uses the language of slave ownership and emancipation, "if Clare was freed" (236)—not "were free" but "was freed."[52]

If Clare was freed by Bellew and therefore were free to spend all her time in Harlem (and perhaps to run off with Brian Redfield), all of the boundaries and rules which Irene has spent her life arranging and enforcing would blur. Hence it is no surprise that the key scenes towards the end of the book are suffused with references to queerness. In her anger towards Brian for inviting Clare to her party for Hugh and towards Clare accepting the invitation, Irene's voice "go[es] queer" (216). Irene begins to suspect sexual foul-play, in the form of Clare and Brian having an affair. Looking at her husband during the party but unable to discern anything from his "half-effaced seeking look,"

Irene finds it "queer, that now she didn't know, couldn't recall" (220) if this was his normal expression. Soon thereafter, when Bellew sees Irene with Felise Freeland and realizes that she must be black, Felise teasingly rebukes Irene, "'Been "passing," have you? Well, I've queered that'" (227). Following Clare's death, "the golden brown of [Felise's] handsome face change[s] to a queer mauve color" (241). "Queer" here signifies blurred boundaries, liminality, transitivity, and internal contradictions. Hence for someone like Irene, a queer situation or exchange produces intense anxiety. Queerness warns of an impending change, the possible blurring, blending, or dissolution of the fixed categories upon which Irene has built her world.

Irene's carefully managed universe does indeed fall apart by the end of the novel, and Irene is intimately involved in the process, as both witness and agent. During the climactic scene in which Bellew discovers Clare at the Freelands's party, everything seems to happen in slow motion. Bellew arrives in a fury, but Clare remains calm, with "a faint smile on her full, red lips, and in her shining eyes" (239). Clare's lack of awareness of, or lack of concern about, her imminent danger pushes Irene over the edge: "It was that smile that maddened Irene. She ran across the room, her terror tinged with ferocity, and laid a hand on Clare's bare arm. One thought possessed her. She couldn't have Clare Kendry cast aside by Bellew. She couldn't have her free" (239). Irene's feelings and motivations are clearly mixed. On the one hand, her actions could be interpreted as race loyalty and an almost maternal urge to protect. Perhaps she meant to place her own body in front of Clare's to take Bellew's wrath herself. But because Bellew's freeing Clare would leave her at liberty to wreck Irene's marriage and her secure life, Irene's actions seem to spring entirely from selfishness. Having been psychologically and metaphorically pushed over the edge, Irene does the same for Clare in reality: Irene cannot allow Bellew to figuratively cast Clare aside, and so Irene literally pushes Clare out the window.

In either case, it is clear that the dynamic which takes place involves more than just Bellew's discovery of his wife's Negro status. Dollimore speaks to the complicated relationship between masquerade, discovery, and identity when he notes that "to be unmasked *is* to be unspirited as well as undone. To lose one's cover is to lose one's soul, to be undone in the sense of socially ruined and spiritually taken apart" (292). While Butler contends that when Bellew detects Clare, we see "her color 'outed'" (*Bodies* 170), it also seems feasible to argue that Irene is outed as well, her true self unmasked and unspirited by an incident which she is incapable of remembering. In the dream-like sequence which follows, Irene steps outside of herself: "in the room there were voices. . . . In the hall below she heard dimly the sound of feet going down the steps, of a door being opened and closed, and of voices far away" (240). Her subsequent loss of consciousness is also a coping mechanism, a retreat from the world of passing, of transitivity and of ambiguity. "Then everything was dark" suggests a return to a black world, one uncomplicated by racial difference or racial fluidity. It also recalls the "immense darkness" of Conrad's *Heart of Darkness,* a central allusion in *Quicksand.* In this way, Larsen's second novel ends up in a similar place as her first—with characters who arrive at the brink of realization and meaningful action but never achieve consummation.

The endings of both of Larsen's novels are considered problematic, but as Kaplan asserts, we need not attribute their perceived flaws solely a lack of skillful writing: "realistic novels have trouble ending because they pose problems they cannot solve, problems that stem from their attempt to imagine and contain social change. . . . The final disjuncture at the ends of novels raises questions about our own expectations of realism: how does a certain order of experience come to be identified as real and another as unreal?" (160). For Nathan Huggins, Larsen's crucial mistake was to conflate and confuse literary approaches, as he explains: "this sharp dichotomy of realist and romantic, etched in both her novels, that makes them seem schizophrenic" (161). DuCille, however, points out that realism and romance are not as incompatible as Huggins supposes because both are literary and fictive constructions (200). Given Larsen's clear engagement with Chopin's *The Awakening,* it is significant that critics found both women's work dissatisfying for similar reasons. George Spangler sees the root of Chopin's failure as "inconsistent characterization, which asks the reader to accept a different and diminished Edna from the one developed so impressively before" (187). Similarly, in her review of *Quicksand,* Eda Lou Walton pronounces to Larsen's discredit "that the young Helga at the beginning of the book 'cannot be the older woman of the latter half'" (Davis 280). Further, Spangler says of Chopin, "one can easily and happily join in the praise that . . . has be given to *The Awakening*—one can, that is, until one reaches the conclusion of the novel, which is unsatisfactory because it is fundamentally evasive" (186). Huggins reaches a similar conclusion about *Passing,* as he declares, "Nella Larsen constructs a perfunctory and entirely unsatisfactory denouement" (160).

The negative assessments of Chopin's and Larsen's endings offered in the 1970s by Spangler and Huggins are by no means representative of current critical opinion. Nevertheless, the difficulties posed by these endings are acknowledged, even as more recent (and, in most cases, more feminist) critics offer alternative readings. Wendy Martin concludes her review of critical responses to Edna's suicide with a statement that acknowledges both the dissent and a certain level of accord: "Clearly, contemporary evaluations of the novel vary markedly in their assessment of the effectiveness of its conclusion, but most critics today agree that *The Awakening* is an important part of the American literary canon" (14). Before attempting to contextualize Larsen's work through "the prism of black female sexuality" (xii), McDowell affirms that "[c]ritics of Larsen have been rightly perplexed by these abrupt and contradictory endings" (xii). More recent Larsen critics have used less negatively charged terms to describe the elusive quality of the endings of her novels. Yohe states that *Quicksand* "ends indecisively" (55), while Clemmen calls the novel enigmatic, "complex enough to conceal its logic" (458). Along similar lines, Cutter describes *Passing*'s conclusion as open-ended and "uncontainable" (97). This critical emphasis on ambiguity recalls yet another reading of *The Awakening*, namely Suzanne Wolkenfeld's pronouncement that "Edna's suicide is not a conscious choice reached through her achievement of self-awareness" (222). This ambiguity is replicated in the uncertainty surrounding "whether Helga Crane is trying to destroy herself" (Berzon 225) and in the murder/ suicide/ accident which brings about Clare Kendry's death.

Clare is only about thirty-one years old when she dies, and Helga immures herself at a young age, as well. Larsen's literary life was also cut off prematurely. Just as we can only speculate what interesting turns Helga's life might have taken had she returned to Harlem or how Irene's and Clare's lives would have changed had Clare lived, "one naturally wonders if Nella Larsen would have taken still more risks had her short, but accomplished, literary career been extended" (McDowell xxxi). While accusations of plagiarism, or passing for authorship (Butler, *Bodies* 185), played the most obvious role in bringing Larsen's career to an abrupt end, Davis offers an equally probable explanation for Larsen's disappearance from the literary scene. To Davis, Larsen falls by the wayside because she slips through a breach between multiple subject positions: "in the psychic split between her individual and group identity (whether that group is defined by gender or race) and in the personality breakdown between her public and private roles, the fiction and the writer herself were lost" (18)

But what does it mean to say that a writer and her fiction are "lost," particularly when the fiction has been in print for years and has been the subject of any number of critical essays and dissertations? Larsen did lose her writing career, her sense of herself as a novelist, and her ability to communicate with an audience via publication (Davis 17). All the same, as Davis acknowledges, Larsen's "novels continue to have a life" (465). So, for that matter, did Larsen. After she stopped writing, Larsen lived a perfectly respectable, if comparatively sequestered life, working as a night nurse and spending the rest of her time in her small apartment. She did not choose suicide, she did not pass for white (Wall 137), and she did not literally disappear (though the term is often used to describe her withdrawal from former friends and acquaintances). Furthermore, Larsen was not unique in her struggles. In their attempts to write with integrity and to live their lives as artists, Cather and Stein also had to negotiate the tension between public and private selves. Cather coped by becoming increasingly reclusive as she got older, though she continued to write up until the end of her life.[53] Stein became even more of a celebrity and a public success as she got older, though none of her later texts equaled *The Autobiography of Alice B. Toklas* in popularity. Although both women are now included in "The Library of America" series and continue to be the subject of conferences, articles, and books, their relative success is open to debate. Shaw, for one, believes that Cather was rewarded for staying in America and facing the tensions that confronted her there head-on (as opposed to taking what he considers the easy way out, expatriation). These tensions made for good literature, and now, Shaw asserts, Cather's work is more read and more highly respected than Stein's ("Victorian" 26). Whether or not one accepts Shaw's valuation, it is clear that both Cather and Stein were concerned with the shape their literary legacy would take. Both actively took part in the publication process throughout their lives and made formal arrangements for the future of their texts. Larsen, on the other hand, quietly accepted the fact that "her old contacts with the publishing world were gone . . . [and] she did not know how to establish new ones" (Davis 463). She responded to adversity with silence and virtual hibernation, "perchance at some point to resume her writing or perhaps writing all the while" (Davis 463), but not sharing her work with anyone. Larsen might not have been able to get past the "Sanctuary" fall-out because the situation threatened her very identity. If, as Wall has suggested, "Larsen tried to 'pass' as a novelist and to an extent succeeded" (138), then "Sanctuary" was her out-ing. Having her authorship called into question destroyed the sense of self which "Nella Larsen, novelist" (Davis 2) had come to rely on. Whereas Cather and Stein were able to re-envision themselves across a lifetime of writing, continually experimenting with new strategies and trying out new personas, Larsen was left in the gap. Gaps are not immutably fixed, however, but shifting, and the pendulum of literary greatness tends to come back around. In literature as in life, Larsen was not really lost—she was just waiting.

Chapter Five
Conclusion: Other Countries,
Other Romances

THIS COUNTRY, TODAY

> "'If you're talking of yourself and Vivaldo—there are other countries—have you ever thought of that?' . . . 'Oh, yes! And in another five or ten years, when we get the loot together, we can pack up and go to one of those countries. . . . And what do you think will have happened to us in those five years? How much will be left?'"
>
> —James Baldwin, *Another Country* (1960)

Questions about who counts in the United States, the benefits and problems associated with immigration, and the meaning/legacy of the melting pot have not disappeared since the great wave of European immigration ended in the 1920s. Indeed, the debates in 2004 are sounding a lot like those in 1904. The stakes are high as would-be residents seek to join the American experience, and a new breed of nativist work to preserve what they consider the nation's threatened integrity. A typical reflection of their efforts is the title of a recent newspaper article: "Immigration to cost states seven seats, study claims" (J. Abrams A15). A spokesman for the anti-immigrant think tank that conducted the study offered such classic nativist scare statements as "[redistribution is a] distortion of the political system in which seats are taken away from citizens and reallocated in effect to noncitizens" and "this can be seen as distorting our democracy." The language of whim and unfairness is consistent throughout: California will "end up" with extra seats, while other states "lost" seats or "failed to get" the ones that were rightfully coming to them. Some states will be "deprived" of their fair representation. New arrivals are jeopardizing the very foundations of the political system.

As early as 1956, Kallen observed that Americans who can trace their ancestry to the Founding Fathers feel that they are somehow more American than their later arriving compatriots: "Our traditional isolationism, our laws respecting immigration and our use of the epithets 'alien,' 'foreign,' our image of the '100 per cent American,' our 'Daughters of the American Revolution,' unheeding of the ideals the Revolution was fought for, their brothers, the Sons, the Ku Klux Klan, all are groups with a creed and code, invidiously setting apart themselves, the elect, from the rest of the nation, somehow the reject" (33). Forty years later, Lowe comments that "in the last century and a half, the American *citizen* has been defined over and against the Asian *immigrant,* legally, economically, and culturally" (4), a point that could easily be applied to other immigrant groups, as well. Berlant notes a recurrent pattern: "every crisis of immigration in U.S. history has involved the claim that something essentially American is being threatened by alien cultural practices" (*Queen* 193).

Ironically, a similar fear is expressed by an African-American resident of the mostly Mexican-American and high immigration town of South Gate, California: "Some people have bought chickens. Others want a shed in the backyard. *We* have laws *here*. Why is it that *they* want to come *here* and *take over?*" (Labi 8; emphasis added). As *Time* magazine reported, the townspeople were squaring off in the debate over colorful expression versus mainstream respectability. The article's subtitle, "A town cloaked in shades of pale shudders as homes cross the color barrier," suggests that plays on racial passing are intentional. The players are different, but the language is similar. The Mexican-American mayor "has resolved to ban what he calls the 'Day-Glo colors—the wild reds, oranges and purples'" from houses in his community. According to the mayor, "the most vocal supporters of a color ordinance are second- and third-generation Latinos." The article's author wonders out loud: "will the melting pot end up with a can of commercial beige paint?" (Labi 8).

Cather, for one, might well have sided with South Gate's color contingent. As Bennett has pointed out, Cather had no patience with second- and third-generation immigrants who were ashamed of their parents and their ancestral traditions (148), a point proven clearly by her satiric treatment of Oscar and Lou Bergson in *O Pioneers!.* Along similar lines, if the individual houses in South Gate are painted a color "that makes your eyes sting on a bright day" (Labi 8), they would probably not have made too great an impression on Stein. Remembering her first visit to 27 rue de Fleurus, "Alice" remarks, "the pictures were so strange that one quite instinctively looked at anything rather than at them just at first" (*ABT* 9). Furthermore, although South Gate might seem a far cry from the fictional Naxos in Larsen's *Quicksand,* the anti-color, pro-homogeneity campaign of ethnic Americans who want to fit in seems similar to the struggle Helga waged in that model school for southern Negro children. In spite of what the Naxos matrons would have her believe, Helga knows that she and her dark-skinned students look good in vibrantly colored clothes (*Q* 18). In South Gate, Patricia Lazalde insists that the situation is "an ethnic thing. . . . Color is passion, emotion. Hey, if you paint your house a beautiful color, what's the crime?" (qtd. in Labi 8).

While "people climb[ing] up the ladder of success" worry that displays by "ranch Mexicans" will ruin everyone's chances for respectability (Labi 8), the upwardly mobile might keep in mind Bourne's contention that assimilation is not the solution: "It is not the Jew who sticks proudly to the faith of his fathers and boasts of that venerable culture who is dangerous to America, but the Jew who has lost the Jewish fire and become a mere elementary, grasping animal. It is not the Bohemian who supports the Bohemian schools in Chicago whose influence is sinister, but the Bohemian who has made money and has got into ward politics" (270). What will become of the Mexican-Americans who use neutral tones on their houses has yet to be seen. Clearly, the relationships between ethnicity, immigration and citizenship are still important. Assimilation has its benefits (including upward mobility) but it also has its costs. "How much will be left?" remains the crucial question in any trade-off between ancestral and adoptive traditions. And, as newly-arrived Mexican-American immigrants might attest, going to another country does not necessarily solve any problems.

ANOTHER COUNTRY

> "All countries were beautiful to Mr. Rosen. He carried a country of his own in his mind, and was able to unfold it like a tent in any wilderness."
> —Willa Cather, "Old Mrs. Harris" (1932)

Although Cather, Stein and Larsen could show American birth certificates and held American passports, each searched for another country (literally and figuratively) in her life and in her art. To this end, all discovered geographical and creative spaces that fostered their work in important ways and betrayed its limitations in other ways. All three occupied the paradoxical position of identifying as American writers and yet finding it difficult to write at home. Cather made many trips to Europe, but did not find the continent congenial to her writing process. As Louise Bogan notes, "she does not like to work away from America. . . . In Paris she misses clear American skies, becomes absorbed in watching the changing soft colors of the Seine, and gets nothing done. She delights in the turns and sound of colloquial American speech" (132). Although she enjoyed hearing American voices and preferred to do her writing within the United States, Cather nevertheless needed physical distance

from her home region (and the one she is most often identified with, popu-
larly and critically), the Nebraska prairie, in order to find her subject matter
and to transform early experiences into mature writing.' Residing in New
York and New England, Cather could once again hear the sounds of
Nebraskan farm women's voices and could rework these memories creatively.[2]
Cather's mentor, Sarah Orne Jewett, had advised her as much: "'Of course,
one day you will write about your own country. In the meantime, get all you
can. One must know the world *so well* before one can know the parish'" (qtd.
in O'Brien, *EV* 345). While Cather liked to hear English around her while she
composed her texts, Stein had an opposite need. Marren suggests that part of
Stein's motivation for living abroad was to establish an exclusive hold on the
English language (174). France was Stein's "other country," and her residence
abroad allowed her to establish her Americanness through distance. Marren
observes that Stein and Toklas considered themselves Americans on the basis
of native-bornness (171), and Spencer adds that "even at the end of her life, .
. . Gertrude Stein not only retained her belief in the ineluctable imprint of nationality but also affirmed the native roots of her own writing" (224). As important as living abroad was for Stein, she needed to identify herself as an
American. Like Cather, Larsen left the scenes of her childhood—both
Chicago and Fisk—at the earliest possible opportunity. She spent time overseas, though her published texts were written in the United States. It is worth
noting, however, that whereas Cather made frequent trips to Nebraska and
Stein visited Baltimore and East Oakland when she finally crossed the ocean
for a lecture tour, Larsen only returned to her childhood memories in fanci-
ful reconstructions.[3] Thus Cather, Stein and Larsen all bore out Urgo's contention that leaving home is a prerequisite to writing about it (56, 65).

   A preoccupation with migration, or movement away from home, places
these writers squarely in an American experiential tradition. As Sollors notes:
"it is hardly an exaggeration to say that the exodus is one of America's central
themes" (43). None of these women was either a first-generation immigrant
or a self-identified expatriate, and yet all experienced immigration or expatriation on some level. Elyse Blankley offers a compelling interpretation of expatriation when she attests that "Stein, literally an 'expatriate' in Paris, was
artistically shaping a distinctly 'ex-patriate' vision (in the word's original Latin
sense of 'away from the father')" (202). Cather also moved away from her literary progenitors, though this departure was not always clear to her critics.
Godfrey St. Peter speaks for Willa Cather as well when he complains that "nobody saw that he was trying to do something quite different—they merely
thought he was trying to do the usual thing, and had not succeeded very well"
(*PH* 32).[4] For her part, Larsen moved away from traditional male models and

laid important foundations for the tradition of twentieth-century African-American women novelists. McDowell includes Ann Allen Shockley, Gayl Jones, Toni Morrison, Alice Walker, Ntozake Shange, and Gloria Naylor in a list of black women who took up the challenges set in motion by Larsen's work (xxxi).

Hence making a literary mark entailed several forms of expatriation for Cather, Stein and Larsen. In addition to leaving home, taking up residence in other countries or regions, and charting new directions in literature, these writers created countries of their own—through their texts and within themselves. These created countries might be considered "imagined communities" of sorts, to use Anderson's term.[5] Some of these countries were envisioned or expressed in texts. Indeed, geography plays an important role in the works under consideration for each writer. In *My Antonia,* young Jim's "old country" is Virginia, while the adult Jim comes to look at Nebraska in the same way. The cosmopolitan Godfrey St. Peter retains his attachment to "*le Michigan*" and "dream[s]" of joining in the "self-sacrificing friendship and disinterested love . . . [of] the day-labourers" in Outland's country (*PH* 31, 172). For Vickie Templeton, the move from the female world of her childhood to the male university world constitutes a relocation to foreign territory.[6]

A similar pattern occurs in Stein's and Larsen's texts. Melanctha Herbert negotiates varied psychological terrain and takes on the demeanor of a world traveler, while Stein's 1930s narratives pose France and America as home and other simultaneously. *The Geographical History of America* responds to the sense that "sometimes one feels there's nothing but geography in this country, and certainly a geographical history is the only kind it can significantly have" (Gass 13).[7] In Larsen's writing, black and white America are presented as intersecting but radically different worlds. *Quicksand* holds Europe up as a counterpoint, but not a solution, to American racism, while *Passing* explores another sort of dual citizenship, the excitement and risks inherent in an individual's attempt to occupy more than one non-intersecting "country" simultaneously (Park 126). Thus all three writers posit complex and multivalent relations between identity and geography.

The search for another country also brought these writers to develop countries in themselves, namely different (and at times seemingly contradictory) aspects of the self. Bifurcation has been a common critical thread in analyzes of their texts. According to this line of thinking, Cather splits herself into Jim and Antonia, Stein splits herself into Melanctha and Jeff, and Larsen splits herself into Clare and Irene. While this kind of oversimplification belies the complexity of their texts and elides significant differences between fiction and life, all three writers did bifurcate themselves into public and private personas.

Cather systematically created a barrier between herself and her public starting in the 1920s when she was becoming well-known (Schroeter 98). Indeed, her public self was formidable at times:

> Her voice is deep and resonant. . . . She stands and moves solidly. She sits with an air of permanence, as though the chair were, and had always been her home. She smokes a cigarette as though she really liked the taste of ignited tobacco and rice paper. . . . Her face, when she detects some affectation in another's words or actions, can lose every atom of warmth and become hostile and set. . . . The remarks 'Oh well' and 'What does it matter?' have never, in all probability, passed her lips. (Bogan 131–32)

While Stein's salon—and eventually her writing—became rather famous, she never really melded her private and public personas. Simon points out that "Stein herself believed that her identity as an artist differed essentially from her social or public personality" (x). For Larsen, writing itself and the identity of "novelist" constituted another country, so to speak. Wanting to act the part of the modern professional woman, "she smoked in public, wore silk stockings and short dresses, mocked the religious conservatives and the racial uplifters, played bridge, and drove a stylish automobile" (Davis 10). All the same, Davis notes that "an outer mask disguised her anxieties about belonging" (10). The identity of "novelist" and the ability to create alternative worlds in her texts served as an important "means of her maintaining her sanity and her balance" (Davis 16). Although Stein's "America" provides the clearest example of an imagined community, Cather and Larsen also offered versions of America and of themselves that allowed them to function, personally and professionally.[8] For these writers, imagination and art jointly became the proverbial tent in any wilderness.

Cather, Stein and Larsen carried a country in their minds and gave voice to that country with their pens. This propensity arguably provides further evidence for considering these women modernist writers. Commenting on the quotation which provides the epigraph for this section, Fetterley and Pryse argue that such an attitude constitutes "a solution—both modern and in many ways modernist—to the problem of 'losing' home" (596). If we see "home" as both a physical location and a centeredness, a sense of self, we might observe that all three women chose to have many homes by negotiating multiple subject positions. Cather's political, religious, geographic, and personal affiliations positioned her inside and outside of multiple categories simultaneously. Similarly, Stein variously chose to emphasize and de-emphasize her sexual orientation, gender, ethnic/religious heritage, and citizenship. Wavering between competing desires to belong and to be different, Larsen and her heroines moved uneasily between bohemianism and social propriety (in both black and white circles). Rather than producing paralysis, however, the ambiguities and fluidities these writers experienced were constructively and beautifully transformed into art.

ROMANCE AND REALITY

> "Mrs. Templeton shrugged. 'You're mistaken, Mrs. Rosen. There ain't a particle of romance in Vickie.'
>
> 'But there are several kinds of romance, Mrs. Templeton. She may not have your kind.'
>
> 'Yes'm, that's so,' said Mrs. Harris in a low, grateful voice. She thought that a hard word Victoria had said of Vickie."
> —Willa Cather, "Old Mrs. Harris" (1932)

The country and the time period Bourne coined "Trans-National America" fostered a particular kind of literary art. Transnationalism, entering the realm of writing, facilitated trans-generic texts. The attempt to break free of confining codes and expectations in literary genres was an important struggle that Cather, Stein and Larsen all waged. In particular, they grappled with the tensions between romance and reality (and a system invested in keeping them separate and unequal). Despite mis-readings which deemed their work "sentimental and nostalgic," "historically conservative," "incoherent," and "lying," these writers have borne out the truth in Mrs. Rosen's statement that "there are several kinds of romance."[9] All three possessed alternative conceptions of what constitutes reality or realistic writing and of how realism works. Cather and Larsen used deceptively simple language in what appeared to be basically mimetic texts, while Stein unhinged concepts of realistic writing (and sometimes unhinged words and their meanings altogether). In any case, all three undermined the notion that realism is straightforward and simple. Lilienfeld argues that "for Cather, seemingly traditional realism became a method to render the safely obvious devious and obscure" (50). In her own critical writing, Cather disagrees with traditional definitions of realism:

> there is a popular superstition that 'realism' asserts itself in the cataloguing of a great number of material objects, in explaining mechanical processes, the methods of operating manufactories and trades, and in minutely and unsparingly describing physical sensations. But is not realism, more than it is anything else, an attitude of mind on the part of the writer toward his material, a vague indication of the sympathy and candour with which he accepts, rather than chooses, his theme?" (*NUF* 45)

Chessman suggests that Stein also had different ideas about reality and realism, and she observes that Stein's texts corroborate the notion that "'reality' is simply what works for us; it is a social construction, socially encoded" (157). Stein explains her own views in "A Trans-Atlantic Interview, 1946": "because the realism of the people who did realism before was a realism of trying to make people real. I was not interested in making the people real but in the essence or, as a painter would call it, value" (Haas 16). In addition, Stein says she derived some inspiration in her task from Cezanne and from Flaubert, both of whom influenced Cather as well.[10] Larsen employs a specific kind of realism for her own ends, too. McDowell notes that "in *Passing* she uses a technique found commonly in narratives by Afro-American women novelists with a 'dangerous' story to tell: 'safe' themes, plots, and conventions are used as the protective cover underneath which lie more dangerous subplots" (xxx). Furthermore, Larsen's *Quicksand* has been mis-read (and summarily dismissed) as a novel of manners because of its careful attention to details such as dress. However, as DuCille explains, these tropes actually serve a symbolic function, reinforcing the novel's thematic explorations of race and gender (205). Thus all three writers moved away from strict demarcations in genre. The same cultural climate that fostered transnationalism encouraged trans-generic experimentation and alternative conceptions of reality and realistic writing.

In fact, on the level both of genre and of culture, the realism/romance divide has never been as clear-cut as some critics would have it: "realism . . . is as much a code as romance, as much artifice as lightening creams and greasepaint" (DuCille 200). Here DuCille delineates the connection between the conscious employment of literary categories or conventions and deliberate alterations of physical appearance towards a social goal. Indeed, observations like DuCille's highlight an important cultural phenomenon of modernity, namely the increasingly coded and simulacral representation of everyday life. Kaplan makes a similar point, agreeing that the generic debate that seeks to clearly demarcate romance from realism (and to privilege realism as more legitimate than romance) ultimately elides the point. Instead Kaplan contends that "fictionality itself—rather than the particular form of the romance—seems to be the underlying enemy of realism, and its danger lies not in its deviance from a normative reality but in the way in which modern life has become indistinguishable from fiction" (19). The notion that life has become collapsed with fiction is consistent with the post-structural tenet that reality is itself a construction, and an unstable one, too, because it is created by inherently slippery language (Eagleton 143–44). Indeed Barthes, along with many others, criticizes traditional realism because of its attempts to pass itself off as an ultimate truth, as Eagleton points out, "the realist or representational sign . . . is for Barthes essentially unhealthy. It effaces its own status as a sign, in order to foster the illusion that we are perceiving reality without its intervention" (136). Clearly, demanding that realistic writing conform to a narrow set of conventional requirements produces neither truth nor great literature.

Cather, Stein and Larsen offered their own versions of reality and realistic writing, and in most cases, their ideas were not consistent with what their audiences and their critics expected. In addition to defying generic expectations by showing the constructed quality of literary realism, all three writers evoked boundary patrol anxieties by blurring lines between fact and fiction—in their lives and in their texts—offering fictionalized versions of themselves which they sometimes presented as fact. Thus trans-generic experimentation was complemented by a willingness or a need to construct personal identities as well. Cather and Larsen both lied about their birth years, an unremarkable and common enough fib, except that critics find this act particularly significant in these authors' cases.[11] Both women also toyed with their given names, while Stein took her beloved's name and voice as her own in *The Autobiography of Alice B. Toklas.* These propensities cause some observers to make value judgments. According to Schroeter, "Miss Cather . . . was a poser, who deliberately constructed an imaginative or dramatized public image" (97), an act, he implies, which is inherently deceptive and false. Stein's voice-swapping in *The Autobiography* generated a fair amount of backlash, as did her questionable assertions uttered as true recollections in a memoir-like confidential tone. Larsen offended fewer people with her emendations to history, but it has come to light that much of the book-jacket biography she submitted to her publisher was as carefully crafted as her fiction and not technically true. Larsen's novels draw on autobiography but the revision process, "the process of reinventing fact" (Davis 296), rendered whatever biographical information one might hope to glean from them obscure. For Cather, Stein and Larsen, identities were consciously constructed and sometimes bore little resemblance to what is conventionally considered fact.

If genre (romance vs. realism) and truth (fact vs. fiction) were subject to loosening or blurring in Trans-National America, gender identity was similarly fluid and ambiguous. Indeed, the "several kinds of romance" alluded to by Mrs. Rosen can also refer to gender identity, possibly hinting at alternatives to heterosexual unions. Vickie Templeton, modeled closely on young Willie Cather, occupies an anomalous position. Carlin argues that she is the outsider in the text and suggests that she might be a lesbian (108). Although Bennett insists that Cather chose not to marry to avoid disappointment (221), O'Brien (among others) has concluded that Cather's primary emotional attachments were to women and identifies her as a lesbian (*EV* 6). Stein chose to marry, but it was another woman whom she took as her wife, a situation which caused her some initial discomfort and which caused a rupture with certain friends and family members (Wagner-Martin, *Favored* 102–03). While Larsen married a man, she was attuned to issues of same-sex love and gender oppression. McDowell argues for a lesbian reading of *Passing*, while Allan surmises that Larsen "must have been tempted to seize the issue and redefine black lesbianism in positive terms. To do so behind a mask must have been as painful for her as it was for [Virginia] Woolf" (107). Because marriage and Americanization have historically been linked, the issues of "another country" and "several kinds of romance" are also joined: "central to both the immigrant and the middle-class narrative is the marriage plot . . . For the native-born American, no less than for the immigrant, marriage is a key site of Americanization" (Wald 279). In the realm of gender, like those of national and professional affiliation, transnationalism facilitated a relaxing of boundaries, a state which had both liberating and dislocating ramifications.

Is the United States a true nation, and does American literature exist as a discrete and recognizable entity? While Sumner thought that a racially and ethnically diverse population meant that "the United States had no claim to the name of nation" (Fairchild 54), Munsterberg conceded that being a country composed of immigrants prevented Americans from developing "a profound feeling of indissoluble unity" (5). He did not, however, conclude that such diversity precluded nationhood. Indeed, Munsterberg seemed to realize ahead of his time that unity is not the point. Concerns about American identity—and influential components such as ethnicity, immigration and gender—are variously ascendant and recessive in national importance. Cather, Stein and Larsen came of age and produced important literary texts during a transitional period in American history and American letters. What they strove to communicate in terms of the fluidity of identity categories and the significance of multiple subject positions retains a lasting relevance, as issues of nationality and geography, ethnicity and race, and gender and sexuality continue to occupy a prominent place in today's socio-cultural landscape. Instead of squeezing themselves and their texts into constricting categories, they opted for dispersal and re-creation, taking the path "that led toward the moon" (Cather, OMH 282). And beyond.

Afterword

"A Time to Every Purpose Under Heaven"

"And if a stranger sojourn with thee in your land, you shall not wrong him. But the stranger that dwells with you shall be to you as one born among you, and thou shalt love him as thyself; for you were strangers in the land of [Egypt]."

—Leviticus 19.33–34 (*Jerusalem Bible*)

"A poem about mushrooms or about a walk with the dog is a more eloquent response to Sept. 11 than a poem that announces that wholesale murder is a bad thing."

—Billy Collins (qtd. in "Poetry and Tragedy")

"Now that 9–11 happened, I'm very careful where I go with my dog. . . . When people ask what kind she is, I just say, 'She's a hound dog.' . . . The only reason I do this is for fear of possible retaliation."

—Lou Guerrero, owner-breeder of the No. 1-ranked Afghan in 2001 (qtd. in Walker)

And the pendulum swings back around. Large numbers of European immigrants came to the United States between 1880 and 1920, and then World War I left an anti-immigration backlash in its wake. Within the resultant nativist climate, some German-Americans "did not feel it was safe to show the hyphen because many Americanizers scorned the newcomers as un-American when they showed pride in things German" (Fuchs 64). Such a climate had broad repercussions, even extending to the world of purebred dogs: "During World War I, the American Kennel Club changed the name of German shepherds to simply shepherd dogs to 'save the breed from prejudice.' They were called Alsatian wolfdogs in Britain, then shifted to merely Alsatians until the late 1970s" (Walker). American nativism climaxed in the 1920s and receded in the 1930s; then ethnicity was again de-emphasized from the 1940s to the

189

early 1960s, when it became a prominent element of personal and national identity (Gleason, *Speaking* 155). By the 1970s, "ethnicity truly was in vogue" (Sollors, *Beyond* 21), starting our culture on the path to such pluralism-friendly melting pot substitutes as the kaleidoscope (Fuchs), the salad bowl or the mosaic (Blair 142).

When I first started this project, in the late 1990s, our country seemed to be all about multiculturalism, globalism, and the dismantling of barriers. The 2000 US Census counted same-sex partners and offered sixty-three categories of racial identification, up from six in 1990 (San Mateo). All-American golfing phenomenon Tiger Woods had been "put[ting] a face—that is reflective of a rich mixture of ethnic heritage—behind the movement for official recognition of Americans who do not fit neatly into a single racial category," identifying himself as "Cablinasian" (San Mateo). Diversity was in.

September 11, 2001 abruptly changed that momentum. Now the bumper stickers emphasize unity over diversity: "United We Stand." And again dogs seem to be on the front line. This time it was the Afghan Hound Club of America contemplating a name change and keeping a low profile at its annual exhibition: "certainly no [other] dogs have come under the kind of scrutiny the breed has faced since the terrorist attacks on the World Trade Center and Pentagon. . . . [and] such bias led to a brief discussion [about] whether the breed's name should be switched to something that would attract less attention" (Walker). Naming is important—and issues of who does the naming and who might (mis)interpret the names seem perpetually relevant.

Issues of legibility have also become increasingly important in the current cultural climate. Soon after September 11, a Sikh man was killed because his vigilante attackers mistook him for an Arab; in fact, he was an Indian immigrant working for his American Dream in Phoenix, Arizona ("Thousands"). And yet what exactly does a terrorist look like? Certainly our country's intensifying efforts at promoting homeland security have failed to protect us from the enemy within, homegrown terrorists such as Timothy McVeigh, Eric Robert Rudolph, and John Allen Muhammed, let alone "the American Taliban," John Walker Lindh. Is American identity ideological or performative? Under what circumstances is it forfeited? Do we need to be more careful about whom we allow to join the "American race"? Xenophobia and isolationism are unmistakably back in style. The Patriot Act has placed severe strains on American civil liberties, and immigrants (legal and otherwise) are being subject to any number of crackdowns.

In the wake of September 11, American writers have tried to make sense of the tragedy, to use art to impose order and foster healing. Robert Pinsky, for example, explains that his poem "Memorial" "tries to meditate death's meaning, its peace, its painful process, the life of the dead in the imagination of the living. It is an effort at remembering and at imagining, and an attempt to register how hard those efforts can be" (qtd. in "Poetry and Tragedy"). Paradoxically, some of this art has engendered additional controversy and discord. Amiri Baraka's divisive poem, "Somebody Blew Up America," for example, generated strong feelings of outrage (culminating in the elimination of New Jersey's poet laureate post) and equally fervent indignation about the perceived dangers to First Amendment rights and artistic expression. Old tensions between blacks and Jews were rekindled by the poem, diverting attention from the poem's larger purpose of protesting the "racist-patriarchal capitalist system" in America: "The First Amendment, it seems, only guarantees freedom of speech to those who can afford a station or a press. . . . The state's revoking of the poet laureate position is a clear message to other cultural workers: Get out of line and you will pay the price" (Ytzhak).

Throughout their lives, Cather, Stein, and Larsen all stepped out of line, to varying degrees, and each paid the price for her aesthetic experimentalism and her American individualism. The decision to move beyond ready-made identity categories in the pursuit of art that validates the complexity of life is not an easy one. But it does lay the groundwork for lasting art. Cather and Stein both accepted and preached the premise that journalism is not great art because it fails to transcend its original context. Literature, on the other hand, retains its relevance across time periods and cultural contexts. Rabbinic tradition comes to a similar conclusion when scrutinizing why, among the many prophets who were active during the times of Kings of Judah and Israel, only the words of Isaiah, Jeremiah, Ezekiel, and the twelve Minor Prophets were anthologized in the Old Testament. The answer provided is that only these fifteen books were written down and passed on because only these prophetic messages have relevance for future generations. In other words, those anthologized are truly literature. The same, I believe, is true of the writings of Cather, Stein, and Larsen. In their struggles with literary, personal, and national identity categories, these writers produced texts that transcend time period, geography, and cultural climate.

Like the Kennedy assassination for my parents' generation and the explosion of the Space Shuttle *Challenger* for my cohort, September 11 will be the flashbulb memory for the Millennials. And yet September 11 has changed the world for all Americans. How do we—as a nation—go on with our lives in the face of such an event? Rabbinic tradition again offers a suggestion, this time in response to the famous third chapter of Ecclesiastes which begins, "To everything there is a season, and a time to every purpose under the heaven" (*Jerusalem Bible,* Ecclesiastes 3.1). This section is read as positing a fundamental realism. There is no predictable order in the pairings that follow (e.g., good before bad or bad before good) because life is not predictable. Instead of trying to pigeonhole the elements of our world into a consistent ordering that makes sense to us, the text suggests, we are much better off tempering our reactions with realism. Life is not always fun; the key to weathering the vicissitudes is knowing what to do in each time and season. And knowing that life works in cycles. The pendulum will come back around.

In the meantime, I will continue to read the great literature that speaks to my spirit. Great literature, by definition, is literature that can be read time and again, and always reveal new meanings to its audience. Post-September 11, I will read these texts that deal with the "the hardest human questions" (Skaggs 64) again, and again get something fresh out of them—not because the texts have changed, but because I have. Perhaps Stein was not so far off when she said "think of the Bible and Homer think of Shakespeare and think of me" (*GH* 109).

Notes

NOTES TO CHAPTER ONE

1. The term "minority" has been applied widely. As Gleason has observed, by the 1970s it included "homosexuals, youth, the aged, the physically handi-capped, the emotionally disturbed, the poor, drug users, alcoholics, convicts and ex-convicts, and others on the margins of society" in addition to ethnic or racial groups and women (*Speaking* 102).

2. The term "matrix of domination" belongs to Patricia Hill Collins, and reflects the fact that oppressions are multiple and not merely additive. Along similar lines, Maxine Baca Zinn and Bonnie Thornton Dill argue for "the importance of race in understanding the social construction of gender" (321).

3. The relationship between women's writing and feminism is complicated and not always clearly defined, although Rosalind Coward's essay, "Are Women's Novels Feminist Novels?" provides an early and compelling discussion of the topic. Noting that feminism is a conscious political movement with definable aims, Coward insists that "it is just not possible to say that woman-centered writings have any necessary relationship to feminism" (230). She further de-nies that "to describe experience typical of women was sufficient to justify call-ing that account 'feminist'" (237). Critics have offered viable feminist readings of Cather, Stein and Larsen, alike. Whether or not we wish to iden-tify these writers as "feminists," their work tackles issues (power relations, gen-der roles, naming, marginality, etc.) central to the concerns of feminism.

4. Although Stein set up a full-time residence abroad, she was kept abreast of activities in American metropolitan centers by the letters and visits of such well-connected friends as Carl Van Vechten, Mabel Dodge Luhan, and the Cone sisters.

5. Berlant observes that "every crisis of immigration in U.S. history has in-volved the claim that something essentially American is being threatened by alien cultural practices" (*Queen* 193).

6. Whether or not Larsen traveled to Denmark as a young adult is a matter of debate among her critics. Wall states that Larsen never really visited

Denmark as she had claimed (92), while Washington accepts the story of
Larsen's studies abroad (161). Davis, Larsen's biographer, endorses neither
version, but suggests that either one could be correct.

7. Cather, like her contemporary, O.E. Rolvaag, was an outspoken critic of
melting pot ideology (Pers 40).

8. Edith Lewis relates the following anecdote told to her by Cather: "she told
once of an old judge who came to call at Willowshade, and who began
stroking her curls and talking to her in the playful platitudes one addressed
to little girls—and of how she horrified her mother by breaking out suddenly: 'I've a dang'ous nigger, I is!'" (13). O'Brien suggests that "we might
interpret this story as Willa Cather's first rebellion against patriarchal authority, represented here by the condescending judge" (*EV* 43). Wagner-Martin
compares Cather and Stein in terms of gender identity: "Unlike Willa
Cather, who called herself 'William Cather, Jr.,' during four years of her adolescence, Stein never wore pants or men's jackets, though she did don derby
hats, ties, and vests later in life" (*Favored* 24).

9. The phrase comes from Adrienne Rich's 1986 collection of poetry, which is
comprised of the following three sections: "Sources," "North American
Time," and "Contradictions: Tracking Poems." Common themes include
identification, ethnicity, and geography.

10. A variety of critics and theorists call attention to the dual nature of identity
formation and attribution. Writing from a cultural perspective like Sollors,
Bottomley points out that "ethnicities are imposed, as well as assumed and
inherited" (60). Berlant discusses the relationship between identity and essentialism in the context of the debate over gays in the military (*Queen* 17).

11. While Sollors discusses turn-of-the-century thinkers such as Randolph
Bourne, Josiah Royce, and Henry Pratt Fairchild in his study of the history
of ethnicity in America, Fuchs calls 1880–1920 "a period of almost continual national debate over the meaning of American identity and unity"
(56–7); Gleason points out that the concept of the melting pot introduced
in Israel Zangwill's 1908 play gave rise to an ideological debate that continued for decades (*Speaking* 5–24).

12. Culley emphasizes that race is usually the most salient axis of identification for
women of color: "black women's 'we' usually has its foundation in race" (15).
It is further worth noting that Stein's Jewishness did not function for her in
the same way that Larsen's identification as African-American shaped her social and geographical milieu. Whereas Larsen lived in Harlem, Stein did not
seek out the company of other Jews and often downplayed her Jewish roots.

13. Gleason observes that "the increasing imprecision of the minority concept re-
sulted largely from its application to more and more elements in American
society" (*Speaking* 101).

14. Pers explains that Cather "could see the significance of their contributions to the
settling of the American Middle West in a wider perspective and not isolated in

specific ethnic groups unrelated to the world outside" and portray it sympathetically to native-born Americans (48). In "The Novel Demeuble," Cather rejects
popular definitions of realism, arguing that the minute details that clutter so-
called realistic writing are extraneous and counterproductive. Instead, Cather
suggests that realism can be found in the author's state of mind, particularly in
her ability to be true to her material (*NUF* 45).

15. Kalaidjian contends that Bourne's forward-looking vision of social diversity
was repressed by modernist cannon formation, noting that
individualism/self-reliance (modernism) is opposed to collectivism/ the social personality (Bourne) (19). In this way, Bourne becomes a victim of the
very process that kept Cather, Stein and Larsen out of books on modernism
for so many years.

16. A book-length study addressing Cather as a modernist writer did not come
out until 1990, with Jo Ann Middleton's *Willa Cather's Modernism: A Study
of Style and Technique.* Carlin's 1992 work, *Cather, Canon, and the Politics of
Reading,* looks at why Cather's later works have persistently been considered
non-canonical.

17. Larsen is not included in lists of high modern writers, perhaps because of her
simple writing style (which has been compared to Cather's) and because
Harlem Renaissance was considered a category of its own. More recent stud-
ies have tried to establish Larsen's writing as modernist, including Bonnie
Kime Scott's *The Gender of Modernism* (1990) and Mary Hairston
McManus's "African-American Modernism in the Novels of Jessie Fauset and
Nella Larsen," which calls for a "re-defining of modernism to include greater
attention to race and gender and less emphasis on form" (190).

18. Raymond Williams observes of modernist writers in general that language
became a crucial source of identification: "liberated or breaking free from
their national or provincial cultures, placed in quite new relations to those
other native languages or native visual traditions, encountering meanwhile a
novel and dynamic common environment from which many of the older
forms were obviously distant, the artists and writers and thinkers of this
phase found the only community available to them: a community of the
medium; of their own practices" (45).

19. The title of Gillian Hanscombe and Virginia Smyers's study suggests as
much: *Writing for their Lives: the Modernist Women, 1910–1940.*

20. Bourne urges acceptance of immigrants who retrace their steps by returning
to their homelands: "Along with dual citizenship we shall have to accept, I
think, that free and mobile passage of the immigrant between America and
his native land again which now arouses so much prejudice among us. . . . To
stigmatize the alien who works in America for a few years and returns to his
own land, only perhaps to seek American fortune again, is to think in narrow nationalistic terms. It is to ignore the cosmopolitan significance of this
migration" (282).

21. Sollors observes that racial passing is sometimes combined with cross-dressing (*Neither* 260). Ginsberg contends that gender passing is "usually effected by deliberate alterations of physical appearance and behavior, including cross-dressing" (3).

22. Davis insists that "there is no indication that Larsen attempted to pass for white" (422). Marren's dissertation title asserts that both Larsen and Stein were "passing for American."

23. Terms like "code" and "mask" abound in discussions of Stein, Cather and Larsen. Kaye devotes a book-length study to explorations of masking in Cather (*Isolation and Masquerade*), while Hively sees Cather's work "as a fascinating puzzle, with . . . many hidden clues" (176), and Lindemann relates queerness and "masking" ("Fear" 31). In reference to Stein, Fifer argues that *The Autobiography of Alice B. Toklas* shows Stein using "another entire personality as a mask" (160) while seeing in *Useful Knowledge* "a sort of secret code" (160); Ruddick contends that Stein employs "a private code" (M. Hoffman 225); Ammons goes so far as to suggest that Stein "could only talk in code" (100). Bettye Williams argues that Larsen's Helga Crane "masks the essence of herself" (53); McManus sees Larsen's use of the mulatta figure as "a mask for the exploration of a female sensibility" (16).

24. Some postmodern and anti-essentialist theory seems to lend itself to this task. For example, Rattansi proposes that we acknowledge that there are racisms as opposed to a single, unitary racism (256); Nicholson and Seidman show how queer theory has built on the concept of fluidity of identity (17); and Balibar urges us to "accept the scattered meaning of the universal" (49). I do not, however, wish to dispense with the depth model entirely, but rather to reconsider some of the valuations we have imposed on its layers. Like Dollimore, I resist the postmodern attempt to see only a surface level as having significance (64).

25. One example is Abraham's *Are Girls Necessary? Lesbian Writing and Modern Histories,* which includes chapters on Woolf, Stein, and Cather.

NOTES TO CHAPTER TWO

1. For a detailed study of the prolonged apprenticeship that preceded Cather's emergence as a mature writer, see Sharon O'Brien's *Willa Cather: the Emerging Voice.*

2. Georg Simmel spells out several defining features of the "metropolitan type of man" (48), including intellectualization (48), an orientation towards money (49), "the blase attitude" (51), "reciprocal reserve and indifference" between acquaintances (55), a high degree of differentiation and specialization (57), and objectivity (58). Although metropolitan man is generally cosmopolitan, a cosmopolite does not necessarily have to be a metropolitan man.

3. Even as she writes a book on Cather's later novels, Skaggs acknowledges that Cather tried a new experiment with each text (2).

4. An important exception to this trend is Cather's dedication and generosity in answering soldiers' letters during World War II (Brown, *Critical Biography* 321).

5. On a wry side note, Cather did not want *My Antonia* taught in high school courses.

6. Although Isabel McClung expressed the fear that cultured east coast readers would misinterpret (or take offense at) the appellation "hired girls," Cather refused to change the term (Moorhead 105). Cather the Midwesterner was in some ways speaking a different language from her eastern compatriots, and if things got lost in the translation, so be it.

7. Jim's reliance on the Widow Steavens's portrayal of a binary moral system anticipates Niel Herbert's inability to comprehend the richness and complexity of a Marian Forrester in *A Lost Lady*. Other parallels include the fact that Elizabeth Sergeant was not completely sure if the "sicilian jar" (Sergeant 13) conversation was meant to refer to Antonia or to Marian and Lee's observation that Wick Cutter anticipates Ivy Peters ("Road" 167).

8. Theodore Dreiser's novel *Sister Carrie* was published in 1900 but suppressed until 1912, the year Cather published her first "first novel," *Alexander's Bridge.*

9. Since Cather does not provide any sex scenes, we have no conclusive evidence that Peter and Pavel engage in homosexual relations; it seems clear, however, that homosocial bonding is a prominent element in their relationship.

10. Carlin sees palimpsest in *Shadows on the Rock,* as well (88).

11. Lee agrees that "to read Jim Burden . . . simply as a mask for lesbian feelings, is a narrowing exercise" ("Road" 167).

12. Jeff Webb further points out that the adult Jim who narrates the story "is also a modern immigrant, having left Nebraska to pursue a career in the East as a railroad executive" (229).

13. Carlin notes that Cather has been "viewed as an antimodernist, [and] an embittered elegiast" (6), while JoAnn Middleton's *Willa Cather's Modernism* fights the uphill battle of contextualizing Cather as a modernist. More recently, Webb reads Cather's portrayal of memory in *My Antonia, A Lost Lady,* and *The Professor's House* as employing modernist modes. From the perspective of a contemporary, Cather fails as an artist because her work (and especially her later work) "fall[s] into supine romanticism because of a refusal to examine life as it is" (Hicks 147).

14. In his attack on the concept of the melting pot, Fairchild suggests, "if we must have a symbol for race mixture, much more accurate than the figure of the melting pot is the figure of the village pound" (125).

15. Karen Hoffman discusses the inter-relationship of language and identity in her essay, which argues that Jim "use[s] . . . narrative to construct his identity" (27).

16. A similar line-up can be found in the Compson family of Faulkner's *The Sound and the Fury:* a suicide (Quentin), a complaining old woman (Mrs. Compson), a ruthless older brother (Jason), a sexually charged sister

(Caddy), and an idiot (Benjy). Although he does not identify the Shimerdas as a Family of Man, Scholes does explicate several Adamic parallels in *My Antonia* (19).

17. Lindemann reports that "*My Antonia* was a USA Pictures production, directed by Joseph Sargent, written for television and produced by Victoria Riskin, 1995" (*Queering* 144–45, n. 13).

18. Fetterley does actually argue that "Lena represents a model of lesbian sexuality" (Bloom 144). We might also apply Adrienne Rich's concept of the lesbian continuum, "a range—through each woman's life and throughout history—of woman-identified experience, not simply the fact that a woman has had or consciously desired genital sexual experience with another woman" ("Compulsory" 51), to our understanding of Tiny's and Lena's relationship.

19. In arguing that Cather was indeed a lesbian, O'Brien notes that the young Cather mourned that "feminine friendship should be unnatural" (*EV* 117).

20. An important exception to this generalization is Lindemann, who includes Marek in her analysis of queerness in Cather (*Queering* 47, 64–65).

21. Shaw provides a detailed analysis of Marek's disorder, focusing on his webbed fingers. He concludes that in creating Marek, Cather combines the symptoms of two types of syndactyly: Cenani and Filippi ("Marek" 29–32).

22. The prototype for Yulka Shimerda actually became a nun. Although Cather chose to leave this event out of her narrative, the parallels between Marek and Yulka are striking. Joining an order is, in fact, a form of incarceration, albeit one that is chosen rather than forced.

23. *The Professor's House* stands out for its complexity and its boldness in formal experimentation; *Death Comes for the Archbishop, Shadows on the Rock,* and *Sapphira and the Slave Girl* all use a more distant historical and geographical settings than the early Nebraska novels which made Cather famous.

24. Gleason observes that two million Eastern European Jews arrived in America between 1870 and 1914 ("American" 108), roughly the period between Cather's birth and the publication of her third novel. Cantor notes that "the era of high Modernism, which stretches from 1900 to 1940 is also the era of the rise of anti-Semitism in the West" (127), so Cather's negative portraits certainly were not created in a vacuum. Cantor also shows how Jewish intellectuals, who played a key role in the modernist movement, were targeted for criticism by both modernist and anti-modernist camps (125–29).

25. Pers points out that Jews were not among the prairie farmers that Cather knew as a child (19, n. 16), and indeed Jews are absent from *O Pioneers!* and *My Antonia.* The Nathanmeyers of *Song of the Lark* and the Ehrlichs of *One of Ours* (avatars of Mr. and Mrs. Charles Wiener) are cultivated German Jews who play a positive but minor role in their respective novels. In Cather's early stories, which tend to be less autobiographical than her early novels, Jews are generally portrayed in a superficial, negative and stereotypical fashion.

Examples include Lichtenstein, "a Jewish picture dealer" marked by a "repulsive personality and innate vulgarity" (53), in "The Marriage of Phaedra" (1905); Miletus Poppas, "the Greek Jew" with an ugly accent, a "foreign" voice, and a "thin lupine face" (103), in "The Diamond Mine" (1920); Siegmund Stein, "one of the most hideous men in New York" (162), in "Scandal" (1920). In "Behind the Singer Tower" (1912), Cather offers "several surprisingly anti-Semitic remarks" (Woodress, *Literary* 216).

26. I am positing that Cather's representations of Jews evolved as she became older and more world-wise. Li Zhu and Tim Bintrim have made a similar argument for Cather's treatment of the Chinese, noting that "no study has treated Cather's three Chinese stories as a record of her developing understanding of the Chinese immigrants in America" and calling for a "reassessment of her Chinese stories" (1, 5).

27. The land is similarly referred to as "the great fact" in Alexandra Bergson's Nebraska (*OP* 11).

28. Appelhoff seems like an old school Cather immigrant, and he anticipates Neighbor Rosicky in his penchant for reflection following a lifetime of hard work: "'When I was young, in de old country, I had it hard to git my wife at all, an' I never had time to t'ink. When I come to dis country I had to work so terrible hard on dat farm to make crops an' pay debts, dat I was like a horse. Now I have it easy, an' I take time to t'ink about all dem t'ings'" (52). His horse-like characterization is also reminiscent of Anton Rosicky's earlier avatar, Anton Cuzak.

29. Joseph Wood Krutch comments that "in spite of many fine touches [*The Professor's House*] does not live up to the promise of the earlier pages. Fragmentary and inconclusive, it starts off in several different directions but never quite arrives at any of the proposed destinations." He faults the inclusion of "Tom Outland's Story" for disrupting the rhythm and integrity of the book, as he continues, "the initial mistake was, I think, the elaboration of the character whose story constitutes the second of the three parts into which the novel is divided" (56).

30. Tom does a better job of presenting information without interpretation than St. Peter does, but Skaggs cautions against taking him at face value either: "a brightest and best young American, Outland seems initially as delightful and as universally adored in his thoroughly masculine way as Marian Forrester was in her feminine. One would be foolish, however, to assume in this increasingly troubled period that Cather would present Tom Outland any less ambivalently than she did Marian Forrester" (66).

31. Karen Hoffman similarly reads *My Antonia* as a study of "identity crossings" and as a "questioning of fixed gender identities" (27).

32. In further corroboration for viewing Louie as one of Cather's mulatto figures, Berlant points out "the analogy between the passing mulatta and the assimilated Jew" (*Queen* 224).

33. All of these examples of the Professor's closetedness draw on the OED definitions of "closet" that Sedgwick provides (65).

34. We might thus conclude that the Professor's passing takes place on at least two levels: sexual and existential. Trapped with a wife and two daughters, the Professor fantasizes about a homosocial universe, "this dream of self-sacrificing friendship and disinterested love . . . among the day-labourers, the men who run the railroad trains and boats and reapers and thrashers and mine-drills of the world" (172); in a materialistic society, the Professor privileges the struggle above the goal but must pretend to enjoy the rewards of his labors.

35. Henry Colbert (*Sapphira and the Slave Girl*) serves as another example in Cather's oeuvre of a man who marries up.

36. In observing the parallels between Cather and St. Peter, Skaggs cautions that Cather "does not suggest, because [she and St. Peter] are similar, that he should therefore be assumed virtuous" (76).

37. Brown reminds us that Cather was confirmed as an Episcopalian on December 27, 1922 (*Critical Biography* 227), and contends that "not by any answers it proposes, but by the problems it elaborates, and by the atmosphere in which they are enveloped, *The Professor's House* is a religious novel" (*Critical Biography* 246).

38. Carlin notes that cross-stitch acts as a metaphor for relationships and for fate (92).

39. Stouck's study was written over twenty-five years ago, but it is still widely quoted and referenced. Stouck first argued his point about the departure represented by Cather's last books in a 1973 article, "Willa Cather's Last Four Books." This essay was expanded in *Willa Cather's Imagination* (1975) and reprinted in *Critical Essays on Willa Cather* (1984). The idea that Cather's early works are qualitatively different from her later texts is the premise on which both Carlin's and Skaggs's book-length studies are based (1992, 1990).

40. In "The Diamond Mine," the Jewish Miletus Poppas is described as having "an indescribably foreign quality in his voice" (103). Further, he has a "lupine" face, along with a "cold, supercilious manner . . . [and] alarming, deep-set eyes,—very close together . . . and always gleaming with something like defeated fury" (103–4). It is interesting that Mrs. Rosen's accent is treated much more sympathetically than Poppas's, while no mention is made of either of the Rosen's noses.

41. As a group, German Jews came to America first, assimilated and succeeded. When their less-educated Russian counterparts arrived and isolated themselves in ghettos, these German Jews tried to distance or distinguish themselves from what they perceived as an embarrassing connection. The stereotype which characterizes Eastern European Jews as backward was a prevalent one during the periods of peak Jewish immigration. Further, as Pers points out, Cather offers particularly positive portrayals of German

Jews: "as a group, Cather's Germans are no doubt more sympathetic than her Scandinavians, and her German Jews in particular are more prominent culturally" (80).

42. Ham and his descendants are subjected to a curse because of the lack of respect Ham shows his father, Noah, by gazing on him drunk and naked (*Jerusalem Bible,* Genesis 9.21–26). Rashi, a rabbinic commentator, explains that Moses demurs from being chosen as the leader of the Jewish people (*Jerusalem Bible,* Exodus 4.10) because he believes that it would be an affront to his older brother, Aaron (Ben Isaiah and Sharfman 31).

43. Skaggs notes Cather's use of the courtly love tradition in other works as well (195, n. 2).

44. Cather lived for several Nebraskan months with her paternal grandfather, a Baptist minister, so it is reasonable to suppose that she would have been familiar with this Scriptural reference.

45. Whether this myth was popular in Cather's lifetime is questionable. It is true, however, that most of the two million Jews who entered the United States between 1870 and 1914 (Gleason, "American" 108) would have come through New York. Furthermore, Cather would have encountered more Jews in her years living in Eastern cities (Pittsburgh and then New York) than she did in Nebraska. In her fiction, Cather seems to connect Jewish cosmopolitans with metropolitan centers.

46. Mrs. Rosen's act of "disavowing difference . . . by reduc[ing] the boys to a single name and a single identity" (Carlin 97) echoes the attempts of Grandmother Burden and Lillian St. Peter to gloss over annoying or painful parts of life.

47. The narrator describes Fair Welcome as "a handsome and pleasant and quite irreproachable young man" (ll. 2763–4) and informs us that he is "the son of generous Courtesy" (ll. 2765–66).

48. Taking Bottomley's definition of ethnicity as "'a consciousness of kind' . . . constructed and reconstituted in relation to specific political and economic circumstances" (57) along with Fuchs's insistence that ethnicity implies ancestral traditions (177), we can argue that the Templetons are southern in all of these ethnic ways.

NOTES TO CHAPTER THREE

1. In *Everybody's Autobiography,* Stein further observes that newspapers are "dull reading because they repeat every day the news of that day and they have to print it as if it were just happening and it always had happened some time ago at least some hours ago and after all a thing is interesting that you see happening or that has happened long enough back so that it has an existence which is romanticism it having happened so long ago that though it is there it is really not happening here" (271).

2. See chapter one, note 14.

3. On a similar note, K. Hoffman argues that the character of Jim Burden in *My Antonia* constitutes "Cather's implicit commentary on the autobiographical act" (28), further suggesting that "through the act of *narrating* the manuscript [. . .] Jim is able to shift continually among different positions" and "enact[. . .] identity crossings" (31). Thus Hoffman sees a redefining of the genre of autobiography in Cather, as well.

4. This microcosmic aspect of the story marks it as particularly modernist, according to the characteristics enumerated by Cantor (36).

5. DeKoven observes that while Jeff can be read as a surrogate for Stein, the story is Melanctha's (*Rich* 82).

6. Sutherland comments that "the equal insistence on the integrity of each component part [in *Three Lives*] is a very important twentieth century thing, obviously in politics, but even more evidently in the arts" (Haas 144).

7. Between the fact that Stein was able to see how people like Melanctha lived firsthand in her medical rotations and the fact that Stein herself juggled wandering and stability, emotion and intellect, we can see Stein as occupying the position of an insider-outsider (as defined by Gambrell). I do not think Stein's goal was in self-nativising for sociological documentation, though, so it does not seem fruitful to push this point too far.

8. Wald (241–42) and Ammons (101,103) take this critical view. Laura Doyle, on the other hand, argues that the racist descriptions "are calculated to offend" (263) and insists that "there is clearly more going on than using black characters to signify transgressive sexuality" (268).

9. Cutter argues that Helga "attempts to use 'passing' as a way of finding a unitary sense of identity—a sense of identity structured around *one* role, a role that somehow corresponds to her 'essential self.' Although Helga Crane passes for many things (an exotic Other, a committed teacher, an art object, a devout Christian, a proponent of racial uplift, a dutiful mother) she is only, at any given point in her career, *one* of these things" (75).

10. Like Ginsberg, Helvie points to the experience of Brandon Teena as an example of "society's violent backlash against those whom it deems 'deviant'" (35) and therefore threatening.

11. Washington points out that the word "passing" can "connote death" (164).

12. As a written legend, the history of the Wandering Jew begins around 1223, in an account telling "of a Jew encountered by pilgrims in Armenia, who had taunted Jesus as he was going to his martyrdom and was told 'I go, and you will await me until I come again'" (Stableford 3). Versions of the story proliferated with the invention of the printing press, and tales flourished throughout Europe, reaching a particularly notable height during the Romantic period (Stableford 4–17, 8). At various times "the Wandering Jew stands as a symbol for the entire Jewish people," "represents the historical misfortune of working men," epitomizes "the doomed wanderer," and is portrayed "as an entirely enviable figure" (Stableford 11, 14, 20, 21). The legend

of the Wandering Jew was alive and well during Stein's literary time period and amongst her fellow writers, as Guillaume Apollinaire's "Le juif errant" (1910) suggests (Stableford 16).

13. For further information on this phenomenon, see Raymond Williams's chapter, "Metropolitan Perceptions and the Emergence of Modernism" (37–48).

14. Rachel Blau DuPlessis identifies "the alternate endings in marriage and death [. . . as a] cultural legacy from nineteenth-century life and letters" (4). Although Melanctha fails to marry and instead dies, we might argue that Stein is already on her way to "offering a different set of choices" (4), a task that DuPlessis connects with twentieth-century women writers of the *bildungsroman*.

15. DeKoven does qualify this assessment by referring to the text as "ostensibly naturalist" (*Rich* 71), and again by noting that Melanctha's wandering "disrupts [the text's] ostensible naturalism" (*Rich* 81).

16. Brown recalls that Cather "always showed impatience at the complaint that *My Antonia* is not precisely a novel. Why should it be?" (*Critical Biography* 199).

17. Rhoda Unger and Mary Crawford describe this phenomenon in their discussion of gender and cognitive developmental theory: "The son's identification with his father [. . .] progresses from identifying with a stereotyped masculine role to identifying with his father's own personification of that role. Feminine identification involves first identifying with a generalized female role, and then with the mother as an example of that role" (45). Chodorow summarizes the "role-training argument" of women's mothering as follows: "Girls [. . . .] 'identify' with their own mothers as they grow up, and this identification produces the girl as a mother" (30–31). She further points out that "girls in contemporary society develop a personal identification with their mother [. . .]. By contrast, boys develop a positional identification with aspects of the masculine role" (175).

18. According to Chodorow, "a girl's father provides a last ditch escape from maternal omnipotence, so a girl cannot risk driving him away" (195). In this light, James Herbert's irregular appearances in Melanctha's life are significant because he provides her with a model for breaking away from her mother (and therefore from the gender roles which female children reproduce).

19. Gail Bederman observes that the turn of the century saw an important ideological shift, one which links gender and race in much the same way that Stein does in "Melanctha": "as the middle class worked to remake manhood, many turned from gender to a related category—one which, like gender, also linked bodies, identities, and power. That category was race" (20).

20. Chodorow points out that "psychological and relational capacities for mothering" are socially transmitted from mothers to daughters. She further remarks that "the reproduction of women's mothering is the basis for the

reproduction of women's location and responsibilities in the domestic sphere" (208).

21. Sollors has similarly observed that "adopted ancestors are elective affinities who may help revolutionaries overcome their physical parents; instead of continuously acting merely as rebellious children, they may play the part of pious heirs" (*Beyond* 227).

22. The female *bildungsroman* generally requires a dead mother (or at the very least, an ineffectual one) as a catalyst for the heroine's coming of age.

23. Cf. the statement which Jim Burden makes to Antonia before separating from her for twenty years: "'Do you know, Antonia, since I've been away, I think of you more often than of anyone else in this part of the world. I'd have liked to have you for a sweetheart, or a wife, or my mother or my sister— anything that a woman can be to a man'" (206). Scholars have found this avowal problematic.

24. DuCille explains that critical standards facing Harlem Renaissance writers like Nella Larsen and Jessie Fauset, for example, insisted that "authentic blacks are southern, rural, and sexually uninhibited" (198). Hence "black women novelists [. . .] whose settings are the urban North and whose sub- jects are middle-class black women are not only dismissed in the name of the vernacular; they are condemned [. . .] for 'historical conservativism'" (195).

25. Benstock observes that Stein came to the conclusion that love was not mono- lithic as she explored her own sexual orientation: "To acknowledge a prefer- ence for women not only involved Stein in a renunciation of her previous beliefs, but urged her toward acceptance of various ways of loving. There was no one way that was 'right' and all others 'wrong'" (163).

26. Benstock points out that Adele in *Q.E.D.* "is described as 'queer' (perhaps original, interesting), accepted by her wealthy, indulged friends because she is different from them" (150). Given that Jeff is a conformist and a proto- proponent of racial uplift, it seems more likely that Stein uses "queer" here to invoke a gay sensibility. Lindemann notes that "during th[e] period [be- tween 1890 and the 1920s], 'queer' became a way of marking the differences between the still emerging categories of 'homosexuality and 'heterosexual- ity,'" further pointing out that early 20th century "queers" were "devoted to middle-class values of 'privacy, self-restraint, and lack of self-disclosure'" (*Queering* 2–3).

27. Other similarities include the ironic distance between the mature female au- thor and a young male character who in some ways seems to represent her view.

28. Burch observes the preponderance of "strong female characters" present in ethnic novels, "often called 'hired girls'" (58). The "hired girls" of *My Antonia* are domestic servants, upwardly-mobile European farm girls who come to town to earn money for their families; Cather was well aware that the term could also suggest prostitutes, but chose not to change it. Abraham also ad-

dresses the multiple meanings of the term "girls," pointing out that it has historically had class and racial overtones (xi-xii).

29. Stein herself had been exposed to such relationships in which one party serves and the other accepts servitude as her due. Indeed, she would eventually experience both sides firsthand, as Benstock observes, "although Alice began to tirelessly wait on Gertrude in the same ways that Etta [Cone] waited on [her sister] Claribel [. . .] the relationship between the Cone sisters already mirrored aspects of the relationship between Gertrude and Leo. Claribel, like Leo, was not attentive to Etta's need to be heard" (167).

30. In my initial discussion of the three lives within "Melanctha," I suggested that Rose Johnson is the third protagonist of the story. Nevertheless, since Jeff and Rose never meet—let alone have a love relationship—I think my interrogation of the love triangle concept stands on solid ground.

31. Reflecting on Stein's work as a whole, William Carlos Williams observes: "she has placed writing on a plane where it may deal unhampered with its own affairs, unburdened with scientific and philosophic lumber" (56).

32. DeKoven underscores the prevalence of naturalism, fatalism, and understatement in "Melanctha" (*Rich* 68).

33. In *Everybody's Autobiography*, Stein recalls the influence Eliot had on her early work: "I read a poem of George Eliot when I was very young I cannot often remember poetry but I can remember that" (119); "I wrote a little story [. . .] when I was at Radcliffe and being still under the influence of George Eliot I called it the Red Deeps" (157).

34. Blackmer, among others, argues that in "Melanctha," Stein "break[s] the deadlock she reached in *Q.E.D.*" (15).

35. This notion that Stein's approachable narrative texts of the 1930s and 1940s are somehow less artistically valuable than her difficult, avant-garde texts has persisted in Stein criticism. Writing in 1995, Marren still feels the need to counter such assumptions, as she asserts that "such sweeping dismissals of Stein's less alienating work [. . .] gloss over its considerable complexity" (150).

36. Chessman avers that *The Autobiography of Alice B. Toklas,* like any autobiography, "compels us to wonder, from the beginning, about the nature of the 'auto,' the self" (62).

37. Stein later notes in *Everybody's Autobiography* that, "it was funny about *The Autobiography of Alice B. Toklas,* writers well I suppose it is because writers write but anyway writers did not really mind anything one said about them, they might have minded something or liked something but since writing is writing and writers know that writing is writing they do not really suffer very much about anything that has been written" (32). Stein knows that writing cannot be truly mimetic, and she appreciates those of her fellow writers who do not hold her to misplaced standards.

38. By using the term "female-oriented" to describe Stein's text, I do not mean to suggest that she wrote for women or that her text is a "women's novel." To

me, "female-oriented" describes the use of cyclical (as opposed to linear) patterns and the inclusion of significant female figures (as opposed to Crusoe's male-only universe).

39. Stein's and Toklas's war stories are of a certain type, however. Marren notes the absence of details about the wounded (177).

40. Dollimore argues that "'I want to be in your place' collapses temporarily into 'I want you'; identification merges with desire, which is then a desire to be/displace the male as other" (267). Thinking about these issues in Larsen's *Passing*, Berlant muses, "I wonder whether Irene's xenophilia isn't indeed a desire to occupy, to experience the privileges of Clare's body, not to love or make love to her, but rather to wear her way of wearing her body, like a prosthesis, or a fetish?" ("National" 111). It would seem that Stein adopts Alice as an adaptive prosthesis. Further, Fuss utilizes Lacanian theory to suggest that "desire *for* the Other often manifests itself as desire to speak as Other, from the place of the Other (some would even say, *instead* of the Other)" (12). Thus we might argue that Stein's speaking as Alice is in fact a sublimation of her desire to possess Alice and/or to write openly about their love.

41. Wagner-Martin suggests that "much of the recognized machismo in Paris's expatriate culture might also have been a disguised anti-Semitism" (*Favored* 185).

42. Stein's brother Leo could be one example of such, according to Gass, who notes that after Alice's arrival in Paris, "Leo at last left to fulfill his promise as a failure, taking the Matisses and the Renoirs with him, and allowing his sister finally her leeway, her chance to define herself" (20).

43. Although the notion that a "Negro [. . .] cannot change" (206) represents a fixed conceptualization of identity, Stein offers a more fluid alternative elsewhere. Indeed, Stein seems to endorse the logic by which Cather's Godfrey St. Peter is thought by some to be a Spaniard. Speaking of an old friend, Stein reflects, "[Harold] Acton is now a Chinaman, he has been teaching in China a long time and I imagine he really does now really look and feel like a Chinaman some people can and do and he will and does and can" (232).

44. Variations on this motif include the following: "this makes propaganda and politics and religion" (47); "communism individualism propaganda politics and women" (77–78); "politics and geography and government and propaganda" (88); "communism and individualism and propaganda" (123); "politics and religion and propaganda and communism and individualism" (124); "propaganda and money and individualism and collectivism" (131).

45. Poirier sees Stein as writing within the tradition of Whitman. He points out that both made "claims to multiple identity" (28), and specifically compares *Song of Myself* to *The Geographical History of America*, noting that "divisions already overelaborated by Whitman are elaborated still further [by Stein]" (28).

46. M.H. Abrams offers the following definition: "a narrative is a story, whether in prose or verse, involving events, characters, and what the characters say

and do" (123). Whether *The Geographical History of America* includes "events," whether its personas are "characters," and whether anyone "does" anything is open to interpretation.

47. These kind of comparisons are also typical of ethnic literature, as Dearborn observes: "Stein's attempt to define the nature of the writer's relationship to language, human experience, and the American identity by writing about and around American heroes places her squarely in the American ethnic tradition [. . .]" (174).

48. The prototype for the "little dog" is eventually unveiled as "Basket a story" (198).

49. Issues of legibility are a hallmark of ethnic writing as well, as Bottomley asserts: "one of the problems [in ethnic literature] is whether and how such messages can be heard, seen and understood by reader" (64).

NOTES TO CHAPTER FOUR

1. Dodge was a friend of Cather's, as well. Woodress speculates that Cather "may have attended Mabel Dodge's famous salon on occasion, as everyone in Greenwich village seems to have gone there, but her friendship with Dodge came after she married Tony Luhan [1923] and was living in New Mexico" (*Literary Life* 236).

2. Speaking through Thea Kronberg's music instructor, Cather insists: "every artist makes himself born" (*SL* 153). Benstock similarly observes of Stein that "she wanted to create herself and the new century through her writing" (192), while Larsen "envisioned herself as a novelist" (Davis 282) and tried to arrange her life and history to fit that role. All three writers yearned towards self creation. First of all, both Cather and Larsen pushed forward the year of their birth. Secondly, all three named themselves: Cather called herself "Willie" and "William Cather, M.D."; Stein was both "Baby" and "Lovey"; Larsen went by many different names in her lifetime (Nellie Walker, Nellie Larson, Nellye Larson, Nella Larsen, Nella Larsen Imes, Nella Imes). Finally all three re-wrote history in their own terms: Cather decided she was named for her confederate soldier uncle as opposed to her aunt who died young; Stein's "autobiographies" are a far cry from non-fiction; and Larsen's dust jacket blurb for Knopf contains questionable and largely unverifiable information.

3. Also like Cather, Larsen would look back at her early stories and pronounce them "hack writing" (Larson xiii).

4. Culley speaks to this issue when she writes, "Black autobiography, and by extension ethnic autobiography, while it may do other things as well, including contesting the sign WOMAN, exhibit—even in its very being—black people in contestation with the content of the dominant culture's sign 'BLACK'" (9). Larsen's work, like Cather's and Stein's, is considered highly autobiographical.

5. Allan has pointed out that Larsen was particularly fluent in the work of her contemporary moderns (99). It is also clear that Larsen read William James and Sigmund Freud (Davis 311, 310).

6. These novels include *A Lost Lady* (1923), *The Professor's House* (1925), *My Mortal Enemy* (1926), and *Death Comes for the Archbishop* (1927).

7. What Nicholson and Seidman observe of Appiah's mixed lines of descent could also be said, with only minor modifications, of Larsen: "as the son of an African father and a European mother, and as someone who grew up in both Ghana and Britain and who now lives in the United States, Appiah was personally troubled by the way individual and national identity has been framed by the African/European binary [. . . which] leaves no 'home' or coherent cultural space for Appiah's own experience" (14).

8. Wall comments that Larsen "scorned purpose novels and mocked the sometimes sententious rhetoric of racial uplift" (117).

9. The Harlemites about and for whom Larsen would eventually write were also the potential customers for a bookshop Larsen contemplated opening. White suggested that the clientele would initially "be interested in keeping abreast of books by and about Negroes," adding that "in time you could get them [. . .] to buy books by Willa Cather [. . .]" (qtd. in Davis 217).

10. McLendon contends that geographical movement in *Quicksand* foregrounds "a recurring pattern of enclosure and escape" (154). Yohe concludes that "Helga's five journeys [. . .] leave her trapped" (55). I would add that a sixth journey, Chicago to Naxos, is implied and significant, even though we do not hear it narrated in the text.

11. Urgo additionally relates geographical crossing to cultural cross-fertilization (62).

12. The epigraph reads, "My old man died in a fine big house./ My ma died in a shack./ I wonder where I'm gonna die,/ Being neither white nor black?"

13. Cutter offers the following list: "an exotic Other, a committed teacher, an art object, a devout Christian, a proponent of racial uplift, a dutiful mother" (75).

14. Helga's restlessness and inability to remain satisfied with any given situation for an extended period of time find an analog in a version of the legend of the Wandering Jew. Stableford notes that "the Wandering Jew most frequently figures in German representations as the most perfect possible embodiment of the weltschmerz (world-weariness) in which Goethe's Werther had taught a whole generation to revel" (10).

15. Helga's growing impatience with Naxos links her to Melanctha Herbert, who seems to go through a pattern of waxing interest for the first year of a relationship, followed by waning interest for the second.

16. Ironically, so is Larsen. Although Larsen mocks the Naxos paradigm, she is not as much of an iconoclast as she might have hoped, as Davis explains: "an assimilationist and a social climber, Larsen took more pride in her inclusion in interracial gatherings than she did in all-black affairs" (232).

17. Davis observes that "Larsen frequently associated with a literary and theater crowd that included lesbians, homosexuals, and bisexuals who were open in their sexual preferences" (325).

18. Cather needed to make money at her art. Indeed, her perception of Houghton Mifflin as not advertising her books aggressively enough was one factor in her decision to switch to Knopf (E. Lewis 108). Lilienfeld further notes that Cather wanted fame in the artistic world, but did not disdain a money-paying audience (50). In *The Professor's House,* however, Cather explores some of the negative ramifications of financial success. Stein had a small inherited income, but was by no means wealthy. She did not make money from her writing until the publication of *The Autobiography of Alice B. Toklas,* and she ponders the effect of money on her art at length in *Everybody's Autobiography.*

19. Larsen definitely knew her Conrad. Davis also suggests that "Larsen depended [. . .] on the modernist concept of the unreliable observer as represented by Joseph Conrad in *Heart of Darkness*" (311).

20. McDowell applies this notion even more broadly, as she observes that "the structure of the novel is a vertical line downward" (xxii).

21. While Helga retrospectively rues the novice teachers' impulse of "doing good to their fellow men" (5), she uses almost exactly the same words to describe her initial approach to the "children" of her husband's church.

22. Jacobs's narrator keeps the welfare of her children foremost in her mind: "I had a woman's pride, and a mother's love for my children; and I resolved that out of the darkness of this hour a brighter dawn should rise for them" (130). Male-authored slave narratives generally emphasize a solitary hero who escapes from slavery and regains his manhood (the classic example being Frederick Douglass) whereas female-authored narratives emphasize interconnectedness and family ties.

23. Clemmen, on the other hand, sees *Quicksand* as a text in diametrical opposition to the *bildungsroman,* and he insists that "instead of a bildungsroman that feeds on experience, we have . . . a narrative that feeds on difference" (460).

24. The phrase belongs to Rachel Blau DuPlessis. See note 14 in chapter three.

25. Cutter disagrees, arguing that Helga "attempts to use 'passing' as a way of finding a unitary sense of identity—a sense of identity structured around *one* role, a role that somehow corresponds to her 'essential self'" (75).

26. Wall notes that in both of Larsen's novels, tragic mulattos discover "the impossibility of self-definition" (89). Carby comments that "her particular use of the figure of the mulatto allowed Larsen to negotiate issues of race as they were articulated by both white and black" (173). Both Washington and Berzon address the mulatto figure in their titles: "The Mulatta Trap" and *Neither White Nor Black.* Yohe argues that Clare is not tragic or pitiful like typical mulatto (71), while McManus sees Larsen's use of the mulatta figure as "a mask for the exploration of a female sensibility" (16).

27. Hall's novel was published the same year as *Quicksand,* and so I am not suggesting influence so much as confluence.

28. The legend of the Wandering Jew also seems to have its roots in the Biblical narrative of Cain's exile (Stableford 1). Furthermore, in Matthew Lewis's *The Monk,* the Wandering Jew bears a Cain-like mark, an "image of a burning cross [. . .] emblazoned on his forehead" (Stableford 11).

29. Lowe similarly observes that "the American nation is founded on myths of mobility that disavow the histories of both the immobility of ghettoization and the forced dislocations of Asian Americans" (82).

30. The epigraph reads, "One three centuries removed/ From the scenes his fathers loved,/ Spicy grove, cinnamon tree,/ What is Africa to me?"

31. From this opening scene, Davis concludes, "the relationship between the concealed and the revealed, announced by Clare's letter to Irene [. . .] is more complex because the central consciousness, though not rendered by means of a first-person narrator, is unreliable" (324). The use of an unreliable, non-first-person narrator links Larsen to Cather, who employed a similar narrative strategy with Niel Herbert (*A Lost Lady*) and Godfrey St. Peter (*The Professor's House*).

32. In the realm of sexual orientation, "gay-dar," the notion that lesbians and gays possess an enigmatic and automatic ability to recognize fellow homosexuals on sight (whereas heterosexuals presumably cannot), works on the same principle. This is similarly embodied in the adage, "it takes one to know one."

33. Cf. Helga's entering Anne Grey's house under questionable pretenses, being accepted warmly, and "feel[ing] like a criminal" (42).

34. In this way, Clare is figured like Stein's Melanctha Herbert, who is mysterious and who wanders like her mother before her (*TL* 50, 52).

35. See Sollors *Neither Black Nor White Yet Both* 248–50 for a thorough elaboration of the double standard.

36. An earlier example is when Helga complains that the Danes look at her, "'as if I had horns'" (70). Gilroy notes that Martin Delany "looks immediately to the Jewish experiences of dispersal as a model for comprehending the history of black Americans" (23). Gilroy also points out that the diaspora concept provides link between Jews and blacks and has ramifications for "the status of ethnic identity, the power of cultural nationalism, and the manner in which carefully preserved social histories of ethnocidal suffering can function to supply ethical and political legitimacy" (207).

37. Several critics raise the possibility that Brian is a homosexual. McDowell reminds the reader that he and Irene have a "sexless marriage" (xxiii), while Blackmer characterizes Brian as "covertly homosexual" (18).

38. Cf. Helga's husband, the Reverend Mr. Pleasant Green, who "consumed his food, even the softest varieties [. . .] audibly" (*Q* 121).

39. Reflecting on the same topic, Fuss offers the following rhetorical questions: "if 'race' is not a biological feature, then what kind of attribute or category is

it: psychological, historical, anthropological, sociological, legal [. . .]? Is race a matter of birth? of culture? both? neither? What, exactly, are the criteria for racial identity?" (73–4).

40. Young adapts Sartre's concept of seriality as a means of talking about "woman" as a category without resorting to essentialism (188).

41. The term "practico-inert" comes from Sartre by way of Jameson.

42. If Irene is like Jeff Campbell and Clare is like Melanctha, then Brian is like Stein herself. Brian is consigned to the life that Stein felt fortunate to be freed from at the eleventh hour: "'Lord! How I hate sick people, and their stupid, meddling families, and smelly, dirty rooms, and climbing filthy steps in dark hallways'" (*P* 186).

43. Sollors makes the following observation: "because the novel's attention is focused on two women, the eroticized gaze that is conventional when male-imagined narrators describe mixed-race women [. . .] here is directed from a *female* center of consciousness toward the mysterious *woman* who passes permanently, and the (otherwise conventional) description therefore calls attention to itself" (*Neither* 276). DuCille sees *Passing* as asking crucial questions about the power politics of the gaze: "who owns the gaze? is the gaze inherently masculine or essentially sexual? what happens when women gaze upon each other? is the very act of gazing upon the female body an appropriation of the masculine and an invocation of the erotic? is there a grammar of the female gaze?" (213).

44. See note 37.

45. See chapter three, note 11.

46. Marren adapts Peter Rabinowitz's concept of social versus rhetorical passing to Larsen's novel, arguing that Irene performs social ("to mislead people into thinking you are something that you are not"), while Clare performs rhetorical ("flaunting your disguise in a context in which you know that it will *fool only some people*") (114).

47. McCoy and others have read Hugh Wentworth as a thinly-disguised representation of Carl Van Vechten (83).

48. Larsen's name was changed when she was a child, and she changed it many times subsequently (see Davis 25, 60, 173, 443).

49. Cf. Antonia's comment to Jim: "'If I live here, like you, that is different. Things will be easy for you. But they will be hard for us'" (*MA* 90).

50. The latter term belongs to Georg Simmel; see chapter two, note 2. Speaking of Larsen herself, Davis comments that she "bore the imprint [. . .] of transformations of identity, possible given the fluidity of western and immigrant lives in an expanding city" (4).

51. Cf. Edna's declaration, "'I would give up the unessential; I would give money, I would give my life for my children; but I wouldn't give myself'" (Chopin 48). Larsen's engagement with Chopin is quite clear. In both *Quicksand* and *Passing*, Larsen explores the tension between a mother's duty to her children

and her quest to achieve self-actualization. Furthermore, Chopin and Larsen share in the attempt to represent an independent, sexual woman. Such a subject position cannot be successfully maintained for any length of time by Edna, Helga, or Clare.

52. McCoy deems *Passing* "the emblematic tale of Irene Redfield's colonization of Clare Kendry" (71), suggesting that we might read Clare as being as much in bondage to Irene as to her husband and "master," John Bellew, in addition to being oppressed by the ideologies or social positions that Irene and Bellew represent.

53. Cather's later novels have finally received critical attention and acclaim within the last ten years, serving as the subject of book-length studies and the focus of academic conferences.

NOTES TO CHAPTER FIVE

1. In "My First Novels [There Were Two]," Cather deems *Alexander's Bridge* "a studio picture . . . made out of 'interesting material'" and assesses that "the impressions . . . were genuine, but they were very shallow." When she wrote *O Pioneers!*, on the other hand, Cather found her authentic voice and her proper subject and setting: "Here there was no arranging or 'inventing'; everything was spontaneous and took its own place, right or wrong. This was like taking a ride through a familiar country on a horse that knew the way, on a fine morning when you felt like riding" (*OW* 91–93).

2. Pers goes so far as to suggest that Cather's phraseology shows that remembered turns of speech "came back as sound rather than in writing" (43).

3. Davis comments that during the 1930s, Larsen's "eccentricities were manifested in a fear of new places, an obsession with wearing a hat at all times, a reliance on medication, a delusion about her whiteness, and a fantasy of her youth in a loving family" (16).

4. Skaggs argues that St. Peter is Cather's mouthpiece in this instance, expressing Cather's thoughts in his statement (11).

5. Anderson defines a nation as "an imagined political community[,] . . . imagined as both inherently limited and sovereign." He elaborates that "imagined" refers to the fact that an image of unity or bondedness exists independent of physical meeting. "Limited" acknowledges that nations have boundaries, while "sovereign" suggests autonomy and freedom. Finally, "community" reflects the ideal of "a deep, horizontal comradeship" (6–7).

6. Fetterley and Pryse observe that "for Cather, the story of Vickie's move outside the home, beyond female community, and into the larger male-dominated world of the university represents the road of development for women of her generation" (596).

7. Bourne offers a similar proposal: "In a world which has dreamed of internationalism, we find that we have all unawares been building up the first international nation. . . . What we have achieved has been rather a cosmopolitan

federation of national colonies, of foreign cultures, from which the sting of devastating competition has been removed" (276).

8. Marren suggests that "expatriation offers Stein the same opportunity to recreate herself as the exemplary citizen of an idealized 'imagined community'" (182).

9. Critics both perpetuate (Carlin 175; Swift 107–120) and react against (Lee, "Bridge" 40) the idea that Cather's work is nostalgic or sentimental. DeKoven classifies Stein's texts as "avant-garde," a category which includes the incoherent (68, 24). DuCille notes that Larsen (and Fauset) were dismissed by many critics for what appeared to be "historical conservativism" in their works (195). Stein came under the most criticism for "lying" by writing Alice's autobiography, but Stimpson points out that the same could be said for just about any text: "*The Autobiography* does lie. What packaging does not?" ("Lie" 153–54).

10. Warren French compares Cather's writing to Cezanne's work (241–42), while Cather acknowledges Flaubert's influence in "A Chance Meeting" (*NUF* 3–42).

11. Bennett states that in Cather's case changing her birth year was symptomatic of "fury—and a resentment that time, her greatest enemy, could effect such changes" as her father's death (28–29). Davis sees Larsen's appropriation of an 1893 birth date as a sign that Larsen wanted to align herself with progress, modernity, and the booming American metropolis, as symbolized by the Chicago World's Fair (4).

Bibliography

Abraham, Julie. *Are Girls Necessary? Lesbian Writing and Modern Histories.* New York: Routledge, 1996.

Abrams, Jim. "Immigration to Cost States Seven Seats, Study Claims." *Atlanta Journal-Constitution* 7 Oct. 1998: A15.

Abrams, M.H. *A Glossary of Literary Terms.* 6th ed. Fort Worth: Harcourt Brace College Publishers, 1993.

Allan, Tuzyline Jita. "The Death of Sex and the Soul in *Mrs. Dalloway* and Nella Larsen's *Passing.*" *Virginia Woolf: Lesbian Readings.* Eds. Eileen Barrett and Patricia Cramer. New York: New York UP, 1997. 95–113.

Ammons, Elizabeth. *Conflicting Stories: American Women Writers at the Turn into the Twentieth Century.* New York: Oxford UP, 1991.

Anderson, Benedict. *Imagined Communities.* 1983. London: Verso, 1995.

Appiah, Kwame Anthony. "African identities." Nicholson and Seidman 103–115.

Arendt, Hannah. Introduction. *Illuminations.* By Walter Benjamin. 1955. Ed. Hannah Arendt. Trans. Harry Zohn. New York: Harcourt, Brace and World, Inc, 1968. 1–55.

Arnold, Marilyn. *Willa Cather's Short Fiction.* Athens, OH: Ohio UP, 1935.

Baldwin, James. *Another Country.* 1960. New York: Vintage Books, 1993.

Balibar, Etienne. "Ambiguous Universality." *differences.* 7.1 (Spring 1995): 48–74.

Baraka, Amiri. "Somebody Blew Up America." *Amiri Baraka* 14 December 2003 <www.amiribaraka.com/somebook.html>

Bederman, Gail. *Manliness and Civilization.* Chicago: University of Chicago Press, 1995.

Ben Isaiah, Rabbi Abraham and Rabbi Benjamin Sharfman. *The Pentateuch and Rashi's Commentary: A Linear Translation into English.* New York: S.S. and R. Publishing, Inc., 1950.

Benjamin, Walter. *Illuminations.* Ed. Hannah Arendt. 1955. Trans. Harry Zohn. New York: Harcourt, Brace and World, Inc, 1968.

Bennett, Mildred R. *The World of Willa Cather.* New York: Dodd, Mead and Co., 1951.

Benstock, Shari. *Women of the Left Bank: Paris, 1900–1940.* Austin: University of Texas Press, 1986.

Berlant, Lauren. "National Brands/ National Body: *Imitation of Life.*" *Comparative American Identities.* Ed. Hortense J. Spillers. New York: Routledge, 1991. 110–140.

—. *The Queen of America Goes to Washington City.* Durham: Duke UP, 1997.

Berzon, Judith. *Neither White Nor Black.* New York: New York UP, 1978.

Bevington, David. Introduction. "The Taming of the Shrew." By William Shakespeare. *The Complete Works of Shakespeare.* 4th ed. Ed. David Bevington. New York: Harper Collins, 1992. 108–110.

Blackmer, Corinne E. "'The Inexplicable Presence of the Thing Not Named': Intersections of Race and Sexuality in Twentieth Century American Women's Writing." Diss. University of California, Los Angeles, 1992.

Blair, John G. *Modular America: Cross-Cultural Perspectives on the Emergence of an American Way.* New York: Greenwood Press, 1988.

Blankley, Elyse. "Beyond the 'Talent of Knowing': Gertrude Stein and the New Woman." M. Hoffman 196–209.

Bloom, Harold, ed. *Antonia.* New York: Chelsea House Publishers, 1991.

____. "Introduction." 1–3.

Bodenheimer, Rosemarie. *The Real Life of Mary Ann Evans: George Eliot, Her Letters and Fiction.* Ithaca, NY: Cornell University Press, 1994.

Bogan, Louise. "American Classic." Schroeter 126–133.

Bottomley, Gillian. *From Another Place: Migration and the Politics of Culture.* Cambridge: Cambridge University Press, 1992.

Bourne, Randolph. "Trans-National America." In*"The History of a Literary Radical" and Other Papers.* New York: S.A. Russell, 1956. 260–84.

Boynton, Percy H. "Percy H. Boynton." Bloom 7–8.

Breslin, James E. "Gertrude Stein and the Problems of Autobiography." M. Hoffman 149–59.

Brown, E.K. *Willa Cather: A Critical Biography.* Completed by Leon Edel. New York: Knopf, 1953.

____. "Willa Cather." Schroeter 72–86.

Burch, Betty Ann. "Us and Them: Personal Reflections on Ethnic Literature." Walch 55–62.

Butler, Judith. *Bodies That Matter.* New York: Routledge,1993.

____. *Gender Trouble: Feminism and the Subversion of Identity.* New York: Routledge, 1990.

Cantor, Norman. *Twentieth-Century Culture: Modernism to Deconstruction.* New York: Peter Lang, 1988.

Carby, Hazel V. *Reconstructing Womanhood: the Emergence of the Afro-American Woman Novelist.* New York: Oxford UP, 1987.

Carlin, Deborah. *Cather, Canon, and the Politics of Reading.* Amherst: U of Massachusetts P, 1992.

Cather, Willa. *The Autobiography of S.S. McClure.* 1914. Lincoln: U of Nebraska P, 1997.

____. "The Best Years." 1948. *Collected Stories*. New York: Vintage Books, 1992. 367–95.

____. *Death Comes for the Archbishop*. 1927. New York: Vintage Books, 1990.

____. "The Diamond Mine."1920. *Collected Stories*. New York: Vintage Books, 1992. 102–36.

____. "Old Mrs. Harris." 1932. *Collected Stories*. New York: Vintage Books, 1992. 262–314.

____. *A Lost Lady*. 1923. New York: Vintage Books, 1990.

____. *Lucy Gayheart*. 1935. New York: Vintage Books, 1976.

____. "The Marriage of Phaedra." 1905. *Collected Stories*. New York: Vintage Books, 1992. 42–59.

____. *My Antonia*. 1918. Boston: Houghton Mifflin Company, 1988.

____. *My Mortal Enemy*. 1926. New York: Vintage Books, 1990.

____. "Neighbour Rosicky." 1932. *Collected Stories*. New York: Vintage Books, 1992. 231–61.

____. *Not Under Forty*. 1936. Lincoln: University of Nebraska Press, 1988.

____. *O Pioneers!* 1913. New York: Signet Classic, 1989.

____. *The Professor's House*. 1925. New York: Vintage Books, 1973.

____. *Sapphira and the Slave Girl*. 1940. New York: Vintage Books, 1975.

____. "Scandal." 1920. *Collected Stories*. New York: Vintage Books, 1992. 153–69.

____. *The Song of the Lark*. 1915. New York: Signet Classic, 1991.

____. *Willa Cather in Person*. Ed. L. Brent Bohlke. Lincoln: University of Nebraska Press, 1986.

____. *Willa Cather on Writing*. Ed. Stephen Tennant. Lincoln: University of Nebraska Press, 1988.

Chessman, Harriet Scott. *The Public is Invited to Dance: Representation, the Body, and Dialogue in Gertrude Stein*. Stanford: Stanford UP, 1989.

Chodorow, Nancy. *The Reproduction of Mothering: Psychoanalysis and the Sociology of Gender*. Berkeley, CA: U of California P, 1978.

Chopin, Kate. *The Awakening*. 1899. Ed. Margaret Culley. New York: W.W. Norton and Co., 1976.

Clemmen, Yves. "Nella Larsen's *Quicksand:* A Narrative of Difference." *CLA Journal* 40.4 (1997): 458–466.

Collins, Patricia Hill. *Black Feminist Thought: Knowledge, Consciousness, and the Politics of Empowerment*. Boston: Unwin Hyman, 1990.

Commons, John. *Races and Immigrants in America*. 1920. New York: Macmillan, 1924.

Conrad, Joseph. *Heart of Darkness*. 1899. *The Norton Anthology of English Literature*. 6th ed. Voume 2. Ed. M.H. Abrams, et al. New York: W. W. Norton and Company, 1993. 1759–1817.

Cooper, Clara B. "Clara B. Cooper." Bloom 32–34.

Coward, Rosalind. "This Novel Changes Women's Lives: Are Women's Novels Feminist Novels?" *Feminist Review* 5 (1980). Rpt. in *The New Feminist Criticism*. Ed. Elaine Showalter. New York: Pantheon Books, 1985. 225–39.

Culley, Margo. "What a Piece of Work is 'Woman'! An Introduction." *American Women's Autobiography: Fea(s)ts of Memory.* Ed. Margo Culley. Madison: the U of Wisconsin P, 1992. 3–31.

Cutter, Martha J. "Sliding Significations: Passing as a Narrative and Textual Strategy in Nella Larsen's Fiction." *Passing and the Fictions of Identity.* Ed. Elaine K. Ginsberg. Durham: Duke UP, 1996. 75–100.

Daiches, David. "The Short Stories." Schroeter 87–95.

Davis, Thadious M. *Nella Larsen, Novelist of the Harlem Renaissance: A Woman's Life Unveiled.* Baton Rouge: Lousiana State UP, 1994.

Dearborn, Mary V. *Pocahontas's Daughters: Gender and Ethnicity in American Culture.* New York: Oxford UP, 1986.

Defoe, Daniel. *The Life and Adventures of Robinson Crusoe.* 1719. New York: Penguin Books, 1985.

DeKoven, Marianne. Introduction to "Gertrude Stein." *The Gender of Modernism.* Ed. Bonnie Kime Scott. Bloomington: Indiana University Press, 1990. 479–488.

_____. *Rich and Strange: Gender, History, Modernism.* Princeton: Princeton UP, 1991.

De Lorris, Guillaume. *The Romance of the Rose.* Ed. Frances Horgan. New York: Oxford UP, 1994.

Dollimore, Jonathan. *Sexual Dissidence.* New York: Clarendon, 1991.

Doyle, Laura. "The Flat, the Round, and Gertrude Stein: Race and the Shape of Modern(ist) History." *Modernism/Modernity* 7 (2000): 249–71.

Dreiser, Theodore. *Sister Carrie.* 1900. ed. Donald Pizer. New York: W.W. Norton, 1991.

DuCille, Ann. "Blues Notes on Black Sexuality: Sex and the Texts of Jessie Fauset and Nella Larsen." *American Sexual Politics.* Ed. John C. Fout and Maura Shaw Tantillo. Chicago: University of Chicago Press, 1993. 193–219.

DuPlessis, Rachel Blau. *Writing Beyond the Ending.* Bloomington: Indiana UP, 1985.

Eagleton, Terry. *Literary Theory.* Minneapolis: U of Minnesota P, 1983.

Edelman, Lee. *Homographesis: Essays in Gay Literary and Cultural Theory.* New York: Routledge, 1994.

Eliot, George. *The Mill on the Floss.* 1860. Boston: Houghton Mifflin Co., 1925.

Emerson, Ralph Waldo. "Self Reliance." *The Heath Anthology of American Literature,* Volume 1. Eds. Paul Lauter, et. al. Lexington, MA: D.C. Heath and Co, 1990. 1511–28.

Ende, Larry. "Inventing Daily Discourse: Gertrude Stein and Invention in Modernist Literature." Diss. State University of New York at Buffalo, 1993.

Fairchild, Henry Pratt. *The Melting-Pot Mistake.* Boston: Little, Brown, and Company, 1926.

Faulkner, William. *Requiem for a Nun.* 1951. New York: Vintage Books, 1975.

_____. *The Sound and the Fury.* 1929. New York: Vintage Books, 1987.

Ferraro, Thomas J. *Ethnic Passages: Literary Immigrants in Twentieth-Century America.* Chicago: University of Chicago Press, 1993.

Fetterley, Judith. "*My Antonia,* Jim Burden and the Dilemma of the Lesbian Writer."
Bloom 132–47.

Fetterley, Judith and Marjorie Pryse, eds. Introduction to Willa Cather. *American Women Regionalists, 1850–1910.* New York: W.W. Norton, 1992. 593–96.

Fifer, Elizabeth. "Guardians and Witnesses: Narrative Technique in Gertrude Stein's *Useful Knowledge.*" M. Hoffman 160–171.

French, Warren. "Directions: Additional Commentary." Slote and Faulkner 238–247.

Frost, Robert. "The Oven Bird." 1916. *The Norton Anthology of Modern Poetry.* 2nd edition. Eds. Richard Ellman and Robert O'Clair. New York: W.W. Norton and Company, 1988. 249.

Fuchs, Lawrence H. *The American Kaleidoscope: Race, Ethnicity, and the Civic Culture.* Hanover: UP of New England, 1990.

Fuss, Diana. *Essentially Speaking.* New York: Routledge, 1989.

Gallup, Donald, ed. *The Flowers of Friendship: Letters Written to Gertrude Stein.* New York: Knopf, 1953.

Gambrell, Alice. *Women Intellectuals, Modernism, and Difference.* Cambridge, Cambridge UP, 1997.

Gass, William H. Introduction. *The Geographical History of America.* By Gertrude Stein. 1936. Baltimore: Johns Hopkins UP, 1995. 3–42.

Gilligan, Carol. *In a Different Voice: Psychological Theory and Women's Development.* Cambridge, MA: Harvard UP, 1982.

Gilroy, Paul. *The Black Atlantic: Modernity and Double Consciousness.* Cambridge: Harvard UP, 1993.

Ginsberg, Elaine K., ed. Introduction. *Passing and the Fictions of Identity.* Durham: Duke UP, 1996. 1–18.

Gleason, Philip. "American Identity and Americanization." In *Concepts of Ethnicity.* Eds. William Petersen, Michael Novak, and Philip Gleason. Cambridge, MA: The Belknap Press of Harvard UP, 1982. 57–143.

____. *Speaking of Diversity: Language and Ethnicity in Twentieth-Century America.* Baltimore: The Johns Hopkins UP, 1992.

Golden, Marita. Foreword. *An Intimation of Things Distant: the Collected Fiction of Nella Larsen.* Ed. Charles Larson. New York: Doubleday, 1992. vii–x.

Grumbach, Doris. Foreword. *My Antonia.* By Willa Cather. 1918. Boston: Houghton Mifflin, 1988.

Haas, Robert Bartlett, ed. *A Primer for the Gradual Understanding of Gertrude Stein.* Los Angeles: Black Sparrow Press, 1971.

Hall, Radclyffe. *The Well of Loneliness.* 1928. New York: Anchor Books. 1990.

Hammond, Thomas. "Paris-New York: Venues of Migration and the Exportation of African-American Culture." *CLA Journal* 41.2 (1997): 135–146.

Hanscombe, Gillian and Virginia L. Smyers. *Writing for their Lives: the Modernist Women, 1910–1940.* London: the Women's Press, 1987.

Heilbrun, Carolyn G. *Reinventing Womanhood.* New York: W.W. Norton and Co., 1979.

Helvie, Sherri. "Willa Cather and Brandon Teena: the Politics of Passing." *Women and Language* 20 (1997): 35–40.

Hicks, Granville. "The Case Against Willa Cather." Schroeter 139–147.

Hively, Evelyn Helmick. *Sacred Fire: Willa Cather's Novel Cycle.* Lanham: UP of America, 1994.

Hoffman, Karen A. "Identity Crossings and the Autobiographical Act in Willa Cather's *My Antonia." Arizona Quarterly* 58 (2002): 25–50.

Hoffman, Michael J., ed. *Critical Essays on Gertrude Stein.* Boston: C. K. Hall & Co., 1986.

Horgan, Frances. Introduction. *The Romance of the Rose.* By Guillaume De Lorris. New York: Oxford UP, 1994.

Huggins, Nathan. *Harlem Renaissance.* New York: Oxford UP, 1971.

Imbs, Bravig. From *Confessions of Another Young Man.* Simon 119–28.

Jackson, Laura Riding. "The Word-Play of Gertrude Stein." M. Hoffman 240–60.

Jacobs, Harriet. *Incidents in the Life of a Slave Girl.* 1861. New York: Oxford UP, 1988.

The Jerusalem Bible. Ed. Harold Fisch. Jerusalem: Koren Publishers, 1992.

Kalaidjian, Walter. *American Culture Between the Wars.* New York: Columbia UP, 1993.

Kallen, Horace M. *Cultural Pluralism and the American Idea: An Essay in Social Philosophy.* Philadelphia: U of Pennsylvania P, 1956.

Kaplan, Amy. *The Social Construction of American Realism.* Chicago: the University of Chicago Press, 1988.

Kaye, Frances W. *Isolation and Masquerade.* New York: Peter Lang, 1993.

Kazin, Alfred. "Willa Cather." Schroeter 161–170.

Kelly, Douglas. *Medieval Imagination: Rhetoric and the Poetry of Courtly Love.* Madison, WI: the U of Wisconsin P, 1978.

Krutch, Joseph Wood. "Second Best: *The Professor's House.*" 1925. Schroeter 54–56.

Labi, Nadya. "Hue Must Be Joking." *Time* 2 Nov. 1998: 8.

Lachman, Arthur. "Gertrude Stein as I Knew Her." Simon 3–9.

Larsen, Nella. "From Nella Larsen." 1 February 1928. Gallup 215–16.

_____. *Quicksand and Passing.* Ed. Deborah McDowell. New Brunswick, NJ: Rutgers UP, 1986.

Larson, Charles R. Introduction. *An Intimation of Things Distant: the Collected Fiction of Nella Larsen.* Ed. Charles Larson. New York: Doubleday, 1992. xi-xxi.

Lee, Hermione. "Cather's Bridge: Anglo-American Crossings in Willa Cather." *Forked Tongues?* Eds. Ann Massa and Alistair Stead. London: Longman, 1994. 38–56.

_____. "The Road of Destiny." Bloom 161–71.

Leeming, David. *James Baldwin: A Biography.* New York: Knopf, 1994.

Lewis, David Levering. *When Harlem Was in Vogue.* New York: Oxford UP, 1979.

Lewis, Edith. *Willa Cather Living.* New York: Alfred A. Knopf, 1953.

Lilienfeld, Jane. Introduction to "Willa Cather." *The Gender of Modernism.* Ed. Bonnie Kime Scott. Bloomington: Indiana University Press, 1990. 46–53.

Lindemann, Marilee. "Fear of a Queer Prairie: Figures of the Body and/as the Nation in Willa Cather's Early Fiction." *Willa Cather Pioneer Memorial Newletter and Review* 42:2 (Fall 1998): 30–35.

____. *Willa Cather: Queering America.* New York: Columbia UP, 1999.

Lowe, Lisa. *Immigrant Acts: On Asian American Cultural Politics.* Durham: Duke UP, 1996.

Marren, Susan Marie. "Passing for American: Establishing American Identity in the Work of James Weldon Johnson, F. Scott Fitzgerald, Nella Larsen and Gertrude Stein." Diss. University of Michigan, 1995.

Martin, Wendy, ed. Introduction. *New Essays on The Awakening.* New York: Cambridge UP, 1988. 1–31.

Massa, Ann and Alistair Stead, eds. Introduction. *Forked Tongues?* London: Longman, 1994. 1–20.

McCoy, Beth A. "'Do I Look Like This or This?': Race, Gender, Class, and Sexuality in the Novels of Jessie Fauset, Carl Van Vechten, Nella Larsen, and F. Scott Fitzgerald." Diss. University of Delaware, 1995.

McDowell, Deborah. Introduction. *Quicksand and Passing.* By Nella Larsen. Ed. Deborah McDowell. New Brunswick, NJ: Rutgers UP, 1986. ix–xxxv.

McLendon, Jacquelyn Y. "Self-Representation as Art in the Novels of Nella Larsen." *Gender and Genre in Literature.* Ed. Janice Morgan and Colette T. Hall. New York: Garland Publishing, Inc., 1991. 149–168.

McManus, Mary Hairston. "African-American Modernism in the Novels of Jessie Fauset and Nella Larsen." Diss. University of Maryland, 1992.

Melville, Herman. "The Paradise of Bachelors and the Tartarus of Maids." 1855. *The Heath Anthology of American Literature,* Volume 1. Eds. Paul Lauter, et al. Lexington, MA: D.C. Heath and Company, 1990. 2447–2464.

Middleton, Jo Ann. *Willa Cather's Modernism: A Study of Style and Technique.* Rutherford, NJ: Farleigh Dickinson UP, 1990.

Moorhead, Elizabeth. "The Novelist." Schroeter 101–13.

Morgan, Janice. "Subject to Subject/ Voice to Voice: Twentieth-Century Autobiographical Fiction by Women Writers." Introduction. *Gender and Genre in Literature.* Ed. Janice Morgan and Colette T. Hall. New York: Garland Publishing, Inc., 1991. 3–19.

Morrison, Toni. *Beloved.* 1987. New York: Plume Books, 1988.

Munsterberg, Hugo. *The Americans.* Trans. Edwin B. Holt. New York: McClure, Phillips, and Co., 1904.

Murphy, John J. "John J. Murphy." Bloom 47–52.

____. "The Modernist Conversion of Willa Cather's Professor." *The Calvinist Roots of the Modern Era.* Eds. Aliki Barnstone, Michael Tomasek Manson and Carol J. Singley. Hanover: UP of New England, 1997. 53–72.

Nelson, Robert J. *Willa Cather and France: in Search of the Lost Language.* Urbana: U of Illinois P, 1988.

Nettels, Elsa. "Gender and First Person Narration in Willa Cather's Fiction." *Speaking the Other Self.* Ed. Jeanne Campbell Reesman. Athens: U of Georgia P, 1997. 165–175.

Nicholson, Linda and Steven Seidman, Eds. *Social Postmodernism: Beyond Identity Politics.* Cambridge: Cambridge UP, 1995.

_____. Introduction. Nicholson and Seidman 1–35.

Novak, Michael. "Pluralism in Humanistic Perspective." In *Concepts of Ethnicity.* Eds. William Petersen, Michael Novak, and Philip Gleason. Cambridge, MA: The Belknap Press of Harvard UP, 1982. 27–56.

O'Brien, Sharon. "Becoming Noncanonical: the Case Against Willa Cather." *Reading in America.* Ed. Cathy Davidson. Baltimore: Johns Hopkins UP, 1989. 240–58.

_____. "Sharon O'Brien." Bloom 52–54.

_____. *Willa Cather: the Emerging Voice.* New York: Oxford UP, 1987.

Palumbo-Liu, David. "Universalisms and Minority Culture." *differences.* 7.1 (Spring 1995): 188–208.

Park, Robert. "The City: Suggestions for the Investigation of Human Behavior in the Urban Environment." *Classic Essays on the Culture of Cities.* Ed. Richard Sennett. New York: Appleton-Century-Crofts, 1969. 91–130.

Pers, Mona. *Willa Cather's Swedes.* Vasteras: Malardalen UP, 1995.

Petersen, William. "Concepts of Ethnicity." In *Concepts of Ethnicity.* Eds. William Petersen, Michael Novak, and Philip Gleason. Cambridge, MA: The Belknap Press of Harvard UP, 1982. 1–26.

Pierpont, Claudia Roth. "The Mother of Confusion." *The New Yorker* 11 May 1998: 80–89.

"Poetry and Tragedy." Editorial. *USA Today* 24 September 2001. 14 December 2003 <http://www.usatoday.com/news/opinion/2001–09–25-ncguest1.htm>.

Poirier, Richard. "Manly Agitations." *The New Republic* 8 June 1998: 25–34.

Porter, Katharine Anne. "Everbody is a Real One." M. Hoffman 49–52.

"Possession." *Webster's Ninth New Collegiate Dictionary.* 1989.

Preston, John Hyde. "A Conversation With Gertrude Stein." Simon 154–65.

Rattansi, Ali. "Just framing: ethnicities and racisms in a 'postmodern' framework." Nicholson and Seidman 250–286.

Redinger, Ruby V. *George Eliot: The Emergent Self.* New York: Alfred A. Knopf, 1975.

Rich, Adrienne. "Compulsory Heterosexuality and Lesbian Existence." 1980. *Blood Bread and Poetry: Selected Prose 1979–1985.* New York: W.W. Norton and Company, 1986. 23–75.

_____. *Your Native Land, Your Life.* New York: W.W. Norton and Company, 1986.

Richards, Grant. "From Grant Richards." 27 September 1911. Gallup 53–54.

Robbins, Bruce. "The Weird Heights: On Cosmopolitanism, Feeling, and Power." *differences.* 7.1 (Spring 1995): 165–187.

Ronnebeck, Arnold. "From Arnold Ronnebeck." 23 April 1941. Gallup 355.

Rosowski, Susan J. *The Voyage Perilous: Willa Cather's Romanticism.* Lincoln: U of Nebraska P, 1986.

Ruddick, Lisa. "A Rosy Charm: Gertrude Stein and the Repressed Feminine." M. Hoffman 225–40.

____. *Reading Gertrude Stein: Body, Text, Gnosis.* Ithaca: Cornell UP, 1990.

Salvaterra, David L. "Becoming American: Assimilation, Pluralism, and Ethnic Identity." Walch 29–54.

San Mateo County Office of Education. *A Report on Multi-Racial Reporting.* 15 December 2003 <http://www.smcoe.k12.ca.us/cspca/MultiRacialReporting Report.doc>

Sapiro, Virginia. *Women in American Society,* 5th edition. Boston: McGraw Hill, 2003.

Scholes, Robert E. "Robert E. Scholes." Bloom 18–22.

Schor, Naomi. "French Feminism is a Universalism." *differences.* 7.1 (Spring 1995): 15–47.

Schroeter, James, ed. *Willa Cather and Her Critics.* Ithaca: Cornell UP, 1967.

____. "Willa Cather and *The Professor's House.*" Schroeter 363–81.

Scott, Bonnie Kime. Introduction. *The Gender of Modernism.* Ed. Bonnie Kime Scott. Bloomington: Indiana University Press, 1990. 1–18.

Sergeant, Elizabeth Shepley. "Elizabeth Shepley Sergeant." Bloom 13.

Sedgwick, Eve Kosofsky. *Epistemology of the Closet.* Berkeley: University of California Press, 1990.

Seidman, Steven. "Deconstructing queer theory or the under-theorization of the social and the ethical." Nicholson and Seidman 116–141.

Shakespeare, William. "The Taming of the Shrew." *The Complete Works of Shakespeare.* 4th ed. Ed. David Bevington. New York: Harper Collins, 1992. 110–146.

Shaw, Patrick. "Marek Shimerda in *My Antonia:* A Noteworthy Medical Etiology." *ANQ* 13.1 (Winter 2000): 29–32.

____. "*My Antonia:* Emergence and Authorial Revelations." Bloom 121–131.

____. "Victorian Rules and Left Bank Rebellion: Willa Cather and Gertrude Stein." *Willa Cather Pioneer Memorial Newsletter* 36.3 (Fall 1992): 23–27.

Showalter, Elaine. "The Death of the Lady (Novelist): Wharton's *House of Mirth.*" *Representations,* 9 (Winter 1985): 133–49. Rpt. in *The House of Mirth.* By Edith Wharton. Ed. Elizabeth Ammons. New York: W.W. Norton and Co, 1990. 357–72.

Simmel, Georg. "The Metropolis and Mental Life." *Classic Essays on the Culture of Cities.* Ed. Richard Sennett. New York: Appleton-Century-Crofts, 1969. 47–60.

Simon, Linda, ed. *Gertrude Stein Remembered.* Lincoln: U of Nebraska P, 1994.

Skaggs, Merrill Maguire. *After the World Broke in Two: the Later Novels of Willa Cather.* Charlottesville: UP of Virginia, 1990.

Slote, Bernice and Virginia Faulkner, eds. *The Art of Willa Cather.* Lincoln: the U of Nebraska P, 1974.

Smith, Liz. "When Love Was the Adventure." *Time*. 14 June 1999: 147–50.

Sollors, Werner. *Beyond Ethnicity: Consent and Descent in American Culture*. New York: Oxford UP, 1986.

_____. *Neither Black Nor White Yet Both: Thematic Explorations of Interracial Literature*. New York: Oxford UP, 1997.

Spangler, George M. "The Ending of the Novel." From "Kate Chopin's *The Awakening*: A Partial Dissent," *Novel* 3 (Spring 1970), 249–55. Rpt. in *The Awakening*. By Kate Chopin. Ed. Maragret Culley. New York: W.W. Norton and Co., 1976. 186–189.

Spencer, Benjamin T. "Gertrude Stein: Non-Expatriate." *Literature and Ideas in America*. Ed. Robert Falk. Ohio: Ohio UP, 1975. 204–27.

Stableford, Brian. Introduction. *Tales of the Wandering Jew*. Ed. Brian Stableford. England: Dedalus Ltd., 1991. 1–25.

Stein, Gertrude. *The Autobiography of Alice B. Toklas*. 1933. New York: Vintage Books, 1990.

_____. *Everybody's Autobiography*. 1937. Cambridge: Exact Change, 1993.

_____. *The Geographical History of America*. 1936. Baltimore: Johns Hopkins UP, 1995.

_____. "Melanctha: Each One as She May." In *Three Lives*. 1909. New York: Dover Publications, Inc., 1994. 47–141.

Stimpson, Catherine R. "Gertrude Stein and the Lesbian Lie." *American Women's Autobiography: Fea(s)ts of Memory*. Ed. Margo Culley. Madison: the U of Wisconsin P, 1992. 152–166.

_____. "The Somagrams of Gertrude Stein." M. Hoffman 183–196.

Stouck, David. *Willa Cather's Imagination*. Lincoln: U of Nebraska P, 1975.

Stuckey, William J. "*My Antonia*: A Rose for Miss Cather." Bloom 97–105.

Sutherland, Donald. "The Elements." M. Hoffman 89–97.

_____. "Gertrude Stein and the Twentieth Century." Haas 139–56.

Swift, John. "Willa Cather's *My Antonia* and the Politics of Modernist Classicism." *Narratives of Nostalgia, Gender and Nationalism*. Eds. Jean Pickering and Suzanne Kehde. London: Macmillan Press Ltd, 1997. 107–120.

"Thousands Mourn Sikh Killed in Hate Rampage." *HoustonChronicle.com* 25 September 2001. 15 December 2003 <http://www.chron.com/cs/CDA/story.hts/special/terror/aftermath/1058610>.

Unger, Rhoda and Mary Crawford. *Women and Gender: A Feminist Psychology*. New York: McGraw-Hill, Inc., 1992.

Urgo, Joseph R. *Willa Cather and the Myth of American Migration*. Urbana: U of Illinois P, 1995.

Wagner-Martin, Linda. *"Favored Strangers": Gertrude Stein and Her Family*. New Brunswick: Rutgers UP, 1995.

_____. "Linda Wagner-Martin." Bloom 62–63.

Walch, Timothy, ed. *Immigrant America: European Ethnicity in the United States*. New York: Garland Publishing, Inc., 1994.

_____. Introduction Part I: "A Clash of Cultures." Walch 3–6.

Wald, Priscilla. *Constituting Americans.* Durham: Duke University Press, 1995.

Walker, Ben. "Miniature poodle wins best-in-show at Westminster." *Boston Globe* 14 February 2002. 14 December 2003 <http://www.boston.com/news/daily/13/westminster.htm>.

Wall, Cheryl A. *Women of the Harlem Renaissance.* Bloomington: Indiana UP, 1995.

Washington, Mary Helen. Introduction. *Invented Lives: Narratives of Black Women 1860–1960.* New York: Anchor Press, 1987. xv-xxxi.

Wasserman, Loretta. *Willa Cather: A Study of the Short Fiction.* Boston: Twayne Publishers, 1991.

Webb, Jeff. "Modernist Memory; or, The Being of Americans." *Criticism* 44 (2002): 227–47.

Wharton, Edith. *The House of Mirth.* 1905. Ed. Elizabeth Ammons. New York: W. W. Norton and Co, 1990.

Whipple, T.K. "Willa Cather." Schroeter 35–51.

Will, Barbara Elizabeth. "Genius and Gender in Gertrude Stein." Diss. Duke University, 1992.

Williams, Bettye J. "Nella Larsen: Shaping African-American Female Representation in *Quicksand* and *Passing*." Diss. Indiana University of Pennsylvania, 1993.

Williams, Raymond. *The Politics of Modernism: Against the New Conformists.* Ed. Tony Pinkney. New York: Verso, 1989.

Williams, William Carlos. "The Work of Gertrude Stein." M. Hoffman 55–58.

Wolkenfeld, Suzanne. "Edna's Suicide: The Problem of the One and the Many." *The Awakening.* By Kate Chopin. Ed. Maragret Culley. New York: W.W. Norton and Co., 1976. 218–224.

Woodress, James. *Willa Cather: Her Life and Art.* Lincoln: U of Nebraska P, 1970.

____. *Willa Cather: A Literary Life.* Lincoln: U of Nebraska P, 1987.

____. "Willa Cather: American Experience and European Tradition." Slote and Faulkner 43–62.

Wussow, Helen. "Language, Gender, and Ethnicity in Three Fictions by Willa Cather." *Women and Language* 18.1 (1995): 52–55.

Yohe, Kristine Anne. "Vainly Seeking the Promised Land: Geography and Migration in the Fiction of Nella Larsen and Toni Morrison." Diss. University of North Carolina at Chapel Hill, 1997.

Young, Iris Marion. "Gender as seriality: thinking about women as a social collective." Nicholson and Seidman 187–215.

Ytzhak. "POV: Amiri Baraka: Whose Free Speech?" *Indymedia.org* 7 July 2003. 14 December 2003 <http://www.indymedia.org.uk/en/2003/07/273925. html>.

Zabel, Morton D. "Willa Cather: the Tone of Time." Schroeter 216–27.

Zhu, Li and Tim Bintrim. "The Chinese Connection: Cather and Pittsburgh's Chinatown." *Willa Cather Pioneer Memorial Newsletter and Review.* 42.1 (Summer 1998): 1–5.

Zinn, Maxine Baca and Bonnie Thornton Dill. "Theorizing Difference From Multiracial Feminism." *Feminist Studies* 22.2 (1996): 321–331.

Index